Dror G. Feitelson Larry Rudolph (Eds.)

Job Scheduling Strategies for Parallel Processing

IPPS/SPDP'98 Workshop
Orlando, Florida, USA, March 30, 1998
Proceedings

 Springer

Series Editors

Gerhard Goos, Karlsruhe University, Germany
Juris Hartmanis, Cornell University, NY, USA
Jan van Leeuwen, Utrecht University, The Netherlands

Volume Editors

Dror G. Feitelson
The Hebrew University of Jerusalem
Institute of Computer Science
91904 Jerusalem, Israel
E-mail: feit@cs.huji.ac.il

Larry Rudolph
Laboratory for Computer Science, MIT
Cambridge, MA 02139, USA
E-mail: rudolph@lcs.mit.edu

Cataloging-in-Publication data applied for

Die Deutsche Bibliothek - CIP-Einheitsaufnahme

Job scheduling strategies for parallel processing : proceedings /
IPPS/SPDP '98 workshop, Orlando, Florida, USA, March 30, 1998.
Dror G. Feitelson ; Larry Rudolph (ed.). - Berlin ; Heidelberg ; New
York ; Barcelona ; Budapest ; Hong Kong ; London ; Milan ; Paris ;
Santa Clara ; Singapore ; Tokyo : Springer, 1998
   (Lecture notes in computer science ; Vol. 1459)
   ISBN 3-540-64825-9

CR Subject Classification (1991): D.4, D.1.3, C.2, F.2.2, C.1.2, B.2.1, B.6.1,
F.1.2

ISSN 0302-9743
ISBN 3-540-64825-9 Springer-Verlag Berlin Heidelberg New York

Typesetting: Camera-ready by author
SPIN 10638279   06/3142 – 5 4 3 2 1 0   Printed on acid-free paper

Springer

Berlin
Heidelberg
New York
Barcelona
Budapest
Hong Kong
London
Milan
Paris
Singapore
Tokyo

Lecture Notes in Computer Science 1459
Edited by G. Goos, J. Hartmanis and J. van Leeuwen

Preface

This volume contains the papers presented at the fourth workshop on Job Scheduling Strategies for Parallel Processing, which was held in conjunction with IPPS/SPDP '98 in Orlando, Florida, on March 30, 1998. All the papers have gone through a complete refereeing process, with the full version being read and evaluated by five or six members of the program committee in most cases. We would like to take this opportunity to thank the program committee, Stephen Booth, Allan Gottlieb, Atsushi Hori, Phil Krueger, Richard Lagerstrom, Miron Livny, Virginia Lo, Reagan Moore, Bill Nitzberg, Uwe Schwiegelshohn, Ken Sevcik, Mark Squillante, John Zahorjan, and Songnian Zhou, for an excellent job. Thanks are also due to the authors for their submissions, presentations, and final revisions for this volume. Finally, we would like to thank the MIT Laboratory for Computer Science and the Computer Science Institute at Hebrew University for the use of their facilities in preparation of these proceedings.

As multi-user parallel supercomputers become more widespread, job scheduling takes on a crucial role. The number of users of parallel supercomputers is growing at an even faster pace and so there is an increasing number of users who must share a parallel computer's resources. Job scheduling strategies must address this need.

There is a spectrum of groups that are interested in job scheduling strategies for parallel processors. At one end are the vendors of parallel supercomputers who supply the scheduling software for managing jobs on their machines. In the middle are researchers in academia, National Labs, and industrial research labs who propose new scheduling strategies and methods for evaluating and comparing them. At the other end of the spectrum are the users and system administrators of parallel processing facilities who have a set of demands and requirements.

The goal of the workshop was to bring together people from all three groups, in order to exchange ideas and discuss ongoing work. Indeed, many interesting discussions took place, and the workshop was quite lively. We were encouraged by this since we believe it is important to increase communication so that academics work on the right problems and vendors and computation centers make the best use of the novel solutions. We hope these proceedings help parallel supercomputing to achieve its fundamental goal of satisfying the needs of the user.

This was the fourth annual workshop in this series, which reflects the continued interest in this field. The previous three were held in conjunction with IPPS '95 through IPPS '97. Their proceedings are available from Springer-Verlag as volumes 949, 1162, and 1291 in the Lecture Notes in Computer Science series.

Jerusalem, May 1998

Dror Feitelson
Larry Rudolph

Table of Contents

Metrics and Benchmarking for Parallel Job Scheduling

Dror G. Feitelson[1] and Larry Rudolph[2]

[1] Institute of Computer Science
The Hebrew University of Jerusalem
91904 Jerusalem, Israel
http://www.cs.huji.ac.il/~feit
[2] Laboratory for Computer Science
MIT
Cambridge, MA 02139
http://www.csg.lcs.mit.edu:8001/Users/rudolph/

Abstract. The evaluation of parallel job schedulers hinges on two things: the use of appropriate metrics, and the use of appropriate workloads on which the scheduler can operate. We argue that the focus should be on on-line open systems, and propose that a standard workload should be used as a benchmark for schedulers. This benchmark will specify distributions of parallelism and runtime, as found by analyzing accounting traces, and also internal structures that create different speedup and synchronization characteristics. As for metrics, we present some problems with slowdown and bounded slowdown that have been proposed recently.

1 Introduction

Since the performance of a computer system depends on the workload which it is processing [3, 18], we argue that a workload benchmark suite is needed in order to evaluate and compare the many features of job schedulers for parallel supercomputers. But unlike standard benchmarks suites that consist of a set of "representative jobs" executed in isolation, a workload benchmark specifies the submission of jobs into the system and characterizes the types of jobs. Part of this characterization may include a description of the internal structure of the jobs themselves. This additional specification allows one to exercise various scheduler features.

A workload benchmark is likely to be useful in quantitative comparisons of two different job schedulers, perhaps even if they are executing on two different machine types. The only requirement is that the same type of generic workload will be relevant to both machines. Moreover, it is useful in evaluating the impact of various scheduler features. For example, it will be possible to evaluate the benefit of a scheduler sensitive to the mass-storage needs of its workload over one that ignores them. It is by far preferable to demonstrate the usefulness of some scheduler feature on a workload that is representative of what may occur on real

Dror G. Feitelson, Larry Rudolph (Eds.): JSSPP'98, LNCS 1459, pp. 1–24, 1998.
© Springer-Verlag Berlin Heidelberg 1998

systems, rather than generating one's own workload tailored to demonstrating the superiority of one's new feature.

There are other approaches to scheduler evaluation. One common method is to use traces of real workloads directly. The problem with this approach is that such traces are not necessarily representative, and that they only provide a single data point. In order to be able to assess the importance of different characteristics of the workload, it is better to use a synthetic benchmark suite. Analytical methods are another common approach. Although this works fine in certain limited domains, most realistic scenarios are too complex. These methods make assumptions about the workload of the scheduler. It is the claim of this paper, that the workload assumptions should be standardized. It does not matter if the synthetic workload is input to analysis, simulation, emulation, or real execution.

We start by explaining the different types of system dynamics that may be assumed, and justifying our focus on on-line, open systems (Section 2). As it seems premature to fully specify a benchmark, we discuss the specifications that are needed and identify topics that require additional research (Section 3). A discussion of metrics then follows since it is the goal of a scheduler to optimize one or more metrics (Section 4). Then we discuss implementation concerns (Section 5) and finally present our conclusions (Section 6).

2   Types of Queueing Systems

A computer system is essentially a *queueing* system: jobs arrive, may wait for some time, receive the required service, and depart. Such systems can be classified as on-line vs. off-line, with the on-line branch being further classified as open or closed (Fig. 1). All of these classes have been used in the analysis of computer systems.

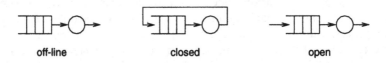

| off-line | closed | open |

Fig. 1. *The three generic types of queueing systems.*

Off-line analysis assumes all the jobs — and maybe also their resource requirements — are available from the outset. There are no additional arrivals later. The scheduler can then pack the jobs together in order to minimize the total processing time. Such a model is often suitable for space slicing, batch job schedulers and their performance can often be predicted using analytical methods [7]. It is also convenient for measuring the execution of real applications as scheduled by real schedulers.

Alternatively, one can assume an *on-line* model where jobs arrive over a period of time. In this case the scheduler must handle new jobs "in real time," without the benefit of prior knowledge about future arrivals. A *closed* on-line system assumes that there is a fixed set of jobs to be handled. Thus arrivals are in effect linked with departures of previous jobs, and there is a bound on the maximum number of jobs in the system at any one time. Although more difficult, such a workload model is still amenable to analytic analysis.

The approach followed in this paper can be characterized as an *open*, on-line system in which there is an endless stream of jobs arriving for service. This most closely models the challenges of real job schedulers, where arrivals are independent of departures and indeed of the current load conditions. However, this type of model is more complex, because the arrival process has to be modeled as well.

Using an open, on-line model implies that the scheduler must be able to handle extreme situations, since in an open system, the tail of a distribution can and will occur. In fact, part of the analysis is to see when the scheduler breaks down because it can no longer handle the incoming load (this always happens when the load approaches the system capacity). Such an analysis is not possible with off-line or closed models.

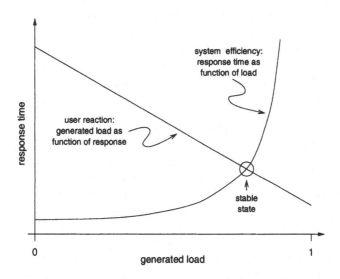

Fig. 2. *User reaction to system performance may be described by supply and demand curves. Only the "system efficiency" curve need be characterized in order to evaluate the system.*

At first blush, it appears that the modeling process is complicated by the fact that users may react to certain "features" (or bugs :-) of the job scheduler. Sophisticated users will learn to exploit imbalances, and cause a bias in the workload. Static workloads, such as those assumed by off-line or closed on-line analysis, cannot capture such user's reactions. Dynamic workloads — as in on-line open systems — allow for a better characterization of the system, but more importantly, they leave the modeling of the user as a separate issue (Fig. 2).

Finally, we note that the use of dynamic workloads captures some second-order effects, whereby feedback due to system characteristics may modify the workload. Examples include jobs that receive preferential treatment, and therefore stay in the system less time, whereas jobs that receive degraded service stay in the system longer than may be expected. As a result the observed mix has more "bad" jobs than the original mix. While it is not clear whether such effects are really significant, it is prudent to be conservative and use a model that does not preclude them.

3   Workload Specifications

A workload description for an on-line, open system can be viewed as consisting of two major components: job arrival and job structure. Each job arrives at a specific time and requires a specific amount of processing time, which we refer to as *work*. Thus, there is a model for the distribution of the arrival process and a separate model for the distribution of each particular job's work requirement. Fortunately, trace data accumulated at various supercomputer computation centers enables realistic models.

The first component describes how jobs are submitted to the system over a period of time. This can be somewhat involved, as a distinction has to be made between short interactive jobs and long batch jobs. In addition, there are daily and weekly cycles in the arrival process, due to the working patterns of the human users of the system.

The second component is that of modeling the work requirements of each job. This can be done in a monolithic manner, or else the internal structure of each job can be specified. As additional internal job structure is modeled, more sophisticated scheduler features can be evaluated, presumably resulting in a more efficient system. Unfortunately, there is not much hard data that has been measured about typical internal structural distributions, but there are common scenarios. The most common and clearly identifiable structures are the computational structure (parallelism and barrier synchronizations), interprocess communication, memory requirements, and I/O needs. The discussion will be limited to only the computational structure because of two reasons: it is the one about which we have some knowledge about typical patterns and it illustrates the specification choices.

The rest of this section addresses possible choices for arrival and computational structure distributions.

3.1   Modeling Job Arrivals

Two broad classes of arrival scenarios can be identified. In one, the arrival process is a memory-less, continuous process. In the other, it is cyclic. The latter case more closely represents observed arrival patterns, where the number of jobs

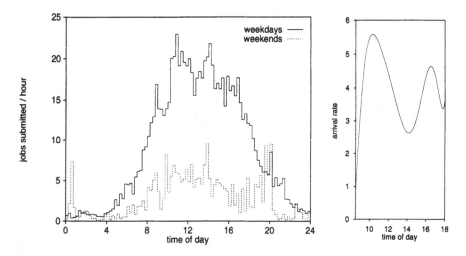

Fig. 3. *Left: cyclic job arrival pattern in the NASA Ames iPSC/860 (from [10]). Right: model of Calzarossa and Serazzi for workload at the University of Pavia [2].*

submitted strongly correlates with the time of day and the day of the week (Fig. 3). However, the simpler continuous model is the one that system performance evaluation almost always uses in practice. This has the unfortunate effect of excluding the evaluation of scheduler optimizations that increase the priority of interactive jobs during the day, at the expense of computational (batch) jobs that are delayed to when more resources are available at night.

It should be noted that a good model of the arrival process is also necessary in order to create various load conditions for the evaluation. If the cyclic structure of the arrival process is acknowledged, it is no longer possible to increase the load by uniformly reducing the interarrival times, because such a practice will also shrink the cycle length. Regrettably, very little work has been done on the derivation of realistic models.

The only detailed model we know of was proposed by Calzarossa and Serazzi [2]. This model uses a polynomial of degree 8 to model the changing arrival rate of interactive work (Fig. 3). The proposed polynomial for "normal" days is

$$\lambda(t) = 3.1 - 8.5t + 24.7t^2 + 130.8t^3 + 107.7t^4 - 804.2t^5 - 2038.5t^6 + 1856.8t^7 + 4618.6t^8$$

where $\lambda(t)$ is the arrival rate at time t, and t is in the range $[-0.5..0.5]$, and should be scaled to the range from 8:30 AM to 6:00 PM. This expression represents the centroid for a set of polynomials that were obtained by fitting measured results for different days. Slightly different polynomials were discovered for abnormal days, in which the administrative office closed early, or were the first day after a weekend or a holiday. While the authors warn against using this data without additional verifications, we propose it as an initial model until more suitable ones are derived.

Much additional work is required in order to better characterize the arrival process of parallel jobs. Specific research questions include

- The possible differentiation between arrival models for batch and interactive jobs. Do both types of jobs arrive according to the same patterns?
- The possible correlation of arrival time with work requirement. Are jobs that arrive at different times of the day and night statistically equivalent, or do they tend to have different structures? For example, do users submit smaller jobs during the morning and larger ones in the afternoon, in anticipation of the resources that will be freed up at night?

3.2   Modeling Rigid Jobs

At the least specific level, no internal computational structure is specified and a job consists of just an amount of work. This work can be processed sequentially or in parallel, with no loss of efficiency. However, such a model is usually too simple minded to be useful.

The simplest useful model is rigid jobs, in which both the work and the degree of parallelism are specified. This is an "external" model, with no details of the internal structure of jobs. It is useful because many parallel supercomputers provide schedulers for this type of jobs, and because this type of workload model can be derived from accounting logs. Indeed, a number of such models have already been derived and used in the evaluation of schedulers for parallel systems [8, 15, 18].

Interestingly, the accounting logs from many diverse systems show several common characteristics, most of which were not anticipated in advance. One such characteristic concerns the distribution of job sizes, i.e. the number of processors that are used. It turns out that even in very large machines, small jobs using only a handful of processors dominate the workload (in terms of number of jobs, though not in terms of runtime). In fact, in machines having more than about 100 processors, there are usually only very few jobs that use the whole system. In addition, there is a strong tendency to use a power-of-two number of processors, even if this is not warranted by the architecture. A representative distribution of job sizes, taken from the 400-node Paragon machine at San-Diego Supercomputer Center, is shown in Fig. 4.

Modeling the distribution of degrees of parallelism is relevant for schedulers that handle rigid jobs. We propose the following approach: first, model the overall distribution as linear in the logarithm of the parallelism, as suggested by Downey [5]. This means that the probability of using fewer than n processors is roughly proportional to $\log n$. Then, modify the distribution by creating steps at powers of two. The size of the steps is determined by a parameter describing the workload, which specifies what percentage of the jobs use power-of-two nodes. The value for the SDSC Paragon cited above is about 81% (including 21% that were serial). More work is required to derive better models, including answers to the following questions:

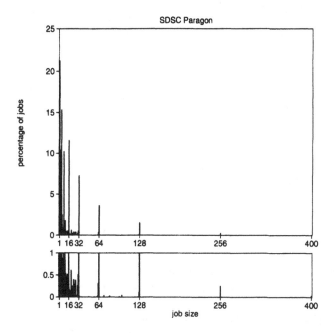

Fig. 4. *Representative distribution of job sizes, showing dominance of small jobs and jobs using a power-of-two processors. (Data from SDSC Paragon.)*

- What is a good representative value for the fraction of jobs that use power-of-two processors?
- Is the use of powers of two a real feature of workloads, or only an artifact resulting from old habits and common interfaces to batch queueing systems?
- Are all powers of two equally likely?

Another potentially important characteristic concerns the correlation between the degree of parallelism and the runtime. In the past, it has been speculated that highly parallel jobs should be shorter, because parallelism is used to achieve speedup. In fact, workload traces indicate that highly parallel jobs run longer (Fig. 5). This has two possible interpretations: either the smaller jobs are development while the larger ones are production runs, or parallelism is used to solve larger problems rather than to achieve speedup on given problems.

A possible model for such a correlation has been proposed by Feitelson [8]. The basis for the model is the observation that job runtimes have a very large variability, manifested by a coefficient of variation that is larger than 1. A plausible model for runtimes is therefore a hyperexponential distribution. For example, a two-stage hyperexponential can be used; intuitively, this means that we first choose at random from two exponential distributions according to a probability p, and then sample the chosen distribution. The correlation with parallelism is achieved by making the probability, p, a function of the parallelism, n. Specifically, Feitelson used

$$p(n) = 0.95 - 0.2(n/N)$$

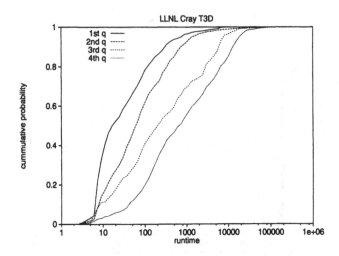

Fig. 5. *Correlation of runtime with parallelism is evident when the distribution of runtimes is plotted for 4 sets of jobs independently, where each set contains jobs with a different degree of parallelism. The weight of the distribution for the set with the smallest jobs is at low values, while jobs with high parallelism tended to have higher runtimes as well. (Data from LLNL Cray T3D.)*

where N is the system size; thus for small n we get that p is near 0.95, and for large n it goes down to 0.75. Given p, sample an exponential distribution with mean 1 with probability p, or a distribution with mean 7 with probability $1 - p$. We are now working on a better model, that will be based on better statistical analysis of workload traces.

Simpler models for job runtime have also been proposed. For interactive jobs (e.g. in a Unix environment), it has been suggested that job runtimes have a cumulative distribution of $F(t) = t^k$, with $k \approx -1$, provided the jobs are longer than a second or so [13]. This means that

$$p(\text{runtime} = t \mid \text{age} = 1sec) = 1/t^2$$

For batch jobs, it has been proposed that the logarithms of the runtimes are uniformly distributed, so their cumulative distribution is linear, $F(t) = a \ln t + b$, with $a \approx 0.1$ [6]. This leads to

$$p(\text{runtime} = t) = 1/10t$$

3.3   Modeling Internal Job Structure

Jobs come in many different shapes, sizes, and styles, and it is important to model much of this internal job structure since models of rigid jobs do not allow for the evaluation of many innovative schedulers. For example, schedulers may wish to change dynamically the degree of parallelism provided to a job, in order to account for various load conditions. The resulting performance depends on the speedup curves of the application [21, 19]. Thus, for each job, it must be possible to compute runtime as a function of partition size. Another example is that a scheduler may want to modify the "gangedness" of an application, that is the degree to which all the processes execute simultaneously on distinct processors. Again, the resulting performance depends on the characteristics of the application [17], and the workload model must specify runtime as a function of skew.

There are two general methods for modelling the "internal" job structure. One is based on equations describing job behavior. This approach has been used for analyzing specific situations, such as how runtime changes with degree of parallelism for adaptive partitioning [20, 4]. However these equations are typically expressed as speedup functions, and imply some assumption about the scheduling, e.g. that all the threads execute simultaneously without interference [19]. A more general approach is to specify the internal structure so that simulation or detailed analytic methods can be used to calculate the runtime from the structure.

A hierarchical model that includes the internal structure of the workload has been proposed by Calzarossa et al [1]. Their model includes the levels of applications, algorithms, and routines, and thus is suitable for the modeling of real applications. We prefer a synthetic workload that only includes certain abstract structures.

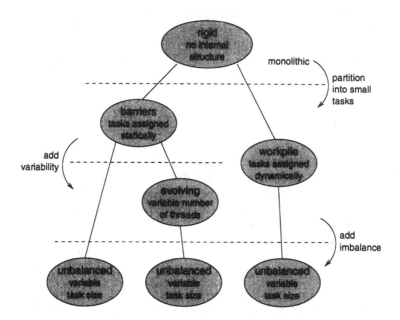

Fig. 6. *The proposed hierarchical workload benchmark suite, in which lower levels add more detail to the internal structure of jobs.*

Our proposal is to capture the "popular" alternative programming styles and scheduler features and is outlined in Fig. 6. The space is deliberately sparse; to keep the set of alternatives manageable, it is necessary to exclude many combinations. At the top level are external models as described above. Lower levels inherit the distributions of total work in the different jobs, and add internal structure. Two basic internal structures are proposed: one in which the computation is organized as communicating threads that synchronize with barriers, and the other in which the computation is organized as an unordered workpile. The barrier structure has a variant in which the number of threads changes from barrier to barrier — this is essentially the fork/join model that represents a sequence of parallel loops. All models are parameterized by their granularity: for barriers, this is the amount of computation each thread does between barriers; for workpile, this is the typical task size. Finally, in all models we may add imbalance by specifying a distribution of task sizes. Workload parameters used to define these workloads are described in Section 5.

One anticipated use of the workload models is that one can choose the model that is most suitable to exercise the scheduler being evaluated. Another important use is to check how the scheduler handles jobs with other characteristics, that are not specifically dealt with in the design of the scheduler. For example, how does a gang scheduler handle a job with evolving parallelism? And how does a two-level scheduler with dynamic partitioning handle a strictly SPMD code with barriers?

While standardization of the job structures that are used to benchmark parallel job schedulers is important, it does not cover the whole workload modeling question. The missing part is creating a job mix from these structures. One must always be careful when evaluating a scheduler with a set of jobs that all have the same structure, because then the likelihood of correlations between the jobs grows. Regrettably, there is no information about typical and realistic job mixes. The definition of good mixes is left as a question for future research.

4   Performance Metrics

As noted in Section 2, computer systems can be modeled in several ways. For each type of system, a different metric is commonly used (Fig. 7). In this section we investigate metrics related to the response time, which is the most suitable for open on-line systems, and explain why we do not use other metrics such as utilization and throughput.

4.1   Metrics and System Types

One problem with selecting a performance metric is that in a real system different metrics may be relevant for different jobs. For example, response time may be the most important metric for interactive jobs, while system utilization is more important for batch jobs. But in an open, on-line system, utilization is largely

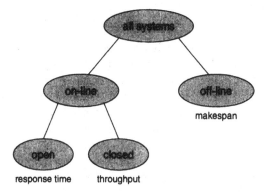

Fig. 7. *Classification of system types and common metric used for each.*

determined by the arrival process and the requirements of the jobs, not by the scheduler. This leaves response time as the main metric.

The way to use response time as a metric is to find its functional dependence on system load, as in Fig. 2. This means that many different load conditions should be checked. With rigid jobs, load and utilization are completely determined by the arrival rate, so it is easy and justifiable to present the results as a function of utilization [11]. But with adaptive or dynamic partitioning schemes, changing the partition size may change the efficiency of job execution and thus change the utilization. The correct load variable is therefore the arrival rate, not the resulting utilization. This has the unfortunate consequence that it becomes harder to compare different schemes, because one needs to understand the workload details to correlate the arrival rates. A standard workload benchmark will solve this problem.

Throughput is a good metric for closed systems, because there the arrival process depends on system performance: each job is re-submitted immediately each time it terminates. The question is then how fast the jobs repeat, i.e. how many times they are executed per unit time. Utilization is also a good metric in this case, because faster job turnaround increases utilization. The power metric is an intriguing variant [16]. It is defined as the throughput divided by the response time, so it goes up when either the throughput goes up or the response time goes down. However, if the throughput is determined by the arrival process, power provides the same information as response time.

Makespan is the metric of choice for off-line scheduling. It can be thought of as an off-line version of response time: it is the time that the whole workload terminates, rather than the (average of the) time that each job terminates. In the off-line scenario, it is directly linked with utilization and throughput, and each can be derived from the others (given information about average requirements of jobs). The same is not true of response time, which depends on the scheduling order.

4.2   Response Time, Slowdown, and Bounded Slowdown

The average response time is a widely accepted metric for open, on-line systems. However, it seems that this metric places greater emphasis on long jobs, as opposed to short jobs, which are much more common. For example, the average response time of 100 1-hour jobs and one 3-week job is 6 hours. A possible solution to this problem is to normalize the reported values by using slowdown rather than raw response time (slowdown is defined as runtime on a loaded system divided by runtime on a dedicated system). Thus all jobs are reduced to the same scale, with 1 indicating good performance, and higher values measuring the degree of degradation. The problem with slowdown is that extremely short jobs with reasonable delays lead to excessive slowdown values. For example, a 1 second job that is delayed for 20 minutes suffers a slowdown of 1200. The proposed solution to this problem is to apply a lower bound on job runtimes, e.g. 10 seconds [12]. Shorter jobs are treated as if their duration is this lower bound; in the above example, the bounded slowdown value is then 120 rather than 1200.

The above "handwaving" arguments indicate that using bounded slowdown should lead to measurements with less variance (and thus quick convergence) that take fair account of all jobs. Regrettably, actual measurements seem to indicate that this is in fact not always the case. The following results are from a simulation of variable partitioning with backfilling, using a realistic model of rigid jobs (similar to the proposal in Section 3.2), and assuming a system of 128 nodes. This is one of the simulations reported in [9], which has been instrumented to collect more data.

Fig. 8 shows the behavior of the three metrics (response time, slowdown, and bounded slowdown) for the first 5000 jobs in the simulation run. The individual value for each job is plotted, as well as a running average. It shows that while response times vary much more than slowdowns, both types of slowdown suffer from bursts of very high values. As a result, the running average of the slowdown converges more *slowly* than that of the response time. Bounded slowdown is somewhat better.

The same effect can be seen in Fig. 9, in which the average values are plotted for a very long simulation. remarkably, the plot for the bounded slowdown is nearly identical to that of the response time, whereas the one for slowdown is much more erratic. Nevertheless, even the "better behaved" response time and bounded slowdown continue to vary even after more than 200000 jobs have been simulated. This is extremely long, considering that typical large supercomputers execute less than 100000 jobs in a whole year.

Some insights can be obtained from Fig. 10, which shows a scatter plots of slowdown and bounded slowdown vs. response time. Two clusters stand out in these plots. In one cluster, jobs have a high response time coupled with a low slowdown. This means that these are long jobs, and the high response time actually reflects their computational demands. In the other cluster the slowdown is proportional to the response time, with much weight concentrated where both slowdown and response time are high. This cluster includes jobs that are actually

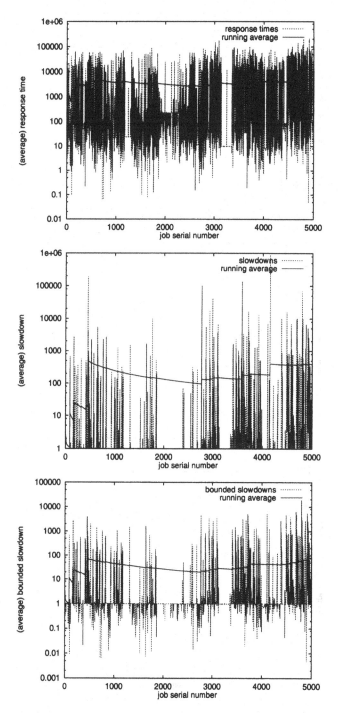

Fig. 8. *Pointwise and running average of metrics for first 5000 jobs in simulation.*

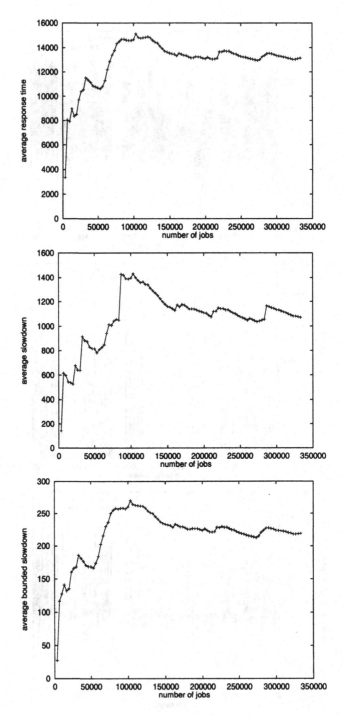

Fig. 9. *Running average of metrics for a very long simulation. Each data point represents an additional 3333 job terminations.*

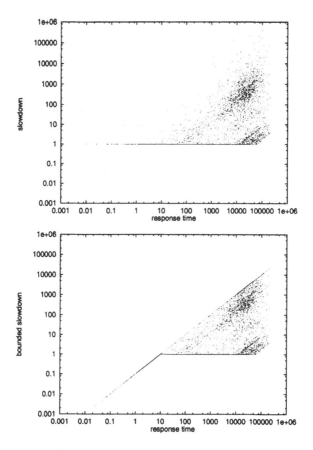

Fig. 10. *Scatter plots of slowdown vs. response time.*

quite short, and their high response time reflects time stuck in the queue waiting for some long job to terminate. Using bounded slowdown trims the most extreme values in this case (bottom plot), where the jobs that are delayed are *very* short. In this cases the denominator in taken as a constant, rather than being the job's runtime, leading to values that are linearly related to the response time — hence the similarity of bounded slowdown and response time.

Nevertheless, this manipulation can't make the problem go away. Due to the high variability of runtimes, at rare intervals a long job comes along and jerks the response time; it also causes multiple short jobs to wait, and thus jerks the slowdown and bounded slowdown. However, this is actually an artifact of the scheduler used in these simulations, which is based on variable partitioning and causes short jobs to be delayed. The behavior of slowdown and bounded slowdown with mechanisms that do not delay jobs, such as gang scheduling or dynamic partitioning, is expected to be different.

In summary, the question of what makes a good metric is still open. More work is required in order to refine our understanding of the relations between response time, slowdown, and bounded slowdown, and maybe additional metrics should also be investigated.

4.3   Workload-Dependent Metrics

Our proposed benchmark suite (Section 3) contains families of programs whose behavior depends on a parameter that specifies their granularity. The results will naturally depend on the value chosen for this parameter. One approach is to report performance results for a range of granularity values. Another is to make such detailed measurements, but report only the following:

1. The best performance that is obtained, at either very high or very low granularity, and

W	Total number of work units in the job
P_l, P_u	lower and upper bounds on the number of processors
B_l, B_u	lower and upper bounds on the number of barriers
$\bar{w}_i, w_{std}$	mean number of work units per barrier, standard deviation of the work units per berrier
$\bar{u}_i, u_{std}$	mean compute time of a work unit, standard deviation of work unit time

Fig. 11. A proposed set of parameters to specify the internal structure of a workload.

The table in Fig. 11 lists the parameters. The idea is that the work done by the job is the sum of many atomic work units, W, which are each computed by a single processor. Precedence constraints between these work units, if any, are expressed by the number B of barrier synchronizations. The number of work units between barriers w_i therefore represents the degree of parallelism in that phase. The mean compute time of a work unit u is used to calibrate the workload across different machines. The variability of u, expressed as its standard variation u_{std}, can be used to add variability among work units.

The next paragraphs explain how to set these parameters to specify the different workloads.

Rigid Jobs Rigid jobs are usually represented by two parameters: the number of processors P and the execution time T. It is assumed that the job is gang scheduled, since if it is not, then there is not enough internal structure to understand the runtime.

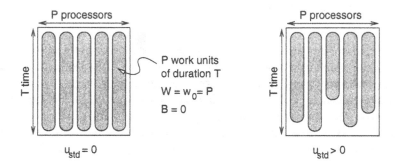

Fig. 12. *Expressing a rigid job structure with the parameters.*

This formulation is expressed using our parameters by creating P work units that execute on P processors for T time, with no additional structure (Fig. 12). The definitions of P and W are then $P_l = P_u = P$ and $W = P$. Since there is no internal structure, the rest of the parameters are easily set too: $B_l = B_u = 0$, $w_0 = P$, $w_{std} = 0$. The mean compute time $\bar{u}$ links with the parameter T normally used to express the duration of rigid jobs: $\bar{u} = T$, $u_{std} = 0$. In fact, we can say that the total work in work units is actually $W = PT/\bar{u}$, but because there is only one work unit on each processor, T and $\bar{u}$ cancel out. The variability of u_{std} can be used to express imbalance among the processors.

Workpile A workpile job has no real internal structure, rather there is a pile of work to be processed. The more processors there are, the faster the work can be processed. However, there is often a minimal number of processors required to meet resource constraints (e.g. to have enough memory). There is also a maximum number of processors that can be assigned to a job. This is trivially bounded by the total number of processors in the system. Therefore the two relevant parameters typically used to describe a workpile are W and P_{min}. It is usually assumed that there is a linear speedup for processing the job.

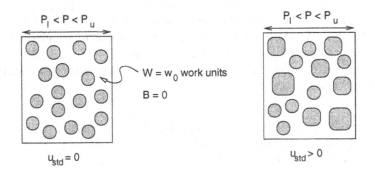

Fig. 13. *Expressing a workpile job structure with the parameters. With $W > P$ there is no internal structure.*

These parameters are easily converted to our job parameters as follows. W is simply the number of work units in the pile. $P_l = P_{min}$ based on resource requirements, and $P_u = P_{max}$. There are no barriers, so $B_l = B_u = 0$, $w_0 = W$, and $w_{std} = 0$. Assuming $W > P_{max}$, there are more work units then processors, and they can therefore be computed on any processor in any order. $\bar{u}$ can be set as desired for calibration, and u_{std} is used to add variability in work unit sizes.

Barriers The main internal job structure feature in this type of job is the number of barriers. The crucial parameter in terms of scheduling and performance is the granularity of each barrier. A secondary issue is how the barrier is implemented: with busy wait, with yielding, with operating system help, or with some combination of these; this affects overhead.

Let us start with a simple case in which each processor performs one unit of work at each barrier (Fig. 14). This is expressed by $w_i = P, 0 \le i \le B$, where B

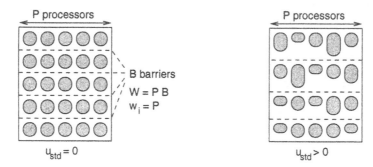

Fig. 14. *Expressing a simple barrier job structure with the parameters.*

is the number of barriers in the job. It then follows that $B = W/P$ (assuming that the number of processors is fixed: $P_l = P_u = P$). Alternatively, it is possible to select B from the range $B_l \leq B \leq B_u$, and then set $W = BP$. This is useful to create a workload of non-identical jobs, representing runs that took a different number of iterations to converge. The granularity of the barriers is expressed by $\bar{u}_i$.

Alternatively, the granularity may be expressed using a "workpiles between barriers" structure. This structure represents a sequence of parallel loops, where the iterations are independent of each other and can be done in any order. In this case $w_i > P$ for all i, so all the processors share all the work units between barriers in a workpile manner. The granularity can then be expressed in work units, rather than in time, as $\bar{w}_i/P$: this is the average number of work units per processor per barrier. The number of barriers is implicitly defined by the formula $B = W/\bar{w}_i$.

Fork-Join There is a large class of jobs in which the amount of parallelism varies during the course of the execution. For example, there may be a sequence of parallel loops with different degrees of parallelism, or separated by sequential phases. It is possible to express such structures by using different values for w_i, the number of work units associated with barrier i (Fig. 15).

If $w_i \leq P$ for all i, then some processors will be idle in some phases, because there are less work units than processors. If $w_i > P$ in some phases, the work units are computed as a workpile in this phase; if it is in all phases, this is the situation discussed above. The number of processors P can be fixed, or else it can vary according to resource requirements and availability, leading to a continuum of possibilities between these two end points.

Creating a Job Mix We note that although it is possible to allow all the parameters to vary, it is doubtful that much meaningful information can be gathered from such cases.

There are two choices for specifying the mean values and their standard deviations: they can be identical for all the jobs (but each job has its own unique

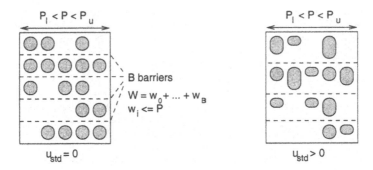

Fig. 15. *Expressing a variable-parallelism job structure with the parameters.*

seed to the random number generator), or they can be generated from some other distribution during job creation. Without any hard evidence from actual workloads, it is impossible to say which is preferable. The mechanisms outlined above easily permit either approach.

5.2 Granularity Issues

Although we leave the actual distribution of the parameters as a subject for future research, there are some interesting points to be noted about the granularity of barriers, or in other words, the length of time of a work unit. It seems to be very important to get this value correct: if it is too big, there is little benefit for gang scheduling and if too small, jobs may never complete.

When there is a large value for a work unit, nearly as long as a time quantum, there is almost no difference between workpile or barrier. Moreover, there is little difference whether or not the system is gang scheduled or not. Similarly, when the work unit is very small the job terminates within the first time quantum, assuming that the processors all begin at the same time.

The number of barriers is also a sensitive issue. If there are too many barriers, the work-unit is short, and the system is not gang-scheduled, many jobs may never terminate. On the other hand, if the are only a few barriers, and the work-unit is short, then jobs may terminate within the first time quantum. Further experimentation is necessary to resolve these issues.

As an example, we experimented with a job with 10,000 barriers executed on an SMP IBM RS/6000 workstation with four PowerPC 604 Processors. The upper table in Fig. 16 shows the execution times on an idle system, as a function of the duration of the work units between barriers and the number of processors. Barriers were implemented by the MPI function. Notice that it is not until the work unit is 10^5 instructions long, that a linear speedup occurs. In the bottom table, the same set of experiments were performed while another 4 node job was executing. Here the four node jobs execute relatively worse than the others until the granularity is even larger.

Another example shows a case of shared memory jobs executed on the same idle system while varying the number of processors from 1 to 4. The barrier

Empty Machine

P	10^0	10^1	10^2	10^3	10^4	10^5	10^6
	granularity of work between barriers						
1	0.013	0.026	0.160	3.494	16.836	150.293	1486.261
2	4.022	4.028	6.720	6.977	12.071	80.657	748.408
3		5.279	7.315	7.736		54.859	500.494
4	5.302	5.122	5.110	7.360	9.211	42.705	382.139

With One Other Job

P	10^0	10^1	10^2	10^3	10^4	10^5	10^6
	granularity of work between barriers						
1	0.013	0.026	0.160	1.697	22.233	228.080	2300.667
2	8.673	6.662	8.967	10.390	21.454	144.723	1418.324
3	10.080	10.015	12.114	11.206	12.696	112.375	1136.834
4	11.462	13.975	11.112	12.166	19.621	104.883	1004.811

Fig. 16. Run-time of an MPI program, with 10,000 barriers, and various values for the granularity between the barriers.

Empty Machine (Shared Memory Program)

P	10^0	10^1	10^2	10^3	10^4	10^5	10^6
	granularity of work between barriers						
1	0.007	0.012	0.057	0.510	5.034	50.279	502.761
2	0.022	0.024	0.047	0.227	2.822	27.188	251.614
3	0.028	0.033	0.047	0.196	1.712	18.815	168.068
4	2.056	0.092	0.064	0.178	1.315	14.703	128.787

Fig. 17. Run-time of a shared-memory program, with 10,000 barriers, and various values for the granularity between the barriers. The barriers were implemented using busy-waiting on a global variable protected by a system mutex lock.

synchronization was executed as a busy-wait by increasing a counter protected by a lock, and there were 10,000 barrier synchronizations. The performance results are shown in Fig. 17. The granularity has a large effect on how the program performs: with a shared memory implementation of barriers, linear speedup occurs for a granularity as small as 10^3.

5.3 Execution Issues

Portability One goal of the benchmarks is that they be executable on a large number of platforms – both hardware and software. But, to be useful, the port to a new system should be as smooth as possible. The problem is that different systems support different features. For example, not many systems provide support for dynamically allocating and deallocating processors to jobs. It has been claimed that this ability dramatically improves overall performance.

The easiest option is for the system to simply ignore the extra specification of the job. If the amount of parallelism per barrier is variable, a system that does not support this feature can simply choose the maximum parallelism.

Length of Execution How long should the benchmark be executed? Given the probabilistic nature, given enough time, anything is likely to happen. That is, the system may get into a saturated state from which it never exits. We also do not have unbounded time in which to execute benchmarks. Experience will have to be teacher.

But we can say that the scheduler will behave differently during warm up and cool down. For this reason, we suggest that measurements only be taken during the steady-state behavior of the system. It is crucially important to ensure that the system does not "dry out" towards the end. For example, if we want to measure performance characteristics of 10000 jobs, we need to keep the arrival process going until all 10000 terminate. When the system is close to saturation, this means that we may have to generate much much more than 10000 jobs.

6 Conclusions

There is still much to be done before a comprehensive workload benchmark can be built. There are many aspects of a job's internal structure for which there is no experimental evidence concerning their actual distributions. It is our hope that this be rectified.

Thus, this paper has only begun the quest for a workload benchmark and for widely accepted and suitable metrics. Although a large design space has been outlined, it is likely that only a small portion of the space is needed to make progress. This portion should be identified and subjected to a focused research effort.

References

[1] M. Calzarossa, G. Haring, G. Kotsis, A. Merlo, and D. Tessera, "*A hierarchical approach to workload characterization for parallel systems*". In *High-Performance Computing and Networking*, pp. 102–109, Springer-Verlag, May 1995. Lect. Notes Comput. Sci. vol. 919.

[2] M. Calzarossa and G. Serazzi, "*A characterization of the variation in time of workload arrival patterns*". *IEEE Trans. Comput.* **C-34(2)**, pp. 156–162, Feb 1985.

[3] M. Calzarossa and G. Serazzi, "*Workload characterization: a survey*". *Proc. IEEE* **81(8)**, pp. 1136–1150, Aug 1993.

[4] S-H. Chiang and M. K. Vernon, "*Dynamic vs. static quantum-based parallel processor allocation*". In *Job Scheduling Strategies for Parallel Processing*, D. G. Feitelson and L. Rudolph (eds.), pp. 200–223, Springer-Verlag, 1996. Lect. Notes Comput. Sci. vol. 1162.

[5] A. B. Downey, *"A parallel workload model and its implications for processor allocation"*. In 6th *Intl. Symp. High Performance Distributed Comput.*, Aug 1997.

[6] A. B. Downey, *"Predicting queue times on space-sharing parallel computers"*. In 11th *Intl. Parallel Processing Symp.*, pp. 209–218, Apr 1997.

[7] M. Drozdowski, *"Scheduling multiprocessor tasks — an overview"*. *European J. Operational Research* **94**, pp. 215–230, 1996.

[8] D. G. Feitelson, *"Packing schemes for gang scheduling"*. In *Job Scheduling Strategies for Parallel Processing*, D. G. Feitelson and L. Rudolph (eds.), pp. 89–110, Springer-Verlag, 1996. Lect. Notes Comput. Sci. vol. 1162.

[9] D. G. Feitelson and M. A. Jette, *"Improved utilization and responsiveness with gang scheduling"*. In *Job Scheduling Strategies for Parallel Processing*, D. G. Feitelson and L. Rudolph (eds.), pp. 238–261, Springer Verlag, 1997. Lect. Notes Comput. Sci. vol. 1291.

[10] D. G. Feitelson and B. Nitzberg, *"Job characteristics of a production parallel scientific workload on the NASA Ames iPSC/860"*. In *Job Scheduling Strategies for Parallel Processing*, D. G. Feitelson and L. Rudolph (eds.), pp. 337–360, Springer-Verlag, 1995. Lect. Notes Comput. Sci. vol. 949.

[11] D. G. Feitelson and L. Rudolph, *"Toward convergence in job schedulers for parallel supercomputers"*. In *Job Scheduling Strategies for Parallel Processing*, D. G. Feitelson and L. Rudolph (eds.), pp. 1–26, Springer-Verlag, 1996. Lect. Notes Comput. Sci. vol. 1162.

[12] D. G. Feitelson, L. Rudolph, U. Schwiegelshohn, K. C. Sevcik, and P. Wong, *"Theory and practice in parallel job scheduling"*. In *Job Scheduling Strategies for Parallel Processing*, D. G. Feitelson and L. Rudolph (eds.), pp. 1–34, Springer Verlag, 1997. Lect. Notes Comput. Sci. vol. 1291.

[13] M. Harchol-Balter and A. B. Downey, *"Exploiting process lifetime distributions for dynamic load balancing"*. In *SIGMETRICS Conf. Measurement & Modeling of Comput. Syst.*, pp. 13–24, May 1996.

[14] R. W. Hockney, *"Performance of parallel computers"*. In *High-Speed Computation*, J. S. Kowalik (ed.), pp. 159–175, Springer-Verlag, 1984. NATO ASI Series Vol. F7.

[15] J. Jann, P. Pattnaik, H. Franke, F. Wang, J. Skovira, and J. Riodan, *"Modeling of workload in MPPs"*. In *Job Scheduling Strategies for Parallel Processing*, D. G. Feitelson and L. Rudolph (eds.), pp. 95–116, Springer Verlag, 1997. Lect. Notes Comput. Sci. vol. 1291.

[16] L. Kleinrock, *"Power and deterministic rules of thumb for probabilistic problems in computer communications"*. In *Intl. Conf. Communications*, vol. 3, pp. 43.1.1–43.1.10, Jun 1979.

[17] W. Lee, M. Frank, V. Lee, K. Mackenzie, and L. Rudolph, *"Implications of I/O for gang scheduled workloads"*. In *Job Scheduling Strategies for Parallel Processing*, D. G. Feitelson and L. Rudolph (eds.), pp. 215–237, Springer Verlag, 1997. Lect. Notes Comput. Sci. vol. 1291.

[18] V. Lo, J. Mache, and K. Windisch, *"A comparative study of real workload traces and synthetic workload models for parallel job scheduling"*. In *Job Scheduling Strategies for Parallel Processing*, D. G. Feitelson and L. Rudolph (eds.), pp. 25–47, Springer Verlag, 1998. Lect. Notes Comput. Sci. vol. 1459.

[19] T. D. Nguyen, R. Vaswani, and J. Zahorjan, *"Parallel application characterization for multiprocessor scheduling policy design"*. In *Job Scheduling Strategies for Parallel Processing*, D. G. Feitelson and L. Rudolph (eds.), pp. 175–199, Springer-Verlag, 1996. Lect. Notes Comput. Sci. vol. 1162.

[20] E. W. Parsons and K. C. Sevcik, "*Multiprocessor scheduling for high-variability service time distributions*". In *Job Scheduling Strategies for Parallel Processing*, D. G. Feitelson and L. Rudolph (eds.), pp. 127–145, Springer-Verlag, 1995. Lect. Notes Comput. Sci. vol. 949.

[21] K. C. Sevcik, "*Application scheduling and processor allocation in multiprogrammed parallel processing systems*". *Performance Evaluation* **19(2-3)**, pp. 107–140, Mar 1994.

A Comparative Study of Real Workload Traces and Synthetic Workload Models for Parallel Job Scheduling *

Virginia Lo, Jens Mache, and Kurt Windisch

Department of Computer and Information Science
University of Oregon, Eugene, OR 97403
{lo, jens, kurtw}@cs.uoregon.edu

Abstract. Two basic approaches are taken when modeling workloads in simulation-based performance evaluation of parallel job scheduling algorithms: (1) a carefully reconstructed trace from a real supercomputer can provide a very realistic job stream, or (2) a flexible synthetic model that attempts to capture the behavior of observed workloads can be devised. Both approaches require that accurate statistical observations be made and that the researcher be aware of the applicability of a given trace for his or her experimental goals.

In this paper, we compare a number of real workload traces and synthetic workload models currently used to evaluate job scheduling and allocation strategies. Our results indicate that the choice of workload model *alone* – real workload trace versus synthetic workload models – did not significantly affect the relative performance of the algorithms in this study (two scheduling algorithms and three static processor allocation algorithms). Almost all traces and models gave the same ranking of algorithms from best to worst. However, two specific workload characteristics were found to significantly affect algorithm performance: (a) proportion of power-of-two job sizes and (b) degree of correlation between job size and job runtime. When used in the experimental evaluation of resource management algorithms, workloads differing in these two characteristics may lead to discrepant conclusions.

1 Introduction

Simulation-based performance evaluation of parallel job scheduling strategies is traditionally carried out using a synthetic workload model to generate a stream of incoming jobs with associated job characteristics. Despite the acknowledged rigor of simulation testing using stochastically generated workloads, there has been a pressing need for more realistic performance evaluation to further validate algorithm performance. Recently, the use of massively parallel machines for high performance computing has grown rapidly, both in numbers and in the maturity of the user communities. Systems administrators at national labs and

---

* This research was sponsored by NSF grant MIP-9108528.

Dror G. Feitelson, Larry Rudolph (Eds.): JSSPP'98, LNCS 1459, pp. 25–46, 1998.
© Springer-Verlag Berlin Heidelberg 1998

supercomputing center sites have collected large amounts of workload trace data and released them for use in the evaluation of new resource management algorithms. Thus, researchers in performance evaluation have at their disposal two valid methods for conducting simulations:

(1) Use of **real workload traces** gathered from scientific production runs on real supercomputers and carefully reconstructed for use in simulation testing.

(2) Use of **synthetic workload models** that use probability distributions to generate workload data. We refer to the earliest synthetic workload models as "naive" because they were based on little or no knowledge of real trace characteristics (due to the fact that real traces didn't exist). Recently, more realistic synthetic models have been developed in which the model and its parameters have been abstracted through careful analysis of real workload data from production machines.

Both approaches require that many assumptions and accurate statistical observations be made, and that the modeler understands well the profile of the targeted, real workload. Inaccurate assumptions or minor perturbations in any proposed model may yield a workload that provides a poor evaluation of scheduling strategies on the targeted system. Yet, there exists very little published literature that offers guidance to researchers concerning the use of real workload traces and synthetic workload models for experimentation with scheduling algorithms.

Our work aims to fill this void. Our goals are to determine the degree of influence of workload choice and workload characteristics on performance and, where possible, to isolate the causes of observed differences in performance results. We will begin to address issues such as those listed below and to propose some rules-of-thumb to help guide the use of these workload traces and models in simulation testing of scheduling algorithms.

- **Real workload traces versus synthetic workload models:** When should one use real traces and when should one use synthetic workloads? Do the results of simulation with these two types of workloads reinforce each other? If not, is it due to biases in the workload traces or inadequacies in the synthetic model?
- **Universality of workload traces:** Given a choice among real workload traces from different sites, how does one know which trace to use? If performance evaluation results are discrepant, how does one know which results are valid?
- **Sensitivity of scheduling algorithm performance to workload characteristics:** What specific workload characteristics might bias performance results?

The experiments reported in this paper compare many real workload traces and synthetic workload models, both analytically and through simulation, observing their effects on the performance evaluation of several classes of scheduling and allocation strategies. Included were two scheduling algorithms: First Come First Served and ScanUp [16], a multi-level queuing algorithm, and three static allocation strategies: First Fit [24], Frame Sliding [3] , and Paging [17].

The real traces were captured from four production machines in use for scientific computing at research labs and supercomputer sites around the world (two IBM SP-2s, an Intel Paragon, and a Cray T3E). The synthetic models include "naive" models and those developed by Downey [6, 5] and Feitelson [7] based on their careful analyses of traces from production machines.

We conducted five distinct experiments: (a) real workload traces versus synthetic workload models; (b) realistic synthetic workload models versus naive synthetic models; (c) a comparison of real workload traces across disjoint time periods (at the same site); (d) a comparison of real workload traces across sites; and (e) effects of specific workload characteristics: power-of-two jobsizes and correlation between jobsize and runtime. These experiments led us to the following general observations; more details are discussed in Section 5.

- The choice of workload *alone* did not significantly affect the relative performance of the resource management algorithms. Almost all workloads (real or synthetic, across sites, and for different time periods at the same site) ranked the scheduling and allocation algorithms in the same order from best to worst with respect to response time and system utilization. The choice of workload did yield differences in more subtle aspects of algorithm performance.
- Two critical workload characteristics were found to significantly affect algorithm performance: (a) proportion of power-of-two job sizes and (b) degree of correlation between job size and job run time. When used in the experimental evaluation of resource management algorithms, workloads differing in these two characteristics may lead to discrepant conclusions.

As we shall see, for both real traces and synthetic models, it is critical that one be aware of specific trace characteristics and the applicability of a given trace for the researcher's experimental goals.

The remainder of this paper is organized as follows: Section 2 gives the background for this study and surveys related work; Section 3 discusses real workload traces and synthetic workload models, and describes the specific traces and models used in this study. In Section 4 we describe our experiments, including the resource management strategies and performance metrics used. Section 5 discusses our experimental results, and Section 6 gives our conclusions.

2   Background and Related Work

This project was motivated by our desire to improve the quality of our own work in performance evaluation of scheduling algorithms and to help facilitate the comparability of (sometimes contradictory) results obtained in the scheduling community. We would like to help develop a benchmark suite of real workload traces and synthetic models for use in the resource management community.

Our focus is on job-oriented resource management for distributed memory parallel machines, and on job-oriented workloads, where a job consists of a collection of one or more computational tasks to be run in parallel. The *job scheduling strategy* involves the decision about which of many queued jobs is next to be allocated resources. Job scheduling policies range from the classic First-Come First Served algorithm to complex, multi-level queue models such as those implemented by scheduling systems such as NQS, Load Leveler, PBS or EASY [4, 14, 12, 13]. The *job allocation strategy* selects the set of processors to be allocated to the job based on its jobsize request. We restrict our attention to static allocation strategies rather than adaptive strategies: the former simply allocate the requested number of processors.[1] Static allocation strategies fall into two classes: contiguous and non-contiguous, based on whether or not the set of allocated processors are directly connected by links in the interconnection network. Research in job scheduling and processor allocation is thoroughly surveyed in [8]; more recent work in this area includes that reported in [10] as well as our own [17, 22, 18]. This project is distinguished from our previous work in that we evaluate the experimental method, not the scheduling techniques themselves.

Some of the first researchers to use real traces from production machines to drive their simulations include [19, 1, 18]. At the same time, analysis of this emerging body of trace data was conducted by Feitelson and Downey in the development of realistic synthetic workload models. Feitelson's model combines observations of five different parallel supercomputers in the evaluation of gang scheduling strategies [7], and Downey's model is based on detailed analysis of the SDSC Paragon, utilized in experiments evaluating adaptive job scheduling algorithms [6, 5]. The synthetic workload models developed by Downey and Feitelson are used in our experiments and are discussed in more detail in Section 4.

Several studies statistically analyzed workload traces from production use of real parallel supercomputers. Feitelson and Nitzberg analyzed the workload from an Intel iPSC/860 located at NASA Ames, providing the first widely available workload measurements from a real system [9]. Windisch et. al. [21] continued this effort by analyzing traces from the Intel Paragon at the San Diego Supercomputer Center (SDSC), and comparing the workload to that of the NASA iPSC/860. The workload characteristics analyzed in these studies included general job mix, resource usage, system utilization and multiprogramming level, runtime distribution, job submission statistics, and interarrival time distributions. Overall, the profiles of the two workloads were surprisingly similar. Hotovy analyzed the evolution of the workload on an IBM SP-2 at the Cornell Theory Center (CTC), concluding that workloads change in significant ways over time, requiring adaptations in the scheduling mechanisms for efficient operation [11].

A few of the many studies of job scheduling and processor allocation algorithms have offered insights into the effects of workload characteristics on those

---

[1] Adaptive allocation strategies for moldable jobs allocate a number of processors that is a function of the number of free processors in the system and of characteristics of the job.

algorithms. Of special interest to our study is Krueger's work on scheduling and allocation performance under workloads exhibiting negative correlations between jobsize and runtimes [16]. As we shall see, our work further explains some of the phenomena he observed. The only recent study that we know of that has focused on the experimental methodology itself, i.e., the effect choice of workload has on scheduling performance results, is that of Chiang et. al. [2]. They compare the performance of several scheduling strategies over a wide range of workload parameters and conclude that the discrepancies among various studies are due to differences in the (synthetic) workloads used for performance evaluation. Neither Krueger nor Chiang studied the effect of real workload traces on performance.

3   Workloads

A workload trace is a record of resource usage data about a stream of parallel and sequential jobs that were submitted to and run on a given message-passing parallel machine. Each job arrives, executes on one or more nodes for a period of time, and then departs the system. The resources requested by these jobs typically include jobsize (the number of requested processors), runtime, memory requirements, I/O devices such as disks or network interfaces, and software resources. Furthermore, every job in a workload is associated with an arrival time, indicating when it was submitted to the scheduler for consideration.

Real workload traces captured from production machines can potentially provide a very high level of realism when used directly in performance evaluation experiments. However, this usage comes with a number of caveats in the interpretation of performance results. A given trace is the product of an existing scheduling policy and thus is biased or affected by that policy. Human factors must be considered when analyzing or utilizing workload data: human users often adapt their resource demands to the system or the scheduling policies, in ways that do not reflect the actual needs of the job. Finally, workload traces may not discriminate between a job's direct resource needs and the resources utilized by the operating system on behalf of the job; furthermore, traces may not distinguish between inherent versus contention-related resource usage.

Synthetic workload models offer the convenience of a much more manageable experimental medium that is free of the idiosyncratic site-specific behavior of production traces. This is both its advantage and a potential point of criticism – the use of a tractable synthetic model provides a neutral, more universal experimental environment but does not yield the realism and pragmatic testing desired by some researchers. Sometimes the mathematical modeling smoothes out perturbations that it is desirable to investigate.

Therefore, researchers should be cognizant of the details surrounding the trace and consider how applicable a given trace is as a model of the target system. They need to be mindful of their specific experimental goals; performance evaluation by a site administrator at one of the supercomputing centers has a much more focused and pragmatic goal than that performed by an academic researcher developing new algorithms for future machines and environments.

3.1 Real Workload Traces

The traces described below were collected from a variety of machines at several national labs and supercomputing sites in the United States and Europe. The type of workload at all the sites consisted of scientific applications ranging from numerical aerodynamic simulations to elementary particle physics. Trace data was collected through a batch scheduling agent such as the Network Queuing System, Load Leveler, PBS, or EASY. Traces that have been used for trace-driven simulation were sanitized to remove user specific information and pre-processed to correct for system downtimes, sporadic missing data, and then reformatted for use in the simulator. In some cases, trace data may also be manipulated in order to study specific phenomena (e.g. selective filtering to remove interactive jobs). We briefly summarize the machine architecture, user environment, and scheduling policies in force at each site. Our experiments used traces from the first four machines in the list.

- **SDSC Intel Paragon**: The San Diego Supercomputer Center houses a 416 node Paragon machine. The scheduling policies are implemented through the Network Queuing System (NQS) which queues jobs according to power-of-two jobsizes, maximum runtime, and memory requirements (16 MB vs. 32 MB nodes). The (static) allocation algorithm is a block-based non-contiguous strategy. The SDSC traces were taken from 1995-1996, in three-month groups. [21, 20]
- **CTC IBM SP-2**: The Cornell Theory Center IBM SP-2 machine has 512 nodes connected by a high performance switch. The traces come from two periods: July 1994-March 1995 with scheduling managed by IBM's LoadLeveller and July 1995-Feb 1996 under LoadLeveller and Easy [11].
- **NASA Ames IBM SP-2**: The NASA Ames IBM SP-2 machine has 160 nodes connected by a high performance switch. The traces cover two years, from August 1995 to August 1997. The scheduling policies are implemented through the Portable Batch System (PBS) [15].
- **KFA Cray T3E**: The Forschungszentrum Jülich has a 512 node CRAY T3E. Jobs are submitted through NQS. Job queues differ in maximum (power-of-two) jobsize and maximum runtime. The (static) allocation algorithm is contiguous. The traces were taken from March 1997 - September 1997.
- Other traces include those from the iPSC/860 at NASA Ames NAS, a 128 node hypercube; the ETH Paragon, a 96 node mesh; the Cray T3D at Pittsburgh Supercomputing Center, a 512 node torus-based machine; Argonne National Laboratory's 128 node IBM SP-1, a 512 node CM-5; and 126 node shared memory BBN Butterfly at Lawrence Livermore National Laboratory's BBN Butterfly.

3.2 Synthetic Workload Models

Workload modeling of the nature required for resource management in distributed memory parallel machines is in its infancy due to prior lack of trace data available for analysis. For the most part, performance evaluation studies have relied on "naive" synthetic models, using classic probability distributions such as exponential and uniform.

Dror Feitelson [7] analyzed trace data from five of the above machines, specifically the NASA iPSC/860, ANL IBM SP-1, SDSC Paragon, LLNL Butterfly, and ETH Paragon. His goal was to derive probabilistic models for use in his experiments with gang scheduling algorithms. Feitelson proposed a harmonic distribution to model jobsizes, and then hand tailored the model to emphasize small job sizes and other "interesting sizes" that he observed across all five machines. These included powers-of-two, squares, multiples of 10, and full system size requests.

He used a two-stage hyperexponential distribution to model runtimes and enforced a linear relationship between jobsize and the probability of using the distribution with the higher mean. This decision was based on observations of a strong correlation between jobsize and job runtime on the NASA iPSC/860 and a weak correlation on the ANL SP-1 and SDSC Paragon. (Our results relating to correlation of jobsize and runtime are discussed in Section 5.)

Feitelson also modeled user job submission behavior, using a Zipf distribution to model repeated submissions of the same job (job *runlength*). We note that Feitelson chose to use an exponential distribution to model interarrival times; our own studies of workload data have shown this assumption to be strongly justified [21].

Allen Downey [6, 5] focused his analysis on two machines, the SDSC Paragon and the CTC SP-2. He proposed a uniform-log distribution for modeling job lifetimes (approximated by the product of runtime and number of processors). From his analysis of the SDSC trace data, he observed that this distribution is accurate except for very small and very large jobs. Downey's curve-fitting analysis eliminated the smallest 10% and largest 10% of jobs. He used this model to predict queue waiting times and verified the accuracy of his model using the SDSC workload data [2]. From his comparison of the SDSC and CTC workloads, he noticed that the same (uniform-log) model is accurate for both machines/sites, but the specific parameters differ significantly. Downey warned that researchers will need to be very careful about use of these models, recommending that a workload derived from one system should not be used to evaluate another. We will discuss this precaution further in Section 5.

In a second study of the same machines, Downey derived a uniform-log distribution for job cluster size (which we call jobsize) by smoothing out the observed step function that characterized the raw trace data. He argued that the power-of-two cluster sizes responsible for the step function reflected the power-of-two NQS job queues, not the actual cluster size requirements of the jobs. This distribution and additional parameters involving variance in job parallelism were used to develop a stochastic model for simulation of several known adaptive

---

[2] Downey acknowledges that his results are prejudiced because he uses the same SDSC trace to derive the prediction model and to evaluate it.

strategies.[3] Downey's goal was to analyze the performance of these strategies in terms of their sensitivity to specific workload characteristics.

Finally, the types of "naive" workload models that have been used over the past decade of scheduling research include the following: The vast majority of researchers have used exponential distributions to model interarrival times. Jobsizes have been modeled using a variety of probabilistic models including uniform, uniform with step functions, normal, geometric, and exponential, while runtimes have been modeled with exponential and hyperexponential distributions.

4   Experiments

4.1   Experimental Method and ProcSimity Simulator

In our experiments we observed the performance of various resource management algorithms through simulation using real workload traces and compared those results with simulations of the same algorithms using synthetic models. The real workload traces that we used were the first four described in Section 3. In all cases, we used batch jobs only, removing the interactive jobs from the trace, since our focus is on batch scheduling. (Interactive jobs tend to have drastically different workload characteristics.) The synthetic models used in these experiments were those of Feitelson, Downey, and two naive models. The specific workload information that was used as input to the scheduling and allocation algorithms included job arrival time, jobsize and job runtime. Our simulator modeled a stream of jobs that arrive, execute for a period of time, and then depart the system. We did not model message-passing behavior in this study.

We conducted five distinct experiments:

- real workload traces versus synthetic workload models
- realistic synthetic workload models versus naive synthetic models
- a comparison of real workload traces across disjoint time periods (at the same site)
- a comparison of real workload traces across sites
- effects of specific workload characteristics: power-of-two jobsizes and correlation between jobsize and runtime.

For all five experiments, we simulated a mesh topology. This mesh was used in all of the experiments involving real workload traces, even if the trace was captured from a machine with a different architecture. For the studies involving the synthetic workloads and the SDSC workloads, we simulated a 16×22 mesh to match the size of the SDSC Paragon batch partition. For studies involving the CTC workload, we used a 16×27 mesh to match the size (but not the

---

[3] The type of allocation strategies studied by Downey are different from those studied in this paper. Downey focused on allocation for moldable jobs, where a job's cluster size is based on the number of available processors or job characteristics. We focus on static allocations in which the jobsize is a fixed request.

topology) of the CTC SP-2 machine. For the experiment investigating power of two jobsizes, we used a 32 × 32 mesh.

All experiments were conducted using ProcSimity [23], a simulation tool we developed for evaluating job scheduling and processor allocation algorithms for distributed memory parallel machines. ProcSimity models a variety of network topologies and several current flow control and routing technologies. ProcSimity supports both synthetic job streams and trace-driven simulation. Our simulator has been in use for several years at the University of Oregon and is currently in use at a number of research sites including the Ministry of International Trade and Industry in Japan, ETH Zurich, and academic institutions in the United States.

4.2 Resource Management Strategies

We evaluated the performance of two scheduling algorithms and three static allocation strategies, varying the type of workload used to drive the simulations. A given job scheduling strategy determines which of many queued jobs is admitted to the system for execution. The allocation strategy selects a subset of the physical processors for allocation to that job. We restricted our attention to static allocation strategies in which the number of processors assigned to a job is fixed for the lifetime of the job.

Job Scheduling Strategies

- **FCFS** is the classic First Come First Served Scheduling Algorithm. FCFS is a simple, single queue algorithm commonly used as a standard of comparison or as a default algorithm.
- **ScanUp** [16] is a multi-queue job scheduling strategy in which jobs are queued by jobsize. The scheduler services one queue at a time, from smallest to largest, serving only those jobs that arrived in a given queue *before* it selected that queue (thereby avoiding starvation). When it completes serving the largest job queue, it begins again with the smallest. ScanUp was shown to outperform a wide range of scheduling algorithms.

Allocation Strategies

Static allocation strategies can be classified as contiguous or non-contiguous, based on whether or not the set of allocated processors are directly connected by communication links in the interconnection network.

- **Frame Sliding** [3] searches for a rectangular block of processors by sliding a window of the desired size across the mesh in horizontal and vertical strides based on the width and height of the requested rectangle. Frame Sliding is a contiguous strategy with marginal performance.
- **First Fit** [24] searches for a contiguous block of processors starting at a reference point (e.g. lower left hand corner of the mesh). First Fit was shown to have the best performance among all contiguous strategies in [17].

- **Paging** allocates processors by scanning the free list of processors in a fixed order and allocating them to the job without regard to their contiguity. Paging was shown to have the best performance among all non-contiguous allocation strategies in [17][4]. Because we do not model message-passing contention in this study, its performance is the same as that of the whole class of purely non-contiguous algorithms.

4.3 Performance Metrics

Performance was measured using the following metrics:

- **average processor utilization**: the percentage of processors allocated to jobs at any given time, averaged over the entire workload.
- **average response time**: the elapsed time from when a job arrives for scheduling to when it completes execution, averaged over the entire workload. Response time includes both time spent in waiting queues and time spent in execution.
- **slowdown ratio**: $\frac{average\ response\ time}{average\ runtime}$. This metric normalizes average response time so that results are more easily compared across workloads. This metric is not the same as average slowdown. The differences and the reason we chose slowdown ratio are discussed below.
- **system load**: $\lambda\ \frac{E[runtime*jobsize]}{N}$ where λ is the arrival rate and N is the system size (total number of processors). This metric measures the offered load relative to the size of the system, and appears as the independent variable in the graphs of experimental results.
- **sustainable load**: the system load value below which average job response times remain within *reasonable* bounds.

While we measured average response times in all experiments, the graphs presented in this paper use *slowdown ratio* as the dependent variable (on the y axis). An alternative metric is *average slowdown*, the expected value of the quotient response time divided by runtime. We found that average slowdown is a heavy-tailed distribution with very large values for outlier data points. These outliers turned out to be jobs with very short runtimes (in the order of seconds) whose response time was huge (in the order of tens of hours) because they were blocked in the waiting queue behind a large and long-running job. We considered using order statistics (e.g. displaying results for the 90% quantile), but found slowdown ratio to be more suitable for this paper.[5]

It is important to realize that sustainable load, the system load value below which average response time remains within *reasonable* bounds, is an important focal point in performance evaluation. This critical point is visible as the "knee" in the graphs of slowdown ratio and system utilization. Below the critical point,

---

[4] Since that time we have developed a superior algorithm called MC [18] that is contiguous when a contiguous block exists, but non-contiguous otherwise.

[5] We plan to look further into the relative merits and utility of various performance metrics.

the system load is at manageable levels so that the increase in job response time is gradual and utilization continues to improve. At the knee, the job response time suddenly begins to grow rapidly toward infinity. By the same token, the system utilization levels off since the system is saturated with work. Thus, in evaluating the relative performance of resource management strategies, we focus our analysis on the phenomena observed near this saturation point.

Table 1. Ranking of Scheduling and Allocation Algorithms

Strategy	Synthetic models				SDSC traces	CTC traces	NAS traces
	N1	N2	D	F	S1 - S8	C1 - C2	N1 - N3
Paging/ScanUp	1	1	1	1	2	1	1
Paging/FCFS	2	2	2	2	1	2	2
FF/ScanUp	3	3	3	3	3	3	3
FS/ScanUp	4	4	4	4	4	4	4
FF/FCFS	5	5	5	5	5	5	5
FS/FCFS	6	6	6	6	6	6	6

5   Results

5.1   Real Workload Traces Versus Synthetic Workload Models

Our experiments showed that the choice of workload trace *alone* did not affect the relative performance of the selected resource management algorithms. Almost all workloads (real or synthetic, across sites, and for different time periods at the same site) ranked the algorithms in the same order from best to worst with respect to slowdown ratio and system utilization. See Table 1. In addition, all workloads strongly discriminated among the three allocation algorithms, with non-contiguous Paging clearly outperforming First Fit, and First Fit clearly outperforming Frame Sliding. The distinctions between the two scheduling algorithms were consistent across workloads but not as pronounced, with ScanUp usually outperforming First Come First Served. In cases where rankings were inconsistent, we conducted further experiments to identify causes for the differences. These are discussed in Section 5.5.

5.2   Realistic Synthetic Models Versus Naive Synthetic Models

Table 2 gives the probability model and values of associated parameters for each of the four synthetic models that we tested. Two of these models, Downey and Feitelson, were realistic models derived through careful analysis of real workload traces; two were naive models widely used in the scheduling literature. Downey did not model job runtimes directly but derived a uniform log model for job

Table 2. Models, means, and parameters for the four stochastic workloads

Model	Jobsize	Runtime	Inter-arrivals
Naive-1	uniform	exponential	exponential
	$\mu = 98.2$ nodes	$\mu = 1.0$-8.0	$\mu = 1.0$
Naive-2	exponential	exponential	exponential
	$\mu = 47.1$ nodes	$\mu = 1.0$-8.0	$\mu = 1.0$
Downey	uniform log	uniform log	exponential
	$\mu = 61.26$ nodes	$\mu = 7142.72$ sec.	observed $\mu = 967$ sec.
			varied
Feitelson	harmonic	2-stage hyper-exponential	exponential
	hand-tailored		
	$\mu = 22.75$ nodes	$\mu = 1289.49$ sec.	$\mu =$ varied

lifetimes. We also determined that a uniform log model was accurate for runtimes by using linear regression over job runtimes from the SDSC Paragon Trace (method of least squares). The maximum runtime was limited to 12 hours, the limit for the trace from which Downey's model was derived. We did not model the repeated job submissions used by Feitelson (runlength).

As shown in Table 1, all four synthetic models ranked the scheduling and allocation algorithms in the same order from best to worst. In Figure 1 it is interesting to note that results from the two realistic synthetic models were similar to each other as were results from the two naive models. This was true despite the fact that each modeled jobsize and job runtime with very different probability distributions. For example, with respect to system utilization, the two Naive models show the noncontiguous allocation strategies clearly outperforming the contiguous ones, with the choice of scheduling algorithm having a lesser effect. This can be seen in Figure 1 in which the algorithms cluster into two groups based on allocation strategy. In contrast, the Downey and Feitelson models show the scheduling algorithm having a more pronounced effect on performance.

The Naive models also differed from Downey and Feitelson's realistic synthetic models with respect to performance under increasing system loads. With the Naive models, performance of the system degrades more gradually as system loads approach 1.0, while with the two realistic synthetic models, slowdown ratios increase much more rapidly and earlier. As discussed in Section 5.5, these differences might be attributed to differences in two specific characteristics of the workload models.

Thus, it appears that the choice of synthetic model *alone* does not affect the overall ranking of scheduling and allocation strategies, despite the fact that they may use very different probability distributions in their models. The choice of synthetic model does affect more subtle aspects of algorithm performance.

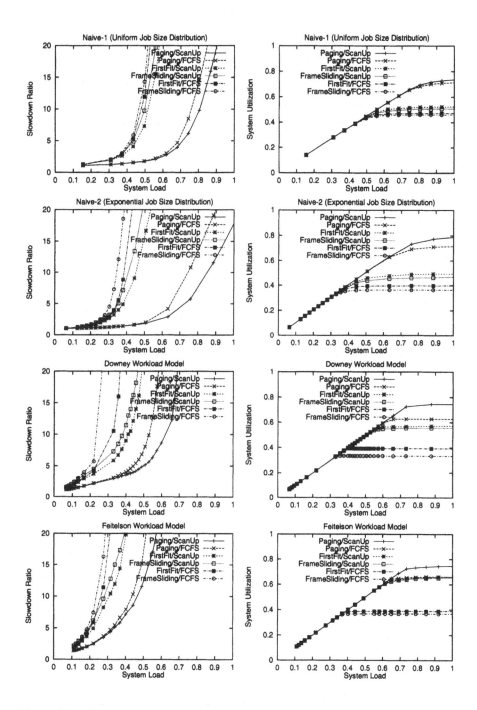

Fig. 1. Four Synthetic Workload Models: Naive1, Naive2, Downey, and Feitelson

5.3   Real Workload Traces over Disjoint Time Periods (at a Single Site)

In this experiment, we compared performance results from the SDSC Paragon traces over eight quarters in 1995 and 1996. We observed highly consistent results for all eight quarters, both in ranking and detailed behavior of scheduling strategies. Due to space limitations we only show graphs for the first quarter of 1995 and the last quarter of 1996 (see Figure 2). The strong consistency in performance results is especially notable given the variation in workload characteristics among the eight quarterly profiles. Table 3 shows the variation in means for jobsize, runtime, and interarrival times and for system load among the quarterly workloads.

We did the same comparison for the CTC SP-2 over two eight month periods in 1994-95 and 1995-96, respectively. The results were similar to those of the SDSC experiments. This is especially interesting because the scheduler changed from LoadLeveller to LoadLeveller/EASY.

We conclude that workload traces from the same site but different time periods are consistent in their evaluation of scheduling algorithms because the workload profile at a given site tend to be fairly stable over time (assuming a mature production site). However, as we discuss below in Section 5.5, there are other workload characteristics that are critical for performance.

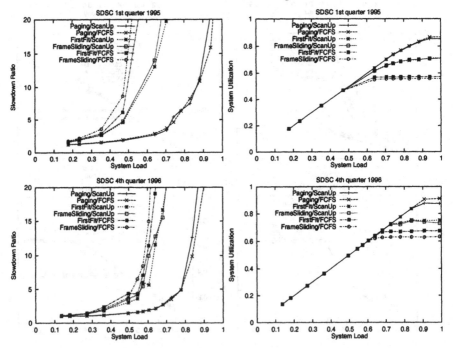

Fig. 2. SDSC 1st Quarter 1995 and 4th Quarter 1996

Table 3. SDSC Workload Characteristics by Quarter

Quarter	Mean Jobsize (nodes)	Mean Runtime (secs)	Mean Interarrival (secs)	Mean Sys.Load
1995 Q1	22	8689	1100	.705
1995 Q2	21	8305	1042	.744
1995 Q3	29	8859	1516	.741
1995 Q4	32	8245	1836	.752
1996 Q1	23	12722	1590	.782
1996 Q2	18	11376	1130	.865
1996 Q3	26	9660	1598	.698
1996 Q4	15	10945	1301	.545

5.4 A Comparison of Real Workload Traces Across Sites and Machines

Our goal for this set of experiments was to compare performance results based on real workload traces from different machines at different sites. The workload traces came from the following machines: SDSC Paragon, NASA Ames NAS IBM SP-2, Cornell Theory Center IBM SP-2, and KFA Cray T3E (see descriptions of each machine and user environment in Section 3).[6]

This set of experiments showed that, with one exception, the ranking of the selected scheduling and allocation algorithms was not affected by the specific workload trace used. (See Table 1.) The exception occurred on the SDSC Paragon for which FCFS slightly outperformed ScanUp as the top ranking algorithm; for the NAS and CTC workloads, ScanUp was the best algorithm as was true for all the synthetic traces as well.

All three workloads showed clear discrimination for non-contiguous allocation algorithms over contiguous algorithms; however, the degree of discrimination varied among the different workloads. It is also interesting to look at the performance of the FCFS algorithm alone. For the contiguous allocation algorithms (First Fit and Frame Sliding), FCFS achieved utilization levels of at best 40% on the NAS and CTC machines, but reached over 60% on the SDSC. See Figure 3.

Looking at the profiles of the workloads in Table 5, we found distinct differences in two areas, motivating the last set of experiments.

5.5 Effects of Specific Workload Characteristics

Effects of Proportion of Power-of-Two Jobsizes. One of the most obvious differences among workloads was the proportion of power-of-two jobsizes. Downey's model smoothed out the power-of-two step function while Feitelson's

---

[6] We are still running experiments with KFA T3E.

emphasized these sizes. Among the production traces, the proportion of power-of-two jobsizes was very high, ranging from 84.2% for SDSC to 100% for the iPSC/860, a hypercube machine.

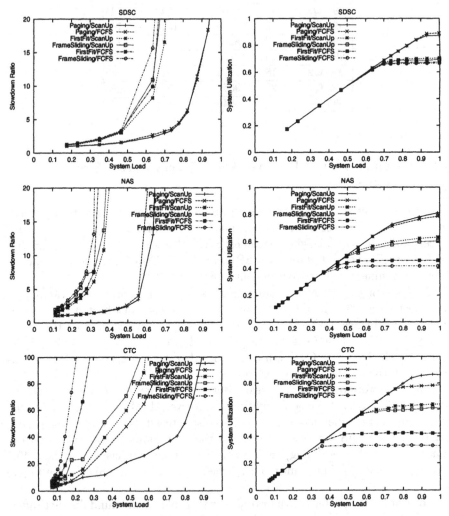

Fig. 3. SDSC Paragon versus NAS SP-2 versus CTC SP-2

We looked into the effect power-of-two jobsizes have on performance evaluation by creating three synthetic traces: one in which jobsize is taken from an exponential distribution, one forced to have a minimum of 50% power-of-two jobsizes, and one forced to have 100% power-of-two jobsizes. The traces for 50% and 100% sets were created so that the step function matched the initial exponential distribution when smoothed. As seen in Table 4, as power-of-two dominance increases, so do utilization levels for all resource management algorithms. As a result, the sustainable load also increases with increasing dominance of power-of-two jobsizes.

Another interesting phenomenon is the fact that with a 100% power-of-two job mix, it is the scheduling strategy (not allocation strategy) that determines performance. ScanUp outperforms First Come First Serve, regardless of allocation strategy. This result is consistent with that of [16] in their experiments with scheduling and allocation algorithms for the hypercube.

Table 4. Effects of Power-of-two Jobsizes on System Utilization and Sustainable Load. Minimum and maximum utilization levels are across all algorithms. Sustainable loads are shown for the worst performing algorithm FS/FCFS and the best performing algorithm Paging/ScanUp.

Percent Power-of-2	Min Util.	Max Util.	Sust.Load FS/FCFS	Sust.Load Paging/ScanUp
3.4%	41%	78%	.36	.74
51.7%	45%	84%	.39	.82
100%	63%	90%	.48	.93

Effects of Degree of Correlation Between Jobsize and Runtime. Degree of correlation between jobsize and runtime is of interest in the scheduling community because it reflects certain assumptions about the work model and the type of scheduling algorithms needed. The *fixed work model* and the notion of adaptive scheduling for *moldable jobs* carry an implicit assumption that jobsize and runtime are negatively correlated since they assume that the more processors given to a job, the more quickly it will finish execution. The *independent work model* presumes that jobsize is unrelated to job runtime (zero correlation).

We note that a common assumption for many large production workloads is that jobsize and runtime are positively correlated. Table 5 shows the range of correlation coefficients relating jobsize to job runtime for some of the real workloads and synthetic models reported in this paper. We used Pearson's r, which presumes a linear relationship between the variables, to compute the correlations. In reality, this relationship does not necessarily hold. Feitelson [7] noted a strong positive correlation for the NAS iPSC/860 trace but found much weaker relationships for other traces.

To test the effect of correlation on performance evaluation, we used the SDSC workload as a base and manipulated the data to achieve correlations of -1, 0, and +1 (see Figure 4). Our experiments show that for highly positively correlated workloads, Krueger's ScanUp algorithm, the best performing strategy in all other studies, performed worse than FCFS for all three allocation strategies!!

Table 5. Trace Characteristics

Trace	Runtime and Jobsize Correlation Coefficient	Percent Power-of-2 Jobs
NAS iPSC/860	strongly pos.	100.0%
SDSC Paragon	0.20 - 0.35	84.2%
CTC SP-2	≈ 0	88.5%
NAS SP-2	≈ 0	51.2%
Feitelson	0.19	84.9%
Downey	0	16.9%
Naive1	0	6.3%
Naive 2	0	20.2%

The explanation lies in the correlation. Recall that ScanUp uses multi-level queues, with each queue associated with a specific jobsize, from small to large. Thus, with a strongly positive correlation, large, long-running jobs arrive in the large-jobs queue while small, short-running jobs arrive in the small-jobs queue. While ScanUp is serving the large-jobs queue, smaller sized jobs arrive at the other queues. However, because all the large jobs are also long-running, these smaller queues fill up and the response time for these smaller jobs increases rapidly, resulting in poor performance. In addition, when ScanUp serves several large jobs in a row, fragmentation of the processor space is high, also diminishing utilization. Thus, for positively correlated workloads, ScanUp suffers.

Looking back at Krueger's performance evaluation experiments for ScanUp, we see that he simulated ScanUp under non-correlated and negatively correlated workload models, the latter based on the fixed work model. Thus, our results are complementary to Krueger's and together show that the performance of algorithms is critically dependent on the correlation.

The effect of correlation between jobsize and runtime on performance results is also illustrated by examining Krueger's statement that "scheduling is more important than allocation." Our results confirm what Krueger concluded, however, only for negatively correlated workloads. In that case, ScanUp did best under all three allocation strategies. However, for non-negatively correlated workloads, scheduling did not dominate.

The key observation is that correlation between jobsize and runtime has strong effects on performance results. Thus, researchers need to take this factor into consideration when choosing or designing workloads and when evaluating algorithm performance.

6   Conclusions and Future Work

In this paper we investigated the use of real workload traces and synthetic workload models for performance evaluation of several parallel job scheduling algorithms. Our long term goal is the development of guidelines for the effective use of traces and models in scheduling research.

Our experiments showed that the choice of workload *alone* – real trace versus synthetic model – did not significantly affect the relative performance of the selected resource management algorithms (FCFS and ScanUp scheduling; First Fit, Frame Sliding, and Paging allocation). Almost all workloads ranked the algorithms in the same order from best to worst with respect to response time, slowdown, and system utilization.

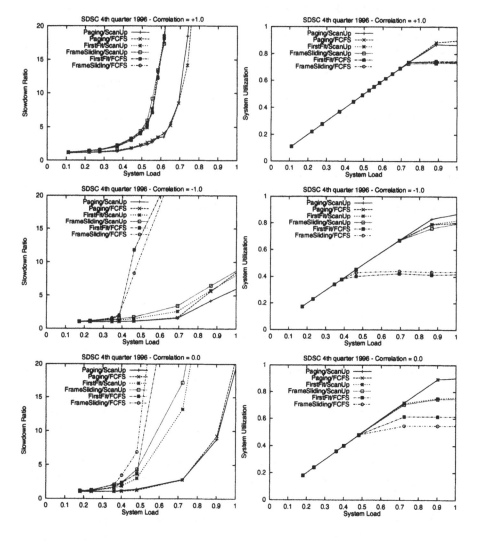

Fig. 4. Effects of Correlation between Jobsize and Runtime

It also appears that the choice of synthetic model *alone* does not affect the overall ranking of these scheduling and allocation strategies, despite the fact that they may use very different probability distributions in their models. The choice of synthetic model does affect more subtle aspects of algorithm performance.

We saw that workload traces from the same site but different time periods are consistent in their evaluation of scheduling algorithms because the workload profile at a given site tends to be fairly stable over time (assuming a mature production site).

However, our experiments revealed clear differences in performance using real workload traces from different machines at different sites. Our investigation of the causes of this inconsistent behavior led us to two factors which significantly affect performance evaluation results:

- As the **proportion of power-of-two jobs** in the workload increases, so does system utilization. As a result, the sustainable load also increases with increasing dominance of power-of-two jobsizes.
- We also found that **correlation between jobsize and runtime** has strong effects on performance results. Scheduling algorithms that did well on a workload with strong positive correlation did worse on a negatively correlated workload, and vice versa.

Taken together, these results show that great care must be taken in the use of both realistic workload traces and synthetic workload models. Naive synthetic workload models are useful in qualitative performance analysis, giving a high level evaluation of algorithm performance. Realistic synthetic workload models provide more detailed performance analysis. Both provide a convenient experimental medium in which parameters are more easily controlled. It is critical, however, that the researcher be aware of the profile of the workload produced by manipulation of the parameters in the context of his experimental goals.

Real workload traces provide a much more realistic simulation testbed but again precautions are necessary. The idiosyncrasies of a trace from one site may make it unsuitable for algorithm testing at another site. In addition, real traces must be carefully prepared for use in simulation testing of algorithms to remove biases that affect performance results.

The experiments reported here open up more questions than they answer. Some specific areas that we plan to investigate further include:

- Extension of these experiments to a broader range of scheduling algorithms. Will these same results hold up when applied to adaptive scheduling? to gang scheduling?
- Extension of these experiments to see if they hold up when evaluating algorithms whose performance is more similar than those we selected for this study? Will the various workloads differ in their ability to discriminate among very similar algorithms?
- Investigation of other workload characteristics that affect performance, such as effect of including interactive jobs and periodic job submissions patterns (such as day/night submissions and repeated submissions).

– Development of a benchmark suite of real workload traces and synthetic workload models for distribution throughout the scheduling community. Use of standardized suites would improve the ability of scheduling researchers to compare experimental results and to reach more solid conclusions about algorithm performance.

7 Acknowledgments

We would like to thank the following people who provided workload traces and information regarding the traces: Reagan Moore, San Diego Supercomputer Center; Steve Hotovy, Cornell Theory Center; James Jones, NASA Ames NAS; and Bernd Mohr, KFA. Thanks to Vimala Appayya and Drina Guzman from the University of Oregon for help with processing the traces. We also would like to thank the referees for their careful reading of the manuscript and their very insightful comments.

References

[1] R. H. Arpaci, A. C. Dusseau, A. M. Vahdat, L. T. Liu, T. E. Anderson, and D. A. Patterson. The interaction of parallel and sequential workloads on a network of workstations. In *Proceedings SIGMETRICS'95*, 1995.

[2] S. H. Chiang, R. K. Mansharamini, and M. K. Vernon. Use of application characteristics and limited preemption for run-to-completion parallel processor scheduling policies. In *Proceedings SIGMETRICS'94*, 1994.

[3] P. J. Chuang and N. F. Tzeng. An efficient submesh allocation strategy for mesh computer systems. In *Proceedings IEEE International Conference on Distributed Computer Systems*, 1991.

[4] Intel Corp. Paragon Network Queuing System manual. October 1993.

[5] A. B. Downey. A parallel workload model and its implications for processor allocation. In *Proceedings HPDC'97*, 1997.

[6] A. B. Downey. Predicting queue times on space-sharing parallel computers. In *Proceedings of the 3rd Workshop on Job Scheduling Strategies for Parallel Processing, IPPS '97*, 1997.

[7] D. Feitelson. Packing schemes for gang scheduling. In *Proceedings of the 2nd Workshop on Job Scheduling Strategies for Parallel Processing, IPPS '96*, 1996.

[8] D. G. Feitelson. A survey of scheduling in multiprogrammed parallel systems. Technical Report RC 19790 (87657), IBM Research Division, T.J. Watson Research Center, Yorktown Heights, NY 10598, October 1994.

[9] D. G. Feitelson and B. Nitzberg. Job characteristics of a production parallel scientific workload on the NASA Ames iPSC/860. In *Proceedings of the 1st. Workshop on Job Scheduling Strategies for Parallel Processing, IPPS '95*, April 1995.

[10] D. G. Feitelson and L. Rudolph, editors. *Job Scheduling Strategies for Parallel Processing*. Springer Lecture Notes in Computer Science, 1995-1997.

[11] S. Hotovy. Workload evolution on the Cornell Theory Center IBM SP2. In *Proceedings of the 2nd Workshop on Job Scheduling Strategies for Parallel Processing, IPPS '96*, 1996.

[12] http://science.nas.nasa.gov/Software/PBS/pbshome.html. PBS portable batch system.

[13] http://www.llnl.gov/liv_comp/dpcs/. LLNL distributed production control system.

[14] http://www.tc.cornell.edu/Papers/abdullah.jul96/index.html. Extensible Argonne scheduler system (EASY).

[15] J. Jones. NASA Ames NAS, Personal communication, 1997.

[16] P. Krueger, T. Lai, and V. A. Dixit-Radiya. Job scheduling is more important than processor allocation for hypercube computers. *IEEE Transactions on Parallel and Distributed Systems*, 5(5):488–497, May 1994.

[17] V. M. Lo, K. Windisch, W. Liu, and B. Nitzberg. Non-contiguous processor allocation algorithms for mesh-connected multicomputers. *IEEE Transactions on Parallel and Distributed Systems*, 8(7):712–726, July 1997.

[18] J. Mache and V. Lo. Minimizing message-passing contention in fragmentation-free processor allocation. In *Proceedings of the 10th International Conference on Parallel and Distributed Computing Systems*, 1997.

[19] J. Subhlok, T. Gross, and T. Suzuoka. Impacts of job mix on optimizations for space sharing schedulers. In *Proceedings of Supercomputing '96*, 1996.

[20] M. Wan, R. Moore, G. Kremenek, and K. Steube. A batch scheduler for the Intel Paragon MPP system with a non-contiguous node allocation algorithm. In *Proceedings of the 2nd Workshop on Job Scheduling Strategies for Parallel Processing, IPPS '96*, 1996.

[21] K. Windisch, V. Lo, D. Feitelson, B. Nitzberg, and R. Moore. A comparison of workload traces from two production parallel machines. In *Proceedings of the Sixth Symposium on the Frontiers of Massively Parallel Computation*, 1996.

[22] K. Windisch, V. M. Lo, and B. Bose. Contiguous and non-contiguous processor allocation algorithms for k-ary n-cubes. In *Proceedings of the International Conference on Parallel Processing*, 1995.

[23] K. Windisch, J. V. Miller, and V. M. Lo. Procsimity: an experimental tool for processor allocation and scheduling in highly parallel systems. In *Proceedings of the Fifth Symposium on the Frontiers of Massively Parallel Computation*, February 1995.

[24] Y. Zhu. Efficient processor allocation strategies for mesh-connected parallel computers. *Journal of Parallel and Distributed Computing*, 16:328–337, 1992.

Lachesis: A Job Scheduler for the Cray T3E

Allen B. Downey

Colby College, Waterville, ME 04901,
downey@colby.edu,
http://www.sdsc.edu/~downey

Abstract. This paper presents the design and implementation of Lachesis, a job scheduler for the Cray T3E. Lachesis was developed at the San Diego Supercomputer Center (SDSC) in an attempt to correct some problems with the scheduling system Cray provides with the T3E.

1   Introduction

The Cray T3E is a distributed-memory multiprocessor consisting of DEC Alpha 21164 processors connected by a bidirectional 3-dimensional torus. The T3E at SDSC has 272 processors, of which 240 are application nodes reserved for parallel applications, 28 are command nodes, which execute sequential commands, and 4 are OS nodes, which provide operating system services like process management and I/O.

Each processor has 128 MB of memory, and is capable of peak performance of 600 MFLOPS. The application (APP) nodes at SDSC are configured with no swap space, because the scheduler does currently allow timesharing between parallel applications. There are, however, 9 GB of swap space for the command (CMD) processors, which do timeshare.

Although the T3E at SDSC can run parallel applications on up to 240 processors, the vast majority run on smaller partitions. These partitions are allocated dynamically by the scheduling system, and must be made up of logically contiguous processors. The contiguity requirement is only one-dimensional, though; each processor has a unique one-dimensional logical address. Thus, the virtual arrangement of processors (linear) is not the same as the virtual topology of the processors on the network (the 3D torus), and the virtual topology does not necessarily reflect the physical arrangement (which can be discontiguous). Unlike on the Cray T3D, partitions on the T3E are not required to be powers of two; jobs can run on any cluster size from 2 to 240.

In the context of this machine, *job scheduling* refers to the following decisions:

Queueing: choosing when each job or application should begin execution.
Preemption/timesharing: deciding when one job should be interrupted (or migrated) to allow another to run.
Allocation: choosing which set of processors to allocate to each parallel application.

Dror G. Feitelson, Larry Rudolph (Eds.): JSSPP'98, LNCS 1459, pp. 47–61, 1998.

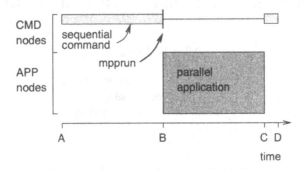

Fig. 1. A chart of the execution of a simple script with several sequential commands and one parallel application.

Section 2 describes the existing scheduler and the problems we encountered at SDSC. Section 3 outlines the goals we would like the scheduler to address; Section 4 proposes an abstract design that might achieve these goals. Section 5 describes two implementations of this design that we considered. Section 6 describes the current status of the project.

1.1 Definitions

Job: A job is a unit of work submitted by a user to the batch system. In most cases, a job executes a single script that contains a sequence of commands (possibly, although not commonly, iterative). Some of these commands are sequential; for example, they might move data between disk and tape or process temporary files. Sequential commands run on the command nodes (CMD nodes). Some commands are parallel; these create parallel applications, which run on the application nodes (APP nodes).

(Parallel) application: A parallel application is a set of sequential processes running concurrently on a set of APP nodes, usually communicating with each other during the execution of a common task. The most common way to spawn a parallel application is to execute the command mpprun on a CMD node. This has the effect of invoking the Global Resource Manager (GRM) to allocate a set of APP nodes, load the named executable on each of the allocated nodes, and begin execution of the application.

Process: A job is made up of a set of processes, including both sequential processes and the processes that make up parallel applications. Accounting information is generally collected on a per-process basis, and later aggregated into per-job reports.

Figure 1 shows the execution of a job with a single parallel application. The job starts at time A and runs a sequential command, possibly moving data from tertiary storage, until time B. During this interval, it runs only on the command node; no APP nodes have been allocated yet. Just before time B, the job executes mpprun, which allocates a set of APP nodes and creates the parallel application that runs from time B to time C. During this interval, the command node is idle, and may begin (or continue) execution of another job. After the application completes, the job executes another sequential command and then completes.

2   Existing Schedulers for the T3E

The scheduler that is shipped with the T3E has two components: NQS, which handles job scheduling, and GRM, which handles process scheduling. When a job arrives, NQS (Network Queueing System) determines when it will begin execution (and whether it might be interrupted or killed). As the job runs and spawns processes, the GRM (Global Resource Manager) decides where to run each process. Cray also provides an optional scheduling daemon, called PScheD, that provides additional features like gang scheduling. The next two sections describe these scheduling components.

2.1   NQS and GRM

Under NQS users submit jobs using the qsub command and specify their resource requirements by choosing the appropriate queue. For example, if a job requires 25 nodes, but does not run for very long, it should be submitted to q32s, where 32 is the smallest cluster size greater than the required 25, and s (short) indicates the user's estimate of the run time of the job, where the exact definition of "short" varies from site to site. Users have the option of providing additional information about their jobs, either on the command line or as pragmas in their scripts, but few users take advantage of this capability.

NQS holds jobs in queue until it sees that there are enough resources available to run the job (on the T3E, the only resource is processors; on many shared-memory machines, NQS also monitors the availability of memory). Once NQS releases the job, it runs as in Figure 1. Since NQS does not release the job until there are enough idle nodes to run the job, it is guaranteed that when the job executes mpprun, it will be able to allocate enough APP nodes from the GRM.

There are several problems with this approach:

– NQS does not communicate directly with the GRM; thus, it often does not know the number of APP nodes that are available. In the example, NQS would reserve 32 nodes for the job, even though it uses only 25. If there were a 7-node job in queue, NQS would not release it, although it would be able to run.

– NQS does not know when the job is running a sequential command or when it is running a parallel application. Thus, it reserves the requested number of APP nodes from the beginning of the job (time A) until the end (time D), although they are only used from the beginning of the parallel application (time B) to the end (time C). As Figure 1 suggests, the duration of the

sequential commands may be large compared to the duration of the parallel application.
- This configuration does not support jobs with multiple parallel applications, if they are not the same size. The user is forced to declare the size of the largest application; again, the system reserves more APP nodes than are needed.

There is another problem with the default scheduler that is due to the queueing discipline used by NQS. Different queues are given different priorities, such that a job submitted to a high-priority queue may run before a lower-priority job that arrived first. Thus, the queueing discipline is non-FIFO (first-in-first-out). The problem with non-FIFO queues is that they are likely to allow *starvation*; that is, there is a class of jobs that might wait in queue indefinitely while other jobs arrive and run.

In the T3E's default configuration, the scheduler gives priority to large jobs (96 or 128 nodes), because otherwise fragmentation might prevent these jobs from running. But if large jobs arrive frequently enough, smaller jobs (64 nodes and smaller) sit in queue indefinitely. At the moment, SDSC addresses this problem with the following ad hoc mechanism:

- After each preventative maintenance shutdown (roughly weekly), the short queues are restarted first, in order to get the starving short jobs out of the queue.
- Over the course of the week, large jobs take up the majority of the nodes, and many small jobs accumulate in queue. Operators sometimes start these jobs manually, by manipulating the NQS queues; otherwise, they run after the next shutdown.

In effect, SDSC runs the system in a weekly cycle: short jobs early in the week, large jobs later. The problems with this system are (1) it requires constant supervision and intervention, (2) the resulting schedules are neither efficient in their use of resources not satisfactory to users, and (3) the system creates incentives for users to modify their workloads (e.g., by submitting only large jobs) in a way that will further reduce the efficient use of the system.

2.2   NQS and GRM and PScheD

PScheD stands for *political scheduling*, which is scheduling that is based on externally-derived priorities (for example, one group of users may outrank another), as opposed to the internal priorities the system might use to improve performance (for example, by giving priority to small or short jobs).

PScheD is a daemon that runs periodically, examines the state of a domain (set) of nodes, and makes scheduling decisions [4]. One of the goals of PScheD is to achieve fair scheduling, where Cray defines "fair" to mean that service is allocated to users according to their priorities, independent of the number of jobs the user is running. The PScheD documentation explains [1]:

With political scheduling, users are allocated a portion of the CPU resource specified by their share. Scheduling *fairly* among users means that users with the same number of shares should be able to consume the same amount of CPU resource, regardless of the number of [jobs] an individual user has active. Scheduling without the political scheduler has a tendency to let users with more [jobs] have a larger share of the machine resources. The political scheduler knows the consumption rate for each user, and users with many active [jobs] consume CPU resources at a higher rate than those with only a few. Therefore, users with many active [jobs] will have their [jobs] positioned lower in the scheduling (run) queue.

This conception of fairness is not an appropriate goal for scheduling at supercomputer centers. In these environments, the resources a researcher needs typically vary over time: during code design and development, a user may consume few node-hours; during production, especially before a deadline, the same user might want the whole machine. Assuming that users' deadlines are not simultaneous, it is desirable to allow a user to dominate the machine at times. When user peaks do coincide, the primary goal of the scheduler will be to avoid starvation, rather than to enforce external priorities.

To find a definition of fairness that is appropriate for supercomputer centers, we divide job scheduling into two separate problems, called "allocation" and "scheduling." The allocation problem is the decision of how many resources should be allocated to each user in a relatively long allocation cycle (typically several months). This decision is made by an Allocation Committee on the basis of the requirements and scientific merit of the project. The scheduling problem is the short-term decision (on the order of minutes or hours) of what job to run and what resources to allocate to it.

The two problems are connected by the liquid currency (node-hours, service units, etc.) that is the unit of allocation. A user's consumption is eventually limited by the allocation, but in the short term there is nothing to prevent a user from allocating a large fraction of the machine.

Even if Cray's notion of fairness were appropriate, their scheduler does not achieve it. Under PScheD, it is possible for an idle user to accumulate such a large priority that when he enters a production phase he is able to dominate the machine for a long time.

A more general problem is that PScheD seems to be based on a scheduling model in which small changes in priority yield gradual changes in quality of service. This model may apply to shared-memory machines with fine-grained time sharing, but on a distributed-memory machine, where time sharing (if it exists) tends to be coarse, with long quanta and significant memory swapping, the tools available to the scheduler are likely to be too blunt for discrimination on the basis of priority to be gradual or subtle.

3   Scheduling Goals

Many of the users of parallel computers at supercomputer centers are working on Grand Challenge Problems; the nature of these problems is that they expand to use the available resources. Given a faster computer (or a larger allocation) researchers increase the size of their problems rather than solve the same problem faster.

In this environment, high system utilization is not the most important goal; it is generally not difficult to keep machines busy, provided that at any given time at least a few users are in a production phase. Instead, we conceive the goals of the scheduler from the users' point-of-view. The scheduler should:

– Allow users to run programs up to the limit of their allocations.
– Create the illusion that each user is running on a dedicated system.

The second goal implies that the scheduler should try to minimize queue times while allowing users to allocate large fractions of the machine when necessary. The scheduler should avoid imposing arbitrary restrictions like time limits and cluster size limits.

Of course, these goals are conflicting; for example, if users can allocate the entire machine for indefinite periods, it will be impossible to avoid long queue times. Addressing this conflict has been the focus of a large body of work on job scheduling.

Based on a survey of this work and observations of the atmosphere and goals of supercomputer centers, we have adopted the following design goals for the scheduler:

– Jobs must not starve. In terms of user satisfaction, avoiding starvation is more important than any other performance metric. It is also one of the most difficult to measure because we seldom see, in real systems, a set of jobs that literally starve. Instead, users typically kill starving jobs and learn not to submit the sort of job that receives poor service. Thus, it is not enough to say that starvation is not a problem because we don't see it. Rather, it is important to choose a queueing strategy that makes starvation impossible. A first-in-first-out queue (FIFO) can make this guarantee. There are, however, serious problems with FIFO queueing. The next section explains these problems and proposes ways to mitigate them.
– Delays should be proportional to run time. It may be acceptable for a 24-hour job to wait in queue for 12 hours, but it is not acceptable for a 1-hour job to wait that long. During testing phases, fast turnaround time for short jobs is critical. In general, the best way to prevent long-running jobs from interfering with short jobs is with preemption. We are considering a form of *lazy time-sharing* that might solve this problem.
– The system should provide a range of quality-of-service. Users should have the option of requesting higher priority (at some cost) or lower priority (in exchange for a discount). Although this feature is desirable, it may be incompatible with the requirement to avoid starvation. It also complicates the

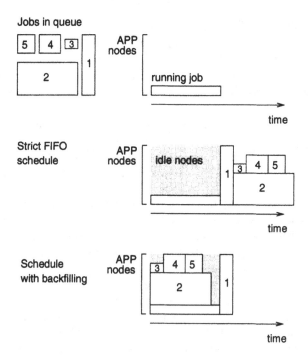

Fig. 2. Backfilling can mitigate the cost of FIFO queueing.

use of accounting to enforce externally-chosen allocations, since a CPU-hour would no longer be a unit of currency.

— Effective accounting is essential in order to control the allocation of the machine, monitor its utilization, and make it possible for users to make informed decisions. The cost of running a job must reflect the resources allocated to the job, rather than the resources used by the job. For parallel application, that means that the relevant measure of a job is the number of processors multiplied by the *wall clock time*. The existing system charges by CPU time, thereby undercharging jobs that perform a lot of I/O or leave processors idle.

The next three sections describe three scheduling features that might achieve these goals: backfilling, lazy timesharing, and support for moldable jobs.

3.1 Backfilling

The benefits of FIFO queueing are the guarantee that no jobs will starve and the ability to make predictions. Predictability is particularly useful in the context of metasystems, in which software agents will need to observe the state of the system (the length of the queue, the jobs already running, etc.) and predict the queue time until a new job can run.

The problems with FIFO queueing are (1) large jobs can impose long queue times on many small jobs, and (2) the system may be underutilized. Figure 2 demonstrates these effects. One way to improve the performance of a FIFO system is to add backfilling. Backfilling allows small jobs to begin execution even if a larger job is waiting, provided that the backfilled jobs do not delay the waiting job.

In the figure, Job 1 is waiting for a large cluster. If the other jobs were forced to wait, many processors would be left idle. We would like to allow the smaller jobs to run, but we can only do so if we can guarantee that they will complete before the running job. There are several variations on this strategy:

- Deterministic backfilling: if the run times of all jobs are known, it is easy to tell when backfilling is safe. In general, though, this is not the case.
- Pessimistic backfilling: we can assume that all jobs will run until their time limits, and backfill accordingly. Observations of other systems indicate that few jobs run until their time limits, so pessimism may not be warranted.
- Non-deterministic backfilling: given the distribution of lifetimes for past jobs, we can make claims about the probability that a job will run for a certain time. We might allow a job to backfill if it has a high probability of completing before the running job. In the occasional event that it exceeds that limit, we would have to delay the waiting job. Although this approach violates the FIFO principle, it can still be shown to avoid starvation, since you can't beat the odds forever.
- Contractual backfilling: we might offer a contract to a waiting job, offering to let it backfill, with the understanding that if it runs longer than the running job it will be killed. For applications that do their own checkpointing, this offer would be attractive. Of course, less robust jobs would decline. Contractual backfilling requires a user interface that allows users to identify killable jobs.

For all kinds of backfilling, the system needs estimates from users about the run times of their jobs. At the moment, users provide this information by choosing a queue with the appropriate time limit. This information is often not very accurate, but it is still useful. One of the features we are planning to add to Lachesis is an interface that solicits two estimates of run time, a best guess and a maximum. The best guess is the user's estimate of how long the job will take; the maximum is the time after which the job may be killed. Users have an incentive to provide accurate information, so that their jobs will be scheduled as soon as possible, with minimal chance of being killed.

The EASY scheduler, developed for the IBM SP at the Argonne National Laboratory, uses pessimistic backfilling [5] [7].

3.2   Lazy Timesharing

The best way to prevent long jobs from imposing queue times on short jobs is to allow preemption. The motivation for preemption is that the longer a job has

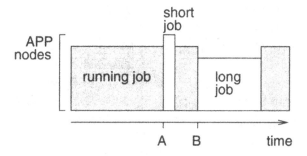

Fig. 3. An example of lazy timesharing.

run the longer we expect it to run. So a newly-arrived job has a shorter expected remaining lifetime than a running job. It is preferable to impose a short delay on the (long) running job than a long delay on the (probably short) arrival.

Figure 3 shows how lazy timesharing might work. At Time A, a job arrives and preempts the running job. Since it turns out to be a short job, as expected, the delay imposed on the running job is not significant, and the turnaround time for the short job is good. The second job, arriving at Time B, turns out to be a long job. In this case, we run the new job until its expected remaining lifetime exceeds that of the original job. At that point, we resume the original job. The new job might migrate to another set of nodes, or continue to timeshare with the original job. Feitelson proposed the name "lazy timesharing" for this kind of preemption [3].

There is consensus in the scheduling research community that gang-scheduling is a necessary feature for timesharing parallel applications with significant communication (although Dusseau et al. argue to the contrary [2]). Gang scheduling is available with PScheD, but not under the vanilla UNICOS/mk scheduler. However, the timesharing strategy used by PScheD is very different from lazy timesharing; it is based on fixed quantum lengths that are shorter than lazy timesharing calls for—on the order of seconds, rather than minutes or hours. It may not be possible to modify PScheD to implement lazy timesharing.

Memory constraints will limit our ability to implement timesharing. Although the T3E memory system implements virtual memory, the T3E at SDSC is currently configured with no swap space. Thus, in order for jobs to timeshare, they must all fit in physical memory. The accounting data for past jobs suggests that there are many jobs (about 60%) that use less than half of the available memory, so some timesharing will be possible. On the other hand, it is not easy to predict before a job begins execution how much memory it will use, and many jobs grow dynamically as they run. Dealing with the allocation of physical memory will significantly complicate the timesharing strategies we can implement (for discussion of this issue, see [6]).

An alternate form of timesharing, checkpointing, may eliminate the problems associated with memory scheduling. Checkpointing differs from standard context-switching in that all of the memory associated with a process is written

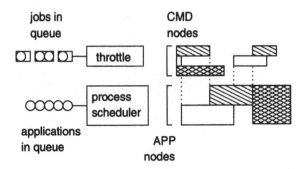

Fig. 4. The abstract design of a two-level job scheduler.

to disk, along with its system state. Of course, the overhead is potentially much greater, but the mechanism has the potential to be more robust, reducing the possibility that one process can interfere with another, and thereby improving the illusion of a dedicated machine. Because we expect context switches to be infrequent, the overhead of checkpointing may not be prohibitive. Checkpointing was not available in UNICOS/mk when we designed Lachesis, but became available with Version 2.0.

3.3   Support for Moldable Applications

Many of the applications running at SDSC are moldable, meaning that they can be configured to run on a range of cluster sizes. In general, this configuration happens once; it is not possible to reconfigure an application once it starts running. We distinguish moldable applications from malleable ones, which can change size dynamically as they execute. Most of the applications running on MPPs are written in SPMD style, which seldom supports dynamic reconfiguration.

Ideally, users should specify the range of cluster sizes on which their applications can run, so that the system can choose the size most appropriate for the current load. In current systems, though, the user interface requires users to choose a specific cluster size. One of the features Lachesis will provide is an interface that allows users to specify a range of cluster sizes (or a set of particular values).

4   Abstract Design

The following is the abstract design of a scheduler that meets the criteria discussed above. This design is based on the goal of separating job-level scheduling from process-level scheduling. In the next section, we will discuss the particular implementation of Lachesis.

Figure 4 shows a diagram of the design. Jobs are represented by small rectangles; the processes (sequential and parallel) that make up jobs are represented by circles. When a new job arrives, the *throttle* controls when and on which CMD node the job begins execution.

Once the job begins execution, it may execute mpprun one or more times, spawning parallel applications. When this happens, the *process scheduler* determines when and on which APP nodes the application runs. Thus, after a job executes mpprun, it may be some time before the spawned application begins execution. In the figure, the first two applications start right away; the third waits in queue until the second completes.

The primary goal of the throttle is to allow as many jobs as possible to begin execution, probably several on each CMD node. Since many of the housekeeping commands that make up a job are I/O bound, multiple jobs may timeshare effectively. Also, the sooner a job arrives at its (first) mpprun, the sooner the spawned application becomes visible to the process scheduler. The only limitations on the number of jobs running simultaneously are (1) available memory on the CMD nodes, (2) the possibility of thrashing at the level of tertiary-secondary storage, and (3) lost state in the event of a crash.

Regarding the first point, accounting information from the first three months of operation (August through October 1997) suggests that more than 99% of jobs use fewer than 4 MB of memory on the CMD nodes. Since each node has 128 MB of memory, we can fit 32 to 64 jobs on each node.

Regarding the second point, it is possible that if many jobs start simultaneously and move data from tertiary storage onto disk, then there might be a long delay between the execution of mpprun and the beginning of a parallel application. During this time, the data moved from tertiary storage might be purged. It is not clear whether this is a serious concern at SDSC.

The last consideration is that it may be wise to limit the number of jobs running simultaneously in order to reduce the amount of work operators and users have to do to restart jobs that are active during a crash. As users gain experience with the T3E, they tend to write scripts that are robust, either by taking advantage of new checkpoint-restart mechanisms, or by using their own application-level checkpointing. Thus, it may not be necessary to worry about the number of jobs running simultaneously.

Since it is not clear that there are any immediate limitations on the number of jobs running simultaneously, an initial implementation of the throttle is likely to be trivial—it should allow all jobs to begin execution immediately.

The more interesting work happens at the level of process scheduling. The process scheduler needs to keep track of the state of the system; thus, it must be notified when a parallel application arrives or completes, and may use status commands to keep track of various system information. The process scheduler is responsible for starting new processes, preempting running applications (if there is timesharing), and killing applications that exceed their time limits. The most appropriate structure for the process scheduler is an *event-driven decision-maker*. That is, the process scheduler should be notified about relevant events and allowed to execute commands to realize its decisions.

If the process scheduler is doing probablistic backfilling, it will need to maintain a database of accounting information from past applications, so that it can predict the resource requirements of new applications. It also needs to generate accounting data of its own and respond to user queries about the state of the system.

A basic principle of this design is that in order to do intelligent scheduling, the scheduler must be aware of the applications that are waiting for service and their attributes. The only way to expose these applications is to get jobs running as quickly as possible until they execute mpprun, and then schedule the spawned applications.

5   Implementation Options

We considered two implementation options, one based on PScheD, the other based on a wrapper around the existing mpprun combined with a scheduling daemon we would write from scratch. We chose not to work with PScheD; the following section explains why.

5.1   PScheD

As discussed in Section 2.2, PScheD implements a scheduling strategy very different from what we want. It does, however, provide a set of hooks where sites can install scheduling modules that implement alternate strategies. Thus, it might be possible to take advantage of the infrastructure provided by PScheD and build our scheduler on top of it.

The primary advantage of a PScheD-based scheduler is the possibility of gang scheduling. ScheD makes it possible to run more than one parallel applications on a given set of nodes, timesharing among them. Without PScheD, the T3E provides no support for gang scheduling; that is, parallel applications can share processors, but there is no guarantee that the processes that make up an application will be scheduled at the same time.

A fundamental problem with PScheD is that it does not address the problems regarding communication between NQS and the GRM. For example, one of the scheduling modules tries to reduce processor fragmentation by migrating applications from one set of nodes to another. It appears that PScheD does not consider the backlog of queued jobs when it makes its packing decisions. But this information is certainly relevant; as a trivial example, it is pointless to reduce fragmentation unless a waiting job requires it.

A second problem is that the interfaces between PScheD and the scheduling modules are narrow—PScheD provides little information and gives the modules little control. In our preliminary designs we realized that we would have to do a lot of work to get the information the scheduler needs into the appropriate modules. We also got the sense that we were not using PScheD in a way that was intended, and feared that we would waste too much effort cutting against the grain.

A final difficulty with the PScheD scheduling modules is that they were not available in the version of UNICOS/mk that was available when we started implementing Lachesis. Although we knew they would be available soon, we decided not to wait.

5.2   Scheduler Daemon and mpprun Wrapper

The design we implemented is based on a scheduler daemon similar to the PScheD daemon, but based on an event-driven paradigm. The daemon works with a wrapper around mpprun that notifies the daemon when applications arrive and complete. The entire system is called Lachesis, after the Fate in Greek mythology that "schedules" the threads of men's lives. The scheduling daemon is called lachd; the wrapper around mpprun is called mppfun.

In order to activate Lachesis, we start lachd and replace mpprun with mppfun. Then, when a user executes mpprun, he actually executes our wrapper, which communicates with lachd through a socket. The wrapper collects information about the application, including the user's name, the location of the executable, and any user-provided information like the cluster size and expected duration, and sends this information to lachd.

When lachd receives a request, it either allocates processors immediately or adds the request to its queue. Eventually, lachd starts the job by sending a message to the mpprun wrapper, telling it which processors (and how many) it can allocate. The wrapper then executes the "real" mpprun, spawning the parallel application.

When the application completes, the wrapper collects the completion code and sends it to lachd. If an application exceeds its time limit, the mpprun wrapper kills it (not, as might be expected, the daemon). Since the wrapper is executed by the owner of the parallel application, it does not need any special permission to kill (or migrate) the application. Furthermore, since lachd does not execute any protected commands, it does not need to run with any special permissions. Thus, at least abstractly, running Lachesis does not introduce any security problems. In the next section, though, we will discuss some implementation problems that undermine what would otherwise be a pleasantly secure system.

An advantage of putting a wrapper around mpprun is that is it is easy to extend the interface to solicit different or additional information from users. In the current implementation, we have not modified the interface, but soon we will make it possible for users to specify a range (or set) of possible cluster sizes, rather than a single choice, and solicit more information about the expected run times of jobs.

We are using an eviscerated configuration of NQS as a throttle. Since users provide information for each application (when they execute mpprun), they no longer have to provide information about jobs when they are submitted. Thus, we do not need a queue for each cluster size and duration. Instead, we have only a few queues, specifying the desired level of service. Within each queue, NQS starts jobs in FIFO order. Some queues have higher priority than others, with correspondingly higher pricing.

5.3 Implementation Difficulties

We ran into several problems building Lachesis, some of which we have still not addressed to our satisfaction. The first is that it is possible on the T3E to start a parallel application without using mpprun. This capability is new, and we did not realize when we designed Lachesis that so many people were using it. Of course, putting a wrapper around mpprun is not as effective if users can circumvent it. So, one user-visible consequence of the new scheduler is that we require users to use mpprun.

Unfortately, in the current version of Lachesis, we have no way to enforce this restriction. Thus, it is possible for users to run *rogue jobs* that never notify Lachesis, and that occupy nodes that Lachesis think are idle. For this reason (and others) Lachesis performs periodic *reality checks* that allow it to detect and monitor rogue jobs.

Because of the reality check mechanism, Lachesis has the ability to start on the fly—that is, while there are already jobs in the system. When Lachesis starts, it collects information about running jobs and monitors them until they complete. Meanwhile, it starts scheduling arriving jobs on the idle processors. The ability to start on the fly has made it possible to test Lachesis in a production environment with a minimal impact on users.

We encountered one other difficulty that is a result of the division of labor between Lachesis and mppfun. Although lachd chooses which processors to allocate to an application, mppfun actually starts the application. Thus, we need a mechanism whereby mppfun specifies where each application runs. In a typical T3E installation, this capability is reserved for system administrators. Users do not have control over the placement of their applications. In order to give users this capability, we had to give all users a special permission bit called DIAG. At the moment, this permbit is not used for anything else, so it does not create a security problem to give it to everyone, but in the future there may be other diagnostic activities we would like to protect, and in that case we would have to create a new permbit.

6 Project Status

A simple version of the Lachesis daemon and the mpprun wrapper ran in production at SDSC from August 1997 to January 1998. During that time, Lachesis did not actually schedule the machine; it only observed and logged system activity. A benefit of the prototype system is that it provides more complete information about parallel applications than is available from the Cray Accouting System. We are currently using that information in our design of a non-deterministic backfilling strategy.

Since January 1998, we have been testing Lachesis version 1.0, which implements a variation of the pessimistic backfilling strategy decribed in Section 3.1. At the time of this writing we do not have enough information to evaluate the performance of the new system.

Along with the development of Lachesis, we have also built a simulator that reads events from the Lachesis logs and simulates the state of the system. The same scheduling module that plugs into the Lachesis daemon also plugs into the simulator, allowing us to test new modules for correctness and to evaluate various scheduling strategies.

Acknowledgements

The primary implementors of Lachesis are Allen Downey and Victor Hazlewood at SDSC. We would also like to thank Larry Diegel from SDSC and Peter Ashford from Cray for all their help.

References

[1] Cray Research, Inc. *UNICOS/mk Resource Administration, SG2602*, 1997.
[2] Andrea C. Dusseau, Remzi H. Arpaci, and David E. Culler. Effective distributed scheduling of parallel workloads. In *Proceedings of the ACM Sigmetrics Conference on Measurement and Modeling of Computer Systems*, pages 25–36, May 1996.
[3] Dror G. Feitelson. Job scheduling in multiprogrammed parallel system. Technical Report RC 19790 (87657), T. J. Watson Research Lab, I.B.M., August 1997. Second revision.
[4] Richard N. Lagerstrom and Stephan K. Gipp. PScheD: Political scheduling on the Cray T3E. In *Job Scheduling Strategies for Parallel Processing, Springer-Verlag LNCS Vol 1291*, pages 117–138, 1997.
[5] David Lifka. The ANL/IBM SP scheduling system. In *Job Scheduling Strategies for Parallel Processing, Springer-Verlag LNCS Vol 949*, pages 295–303, 1995.
[6] Eric W. Parsons and Kenneth C. Sevcik. Coordinated allocation of memory and processors in multiprocessors. In *Proceedings of the ACM Sigmetrics Conference on Measurement and Modeling of Computer Systems*, pages 57–67, May 1996.
[7] Joseph Skovira, Waiman Chan, Honbo Zhou, and David Lifka. The EASY – LoadLeveler API project. In *Job Scheduling Strategies for Parallel Processing, Springer-Verlag LNCS Vol 1162*, pages 41–47, 1996.

A Resource Management Architecture for Metacomputing Systems

Karl Czajkowski[1], Ian Foster[2], Nick Karonis[2], Carl Kesselman[1], Stuart Martin[2], Warren Smith[2], and Steven Tuecke[2]

{karlcz, itf, karonis, carl, smartin, wsmith, tuecke}@globus.org
http://www.globus.org

[1] Information Sciences Institute
University of Southern California
Marina del Rey, CA 90292-6695
http://www.isi.edu
[2] Mathematics and Computer Science Division
Argonne National Laboratory
Argonne, IL 60439
http://www.mcs.anl.gov

Abstract. Metacomputing systems are intended to support remote and/or concurrent use of geographically distributed computational resources. Resource management in such systems is complicated by five concerns that do not typically arise in other situations: site autonomy and heterogeneous substrates at the resources, and application requirements for policy extensibility, co-allocation, and online control. We describe a resource management architecture that addresses these concerns. This architecture distributes the resource management problem among distinct local manager, resource broker, and resource co-allocator components and defines an extensible resource specification language to exchange information about requirements. We describe how these techniques have been implemented in the context of the Globus metacomputing toolkit and used to implement a variety of different resource management strategies. We report on our experiences applying our techniques in a large testbed, GUSTO, incorporating 15 sites, 330 computers, and 3600 processors.

1   Introduction

Metacomputing systems allow applications to assemble and use collections of computational resources on an as-needed basis, without regard to physical location. Various groups are implementing such systems and exploring applications in distributed supercomputing, high-throughput computing, smart instruments, collaborative environments, and data mining [10, 12, 18, 20, 22, 6, 25].

This paper is concerned with *resource management* for metacomputing: that is, with the problems of locating and allocating computational resources, and with authentication, process creation, and other activities required to prepare a

Dror G. Feitelson, Larry Rudolph (Eds.): JSSPP'98, LNCS 1459, pp. 62–82, 1998.

resource for use. We do not address other issues that are traditionally associated with scheduling (such as decomposition, assignment, and execution ordering of tasks) or the management of other resources such as memory, disk, and networks.

The metacomputing environment introduces five challenging resource management problems: site autonomy, heterogeneous substrate, policy extensibility, co-allocation, and online control.

1. The *site autonomy* problem refers to the fact that resources are typically owned and operated by different organizations, in different administrative domains [5]. Hence, we cannot expect to see commonality in acceptable use policy, scheduling policies, security mechanisms, and the like.
2. The *heterogeneous substrate* problem derives from the site autonomy problem and refers to the fact that different sites may use different local resource management systems [16], such as Condor [18], NQE [1], CODINE [11], EASY [17], LSF [28], PBS [14], and LoadLeveler [15]. Even when the same system is used at two sites, different configurations and local modifications often lead to significant differences in functionality.
3. The *policy extensibility* problem arises because metacomputing applications are drawn from a wide range of domains, each with its own requirements. A resource management solution must support the frequent development of new domain-specific management structures, without requiring changes to code installed at participating sites.
4. The *co-allocation* problem arises because many applications have resource requirements that can be satisfied only by using resources simultaneously at several sites. Site autonomy and the possibility of failure during allocation introduce a need for specialized mechanisms for allocating multiple resources, initiating computation on those resources, and monitoring and managing those computations.
5. The *online control* problem arises because substantial negotiation can be required to adapt application requirements to resource availability, particularly when requirements and resource characteristics change during execution. For example, a tele-immersive application that needs to simulate a new entity may prefer a lower-resolution rendering, if the alternative is that the entity not be modeled at all. Resource management mechanisms must support such negotiation.

As we explain in Section 2, no existing resource management systems addresses all five problems. Some batch queuing systems support co-allocation, but not site autonomy, policy extensibility, and online control [16]. Condor supports site autonomy, but not co-allocation or online control [18]. Gallop [26] addresses online control and policy extensibility, but not the heterogeneous substrate or co-allocation problem. Legion [12] does not address the heterogeneous substrate problem.

In this paper, we describe a resource management architecture that we have developed to address the five problems. In this architecture, developed in the context of the Globus project [10], we address problems of site autonomy and heterogeneous substrate by introducing entities called *resource managers* to provide a well-defined interface to diverse local resource management tools, policies, and security mechanisms. To support online control and policy extensibility, we define an extensible *resource specification language* that supports negotiation between different components of a resource management architecture, and we introduce *resource brokers* to handle the mapping of high-level application requests into requests to individual managers. We address the problem of co-allocation by defining various co-allocation strategies, which we encapsulate in *resource co-allocators*.

One measure of success for an architecture such as this is its usability in a practical setting. To this end, we have implemented and deployed this architecture on GUSTO, a large computational grid testbed comprising 15 sites, 330 computers, and 3600 processors, using LSF, NQE, LoadLeveler, EASY, Fork, and Condor as local schedulers. To date, this architecture and testbed have been used by ourselves and others to implement numerous applications and half a dozen different higher-level resource management strategies. This experiment represents a significant step forward in terms of number of global metacomputing services implemented and number and variety of commercial and experimental local resource management systems employed. A more quantitative evaluation of the approach remains as a significant challenge for future work.

The rest of this paper is structured as follows. In the next section, we review current distributed resource management solutions. In subsequent sections we first outline our architecture and then examine each major function in detail: the resource specification language, local resource managers, resource brokers, and resource co-allocators. We summarize the paper and discuss future work in Section 8.

2   Resource Management Approaches

Previous work on resource management for metacomputing systems can be broken into two broad classes:

- *Network batch queuing systems.* These systems focus strictly on resource management issues for a set of networked computers. These systems do not address policy extensibility and provide only limited support for online control and co-allocation.
- *Wide-area scheduling systems.* Here, resource management is performed as a component of mapping application components to resources and scheduling their execution. To date, these systems do not address issues of heterogeneous substrates, site autonomy, and co-allocation.

In the following, we use representative examples of these two types of system to illustrate the strengths and weaknesses of current approaches.

2.1   Networked Batch Queuing Systems

Networked batch queuing systems, such as NQE [1], CODINE [11], LSF [28], PBS [14], and LoadLeveler [15], handle user-submitted jobs by allocating resources from a networked pool of computers. The user characterizes application resource requirements either explicitly, by some type of job control language, or implicitly, by selecting the queue to which a request is submitted. Networked batch queuing systems typically are designed for single administrative domains, making site autonomy difficult to achieve. Likewise, the heterogeneous substrate problem is also an issue because these systems generally assume that they are the only resource management system in operation. One exception is the CODINE system, which introduces the concept of a *transfer queue* to allow jobs submitted to CODINE to be allocated by some other resource management system, at a reduced level of functionality. An alternative approach to supporting substrate heterogeneity is being explored by the PSCHED [13] initiative. This project is attempting to define a uniform API through which a variety of batch scheduling systems may be controlled. The goals of PSCHED are similar in many ways to those of the Globus Resource Allocation Manager described in Section 5.

Batch scheduling systems provide a limited form of policy extensibility in that resource management policy is set by either the system or the system administrator, by the creation of scheduling policy or batch queues. However, this capability is not available to the end users, who have little control over how the batch scheduling system interprets their resource requirements.

Finally, we observe that batch queuing systems have limited support for online allocation, as these systems are designed to support applications in which the requirements specifications are in the form "get X done soon", where X is precisely defined but "soon" is not. In metacomputing applications, we have more complex, fluid constraints, in which we will want to make tradeoffs between time (when) and space (physical characteristics). Such constraints lead to a need for the resource management system to provide capabilities such as negotiation, inquiry interfaces, information-based control, and co-allocation, none of which are provided in these systems.

In summary, batch scheduling systems do not provide in themselves a complete solution to metacomputing resource management problems. However, clearly some of the mechanisms developed for resource location, distributed process control, remote file access, to name a few, can be applied to wide-area systems as well. Furthermore, we note that network batch queuing systems will necessarily be part of the local resource management solution. Hence, any metacomputing resource management architecture must be able to interface to these systems.

2.2   Wide-Area Scheduling Systems

We now examine how resource management is addressed within systems developed specifically to schedule metacomputing applications. To gain a good perspective on the range of possibilities, we discuss four different schedulers, designed variously to support specific classes of applications (Gallop [26]), an extensible object-oriented system (Legion [12]), general classes of parallel programs (PRM [22]), and high-throughput computation (Condor [18]).

The **Gallop** [26] system allocates and schedules tasks defined by a static task graph onto a set of networked computational resources. (A similar mechanism has been used in Legion [27].) Resource allocation is implemented by a scheduling manager, which coordinates scheduling requests, and a local manager, which manages the resources at a local site, potentially interfacing to site-specific scheduling and resource allocation services. This decomposition, which we also adopt, separates local resource management operations from global resource management policy and hence facilitates solutions to the problems of site autonomy, heterogeneous substrates, and policy extensibility. However, Gallop does not appear to handle authentication to local resource management services, thereby limiting the level of site autonomy that can be achieved.

The use of a static task-graph model makes online control in Gallop difficult. Resource selection is performed by attempting to minimize the execution time of task graph as predicted by a performance model for the application and the prospective resource. However, because the minimization procedure and the cost model is fixed, there is no support for policy extensibility. **Legion** [12] overcomes this limitation by leveraging its object-oriented model. Two specialized objects, an application-specific `Scheduler` and a resource-specific `Enactor` negotiate with one another to make allocation decisions. The `Enactor` can also provide co-allocation functions.

Gallop supports co-allocation for resources maintained within an administrative domain, but depends for this purpose on the ability to reserve resources. Unfortunately, reservation is not currently supported by most local resource management systems. For this reason, our architecture does not rely on reservation to perform co-allocation, but rather uses a separate co-allocation management service to perform this function.

The **Prospero Resource Manager** [22] (PRM) provides resource management functions for parallel programs written by using the PVM message-passing library. PRM consists of three components: a system manager, a job manager, and a node manager. The job manager makes allocation decisions, while the system and node manager actually allocate resources. The node manager is solely responsible for implementing resource allocation functions. Thus, PRM does not address issues of site autonomy or substrate heterogeneity. A variety of job managers can be constructed, allowing for policy extensibility, although there is no provision for composing job managers so as to extend an existing management policy. As in our architecture, PRM has both an information infrastructure (Prospero [21]) and a management API, providing the infrastructure needed to perform online control. However, unlike our architecture, PRM does not support co-allocation of resources.

Condor [18] is a resource management system designed to support high-throughput computations by discovering idle resources on a network and allocating those resources to application tasks. While Condor does not interface with existing resource management systems, resources controlled by Condor are deallocated as soon as the "rightful" owner starts to use them. In this sense, Condor supports site autonomy and heterogeneous substrates. However, Condor currently does not interoperate with local resource authentication, limiting the degree of autonomy a site can assert. Condor provides an extensible resource description language, called *classified ads*, which provides limited control over resource selection to both the application and resource. However, the matching of application component to resource is performed by a system *classifier*, which defines how matches—and consequently resource management—take place, limiting the extensibility of this selection policy. Finally, Condor provides no support for co-allocation or online control.

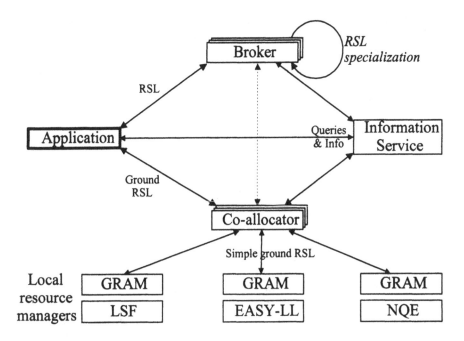

Fig. 1. The Globus resource management architecture, showing how RSL specifications pass between application, resource brokers, resource co-allocators, and local managers (GRAMs). Notice the central role of the information service.

In summary, our review of current resource management approaches revealed a range of valuable services, but no single system that provides solutions to all five metacomputing resource management problems posed in the introduction.

3 Our Resource Management Architecture

Our approach to the metacomputing resource management problem is illustrated in Figure 1. In this architecture, an extensible *resource specification language* (RSL), discussed in Section 4 below, is used to communicate requests for resources between components: from applications to resource brokers, resource co-allocators, and resource managers. At each stage in this process, information about resource requirements, coded as an RSL expression by the application, is refined by one or more resource brokers and co-allocators; information about resource availability and characteristics is obtained from an information service.

Resource brokers are responsible for taking high-level RSL specifications and transforming them into more concrete specifications through a process we call *specialization*. As illustrated in Figure 2, multiple brokers may be involved in servicing a single request, with application-specific brokers translating application requirements into more concrete resource requirements, and different resource brokers being used to locate available resources that meet those requirements.

Transformations effected by resource brokers generate a specification in which the locations of the required resources are completely specified. Such a *ground request* can be passed to a *co-allocator*, which is responsible for coordinating the allocation and management of resources at multiple sites. As we describe in Section 7, a variety of co-allocators will be required in a metacomputing system, providing different co-allocation semantics.

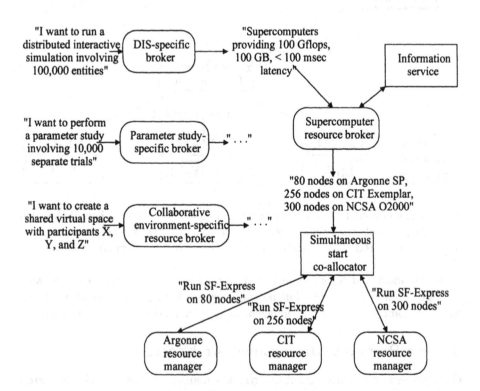

Fig. 2. This view of the Globus resource management architecture shows how different types of broker can participate in a single resource request

Resource co-allocators break a multirequest—that is, a request involving resources at multiple sites—into its constituent elements and pass each component to the appropriate *resource manager*. As discussed in Section 5, each resource manager in the system is responsible for taking an RSL request and translating it into operations in the local, site-specific resource management system.

The *information service* is responsible for providing efficient and pervasive access to information about the current availability and capability of resources. This information is used to locate resources with particular characteristics, to identify the resource manager associated with a resource, to determine properties of that resource, and for numerous other purposes as high-level resource specifications are translated into requests to specific managers. We use the Globus system's Metacomputing Directory Service (MDS) [8] as our information service. MDS uses the data representation and application programming interface (API) defined on the Lightweight Directory Access Protocol (LDAP) to meet requirements for uniformity, extensibility, and distributed maintenance. It defines a data model suitable for distributed computing applications, able to represent computers and networks of interest, and provides tools for populating this data model. LDAP defines a hierarchical, tree-structured name space called a *directory information tree* (DIT). Fields within the namespace are identified by a unique *distinguished name* (DN). LDAP supports both distribution and replication. Hence, the local service associated with MDS is exactly an LDAP server (or a gateway to another LDAP server, if multiple sites share a server), plus the utilities used to populate this server with up-to-date information about the structure and state of the resources within that site. The global MDS service is simply the ensemble of all these servers. An advantage of using MDS as our information service is that resource management information can be used by other tools, as illustrated in Figure 3.

4   Resource Specification Language

We now discuss the resource specification language itself. The syntax of an RSL specification, summarized in Figure 4, is based on the syntax for filter specifications in the Lightweight Directory Access Protocol and MDS. An RSL specification is constructed by combining simple parameter specifications and conditions with the operators &; to specify conjunction of parameter specifications, |; to express the disjunction of parameter specifications, +; or to combine two or more requests into a single compound request, or multirequest.

The set of **parameter-name** terminal symbols is extensible: resource brokers, co-allocators, and resource managers can each define a set of parameter names that they will recognize. For example, a resource broker that is specialized for tele-immersive applications might accept as input a specification containing a **frames-per-second** parameter and might generate as output a specification containing an **mflops-per-second** parameter, to be passed to a broker that deals with computational resources. Resource managers, the system components that

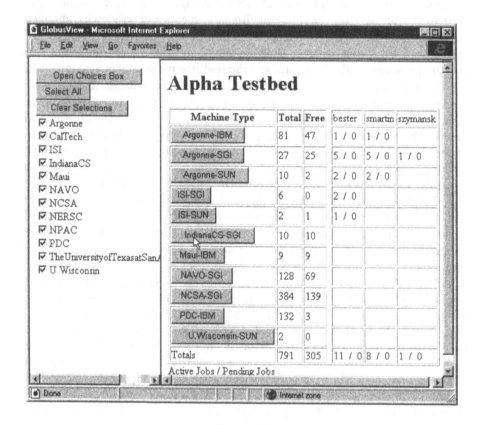

Fig. 3. The GlobusView tool uses MDS information about resource manager status to present information about the current status of a metacomputing testbed. On the left, we see the sites that are currently participating in the testbed; on the right is information about the total number of nodes that each site is contributing, the number of those nodes that are currently available to external users, and the usage of those nodes by Globus users.

specification	:= request
request	:= multirequest | conjunction | disjunction | parameter
multirequest	:= + request-list
conjunction	:= & request-list
disjunction	:= | request-list
request-list	:= (request) request-list | (request)
parameter	:= parameter-name op value
op	:= = | > | < | >= | <= | !=
value	:= ([a..Z][0..9][_])+

Fig. 4. BNF grammar describing the syntax of an RSL request

actually talk to local scheduling systems, recognize two types of `parameter-name` terminal symbols:

- *MDS attribute names*, used to express constraints on resources: for example, `memory>=64` or `network=atm`. In this case, the parameter name refers to a field defined in the MDS entry for the resource being allocated. The truth of the parameter specification is determined by comparing the value provided with the specification with the current value associated with the corresponding field in the MDS. Arbitrary MDS fields can be specified by providing their full distinguished name.
- *Scheduler parameters*, used to communicate information regarding the job, such as `count` (number of nodes required), `max_time` (maximum time required), `executable`, `arguments`, `directory`, and `environment` (environment variables). Schedule parameters are interpreted directly by the resource manager.

For example, the specification

```
&(executable=myprog)
 (|(&(count=5)(memory>=64))(&(count=10)(memory>=32)))
```

requests 5 nodes with at least 64 MB memory, or 10 nodes with at least 32 MB. In this request, `executable` and `count` are scheduler attribute names, while `memory` is an MDS attribute name.

Our current RSL parser and resource manager disambiguate these two parameter types on the basis of the parameter name. That is, the resource manager knows which fields it will accept as scheduler parameters and assumes all others are MDS attribute names. Name clashes can be disambiguated by using the complete distinguished name for the MDS field in question.

The ability to include constraints on MDS attribute values in RSL specifications is important. As we discuss in Section 5, the state of resource managers is stored in MDS. Hence, resource specifications can refer to resource characteristics such as queue-length, expected wait time, and number of processors available. This technique provides a powerful mechanism for controlling how an RSL specification is interpreted.

The following example of a multirequest is derived from the example shown in Figure 2.

```
+(&(count=80)(memory>=64M)(executable=sf_express)
   (resourcemanager=ico16.mcs.anl.gov:8711))
 (&(count=256)(network=atm)(executable=sf_express)
   (resourcemanager=neptune.cacr.caltech.edu:755))
 (&(count=300)(memory>=64M)(executable=sf_express)
   (resourcemanager=modi4.ncsa.edu:4000))
```

This is a ground request: every component of the multirequest specifies a resource manager. A co-allocator can use the `resourcemanager` parameters specified in this request to determine to which resource manager each component of the multirequest should be submitted.

Notations intended for similar purposes include the Condor "classified ad" [18] and Chapin's "task description vector" [5]. Our work is novel in three respects: the tight integration with a directory service, the use of specification rewriting to express broker operations (as described below), and the fact that the language and associated tools have been implemented and demonstrated effective when layered on top of numerous different low-level schedulers.

We conclude this section by noting that it is the combination of resource brokers, information service, and RSL that makes online control possible in our architecture. Together, these services make it possible to construct requests dynamically, based on current system state and negotiation between the application and the underlying resources.

5 Local Resource Management

We now describe the lowest level of our resource management architecture: the local resource managers, implemented in our architecture as Globus Resource Allocation Managers (GRAMs). A GRAM is responsible for

1. processing RSL specifications representing resource requests, by either denying the request or by creating one or more processes (a "job") that satisfy that request;
2. enabling remote monitoring and management of jobs created in response to a resource request; and
3. periodically updating the MDS information service with information about the current availability and capabilities of the resources that it manages.

A GRAM serves as the interface between a wide area metacomputing environment and an autonomous entity able to create processes, such as a parallel computer scheduler or a Condor pool. Hence, a resource manager need not correspond to a single host or a specific computer, but rather to a service that acts on behalf of one or more computational resources. This use of local scheduler interfaces was first explored in the software environment for the I-WAY networking experiment [9], but is extended and generalized here significantly to provide a richer and more flexible interface.

A resource specification passed to a GRAM is assumed to be ground: that is, to be sufficiently concrete that the GRAM can identify local resources that meet the specification without further interaction with the entity that generated the request. A particular GRAM implementation may achieve this goal by scheduling resources itself or, more commonly, by mapping the resource specification into a request to some local resource allocation mechanism. (To date, we have interfaced GRAMs to six different schedulers or resource allocators: Condor, EASY, Fork, LoadLeveler, LSF, and NQE.) Hence, the GRAM API plays for resource management a similar role to that played by IP for communication: it can co-exist with local mechanisms, just as IP rides on top of ethernet, FDDI, or ATM networking technology.

The GRAM API provides functions for submitting and for canceling a job request and for asking when a job (submitted or not) is expected to run. An implementation of the latter function may use queue time estimation techniques [24]. When a job is submitted, a globally unique *job handle* is returned that can then be used to monitor and control the progress of the job. In addition, a job submission call can request that the progress of the requested job be signaled asynchronously to a supplied *callback URL*. Job handles can be passed to other processes, and callbacks do not have to be directed to the process that submitted the job request. These features of the GRAM design facilitate the implementation of diverse higher-level scheduling strategies. For example, a high-level broker or co-allocator can make a request on behalf of an application, while the application monitor the progress of the request.

5.1   GRAM Scheduling Model

We discuss briefly the scheduling model defined by GRAM because this is relevant to subsequent discussion of co-allocation. This model is illustrated in Figure 5, which shows the state transitions that may be experienced by a GRAM job.

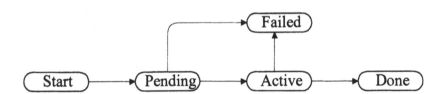

Fig. 5. State transition diagram for resource allocation requests submitted to the GRAM resource management API

When submitted, the job is initially **pending**, indicating that resources have not yet been allocated to the job. At some point, the job is allocated the requested resources, and the application starts running. The job then transitions to the **active** state. At any point prior to entering the **done** state, the job can be terminated, causing it to enter the **failed** state. A job can fail because of explicit termination, an error in the format of the request, a failure in the underlying resource management system, or a denial of access to the resource. The source of the failure is provided as part of the notification of state transition. When all of the processes in the job have terminated and resources have been deallocated, the job enters the **done** state.

5.2   GRAM Implementation

The GRAM implementations that we have constructed have the structure shown
in Figure 6. The principal components are the GRAM client library, the gatekeeper, the RSL parsing library, the job manager, and the GRAM reporter. The
Globus security infrastructure (GSI) is used for authentication and for authorization.

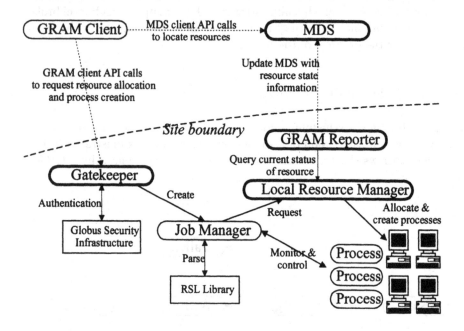

Fig. 6. Major components of the GRAM implementation. Those represented by
thick-lined ovals are long-lived processes, while the thin-lined ovals are short-
lived processes created in response to a request.

The *GRAM client library* is used by an application or a co-allocator acting
on behalf of an application. It interacts with the GRAM gatekeeper at a remote
site to perform mutual authentication and transfer a request, which includes a
resource specification and a callback (described below).

The *gatekeeper* is an extremely simple component that responds to a request
by doing three tasks: performing mutual authentication of user and resource,
determining a local user name for the remote user, and starting a job manager
which executes as that local user and actually handles the request. The first two
security-related tasks are performed by calls to the Globus security infrastructure (GSI), which handles issues of site autonomy and substrate heterogeneity

in the security domain. To start the job manager, the gatekeeper must run as a privileged program: on Unix systems, this is achieved via suid or inetd. However, because the interface to the GSI is small and well defined, it is easy for organizations to approve (and port) the gatekeeper code. In fact, the gatekeeper code has successfully undergone security reviews at a number of large supercomputer centers. The mapping of remote user to locally recognized user name minimizes the amount of code that must run as a privileged program; it also allows us to delegate most authorization issues to the local system.

The *job manager* is responsible for creating the actual processes requested by the user. This task typically involves submitting a resource allocation request to the underlying resource management system, although if no such system exists on a particular resource, a simple fork may be performed. Once processes are created, the job manager is also responsible for monitoring the state of the created processes, notifying the callback contact of any state transitions, and implementing control operations such as process termination. The job manager terminates once the job for which it is responsible has terminated.

The *GRAM reporter* is responsible for storing into MDS various information about scheduler structure (e.g., whether the scheduler supports reservation and the number of queues) and state (e.g., total number of nodes, number of nodes currently available, currently active jobs, and expected wait time in a queue). An advantage of implementing the GRAM reporter as a distinct component is that MDS reports can continue even when no gatekeeper or job manager is running: for example, when the gatekeeper is run from inetd.

As noted above, GRAM implementations have been constructed for six local schedulers to date: Condor, LSF, NQE, Fork, EASY, and LoadLeveler. Much of the GRAM code is independent of the local scheduler, and so only a relatively small amount of scheduler-specific code needed to be written in each case. In most cases, this code comprises shell scripts that use the local scheduler's user-level API. State transitions are handled mostly by polling, because this proved to be more reliable than monitoring job processes by using mechanisms provided by the local schedulers.

6 Resource Brokers

As noted above, we use the term *resource broker* to denote an entity in our architecture that translates abstract resource specifications into more concrete specifications. As illustrated in Figure 2, this definition is broad enough to encompass a variety of behaviors, including application-level schedulers [3] that encapsulate information about the types of resource required to meet a particular performance requirement, resource locators that maintain information about the availability of various types of resource, and (ultimately) traders that create markets for resources. In each case, the broker uses information maintained locally, obtained from MDS, or contained in the specification to *specialize* the specification, mapping it into a new specification that contain more detail. Requests can be passed to several brokers, effectively composing the behaviors of those brokers, until eventually the specification is specialized to the point that it identifies a specific resource manager. This specification can then be passed to the appropriate GRAM or, in the case of a multirequest, to a resource co-allocator.

fault tolerance, so that errors reported by GRAM would result in a task being resubmitted elsewhere.

6.3 A Graphical Resource Selector

The graphical resource selector (GRS) illustrated in Figure 7 is an example of an interactive resource selector constructed with our services. This Java application allows the user to build up a network representing the resources required for an application; another network can be constructed to monitor the status of candidate physical resources. A combination of automatic and manual techniques is then used to guide resource selection, eventually generating an RSL specification for the resources in question. MDS services are used to obtain the information used for resource monitoring and selection, and resource co-allocator services are used to generate the GRAM requests required to execute a program once a resource selection is made.

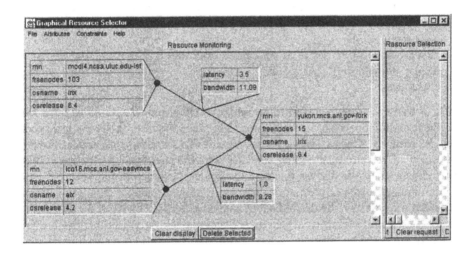

Fig. 7. A screen shot of the Graphical Resource Selector. This network shows three candidate resources and associated network connections. Static information regarding operating system version and dynamically updated information regarding the number of currently available nodes (**freenodes**) and network latency and bandwidth (in msec and Mb/s, respectively) allows the user to select appropriate resources for a particular experiment.

7   Resource Co-allocation

Through the actions of one or more resource brokers, the requirements of an application are refined into a ground RSL expression. If the expression consists of a single resource request, it can be submitted directly to the manager that controls that resource. However, as discussed above, a metacomputing application often requires that several resources—such as two or more computers and intervening networks—be allocated simultaneously. In these cases, a resource broker produces a multirequest, and co-allocation is required. The challenge in responding to a co-allocation request is to allocate the requested resources in a distributed environment, across two or more resource managers, where global state, such as availability of a set of resources, is difficult to determine.

Within our resource management architecture, multirequests are handled by an entity called a resource co-allocator. In brief, the role of a co-allocator is to split a request into its constituent components, submit each component to the appropriate resource manager, and then provide a means for manipulating the resulting set of resources as a whole: for example, for monitoring job status or terminating the job. Within these general guidelines, a range of different co-allocation services can be constructed. For example, we can imagine allocators that

- mirror current GRAM semantics: that is, require all resources to be available before the job is allowed to proceed, and fail globally if failure occurs at any resource;
- allocate at least N out of M requested resources and then return; or
- return immediately, but gradually return more resources as they become available.

Each of these services is useful to a class of applications. To date, we have had the most experience with a co-allocator that takes the first of these approaches: that is, extends GRAM semantics to provide for simultaneous allocation of a collection of resources, enabling the distributed collection of processes to be treated as a unit. We discuss this co-allocator in more detail.

Fundamental to a GRAM-style concurrent allocation algorithm is the ability to determine whether the desired set of resources is available at some time in the future. If the underlying local schedulers support reservation, this question can be easily answered by obtaining a list of available time slots from each participating resource manager, and choosing a suitable timeslot [23]. Ideally, this scheme would use transaction-based reservations across a set of resource managers, as provided by Gallop [26]. In the absence of transactions, the ability either to make a tentative reservation or to retract an existing reservation in needed. However, in general, a reservation-based strategy is limited because currently deployed local resource management solutions do not support reservation.

In the absence of reservation, we are forced to use indirect methods to achieve concurrent allocation. These methods optimistically allocate resources in the hope that the desired set will be available at some "reasonable" time in the future. Guided by sources of information, such as the current availability of resources (provided by MDS) or queue-time estimation [24, 7], a resource broker can construct an RSL request that is *likely*, but not guaranteed, to succeed. If for some reason the allocation eventually fails, all of the started jobs must be terminated. This approach has several drawbacks:

- It is inefficient in that computational resource are wasted while waiting for all of the requested to become available.
- We need to ensure that application components do not start to execute before the co-allocator can determine whether the request will succeed. Therefore, the application must perform a barrier operation to synchronize startup across components, meaning that the application must be altered beyond what is required for GRAM.
- Detecting failure of a request can be difficult if some of the request components are directed to resource managers that interface to queue-based local resource management systems. In these situations, a timeout must be used to detect failure.

However, in spite of all of these drawbacks, co-allocation can frequently be achieved in practice as long as the resource requirements are not large compared with the capacity of the metacomputing system.

We have implemented a GRAM-compatible co-allocator that implements a job abstraction in which multiple GRAM subjobs are collected into a single distributed job entity. State information for the distributed job is synthesized from the individual states of each subjob, and job control (e.g., cancellation) is automatically propagated to the resource managers at each subjob site. Subjobs are started independently and as discussed above must perform a runtime check-in operation. With the exception of this check-in operation, the co-allocator interface is a drop-in replacement for GRAM.

We have used this co-allocator to manage resources for SF-Express [19, 4], a large-scale distributed interactive simulation application. Using our co-allocator and the GUSTO testbed, we were able to simultaneously obtain 852 compute nodes on three different architectures located at six different computer centers, controlled by three different local resource managers. The use of a co-allocation service significantly simplified the process of resource allocation and application startup.

Running SF-Express "at scale" on a realistic testbed allowed us to study the scalability of our co-allocation strategy. One clear lesson learned is that the strict "all or nothing" semantics of the distributed job abstraction severely limits scalability. Even if each individual parallel computer is reasonably reliable and well understood, the probability of subjob failure due to improper configuration, network error, authorization difficulties, and the like. increases rapidly as the number of subjobs increases. Yet many such failure modes resulted simply from a failure to allocate a specific instance of a commodity resource, for which an equivalent resource could easily have been substituted. Because such failures frequently occur after a large number of subjobs have been successfully allocated, it would be desirable to make the substitution dynamically, rather than to cancel all the allocations and start over.

We plan to extend the current co-allocation structure to support such dynamic job structure modification. By passing information about the nature of the subjob failure out of the co-allocator, a resource broker can edit the specification, effectively implementing a backtracking algorithm for distributed resource allocation. Note that we can encode the necessary information about failure in a modified version of the original RSL request, which can be returned to the component that originally requested the co-allocation services. In this way, we can iterate through the resource-broker/co-allocation components of the resource management architecture until an acceptable collection of resources has been acquired on behalf of the application.

8   Conclusions

We have described a resource management architecture for metacomputing systems that addresses requirements of site autonomy, heterogeneous substrates, policy extensibility, co-allocation, and online control. This architecture has been deployed and applied successfully in a large testbed comprising 15 sites, 330 computers, and 3600 processors, within which LSF, NQE, LoadLeveler, EASY, Fork, and Condor were used as local schedulers.

The primary focus of our future work in this area will be on the development of more sophisticated resource broker and resource co-allocator services within our architecture, and on the extension of our resource management architecture to encompass other resources such as disk and network. We are also interested in the question of how policy information can be encoded so as to facilitate automatic negotiation of policy requirements by resources, users, and processes such as brokers acting as intermediaries.

Acknowledgments

We gratefully acknowledge the contributions made by many colleagues to the development of the GUSTO testbed and the Globus resource management architecture: in particular, Doru Marcusiu at NCSA and Bill Saphir at NERSC. This work was supported by DARPA under contract N66001-96-C-8523, and by the Mathematical, Information, and Computational Sciences Division subprogram of the Office of Computational and Technology Research, U.S. Department of Energy, under Contract W-31-109-Eng-38.

References

[1] Cray Research, 1997. Document Number IN-2153 2/97.

[2] D. Abramson, R. Sosic, J. Giddy, and B. Hall. Nimrod: A tool for performing parameterised simulations using distributed workstations. In *Proc. 4th IEEE Symp. on High Performance Distributed Computing*. IEEE Computer Society Press, 1995.

[3] F. Berman, R. Wolski, S. Figueira, J. Schopf, and G. Shao. Application-level scheduling on distributed heterogeneous networks. In *Proceedings of Supercomputing '96*. ACM Press, 1996.

[4] S. Brunett and T. Gottschalk. Scalable ModSAF simulations with more than 50,000 vehicles using multiple scalable parallel processors. In *Proceedings of the Simulation Interoperability Workshop*, 1997.

[5] S. Chapin. Distributed scheduling support in the presence of autonomy. In *Proc. Heterogeneous Computing Workshop*, pages 22–29, 1995.

[6] Joseph Czyzyk, Michael P. Mesnier, and Jorge J. Moré. The Network-Enabled Optimization System (NEOS) Server. Preprint MCS-P615-0996, Argonne National Laboratory, Argonne, Illinois, 1996.

[7] A. Downey. Predicting queue times on space-sharing parallel computers. In *Proceedings of the 11th International Parallel Processing Symposium*, 1997.

[8] S. Fitzgerald, I. Foster, C. Kesselman, G. von Laszewski, W. Smith, and S. Tuecke. A directory service for configuring high-performance distributed computations. In *Proc. 6th IEEE Symp. on High Performance Distributed Computing*, pages 365–375. IEEE Computer Society Press, 1997.

[9] I. Foster, J. Geisler, W. Nickless, W. Smith, and S. Tuecke. Software infrastructure for the I-WAY metacomputing experiment. *Concurrency: Practice & Experience*, 1998. to appear.

[10] I. Foster and C. Kesselman. Globus: A metacomputing infrastructure toolkit. *International Journal of Supercomputer Applications*, 11(2):115–128, 1997.

[11] GENIAS Software GmbH. CODINE: Computing in distributed networked environments, 1995. http://www.genias.de/genias/english/codine.html.

[12] A. Grimshaw, W. Wulf, J. French, A. Weaver, and P. Reynolds, Jr. Legion: The next logical step toward a nationwide virtual computer. Technical Report CS-94-21, Department of Computer Science, University of Virginia, 1994.

[13] The PSCHED API Working Group. PSCHED: An API for parallel job/resource management version 0.1, 1996. http://parallel.nas.nasa.gov/PSCHED/.

[14] R. Henderson and D. Tweten. Portable Batch System: External reference specification. Technical report, NASA Ames Research Center, 1996.

[15] International Business Machines Corporation, Kingston, NY. *IBM Load Leveler: User's Guide*, September 1993.

[16] J. Jones and C. Brickell. Second evaluation of job queuing/scheduling software: Phase 1 report. NAS Technical Report NAS-97-013, NASA Ames Research Center, Moffett Field, CA 94035-1000, 1997. http://science.nas.nasa.gov/Pubs/TechReports/NASreports/NAS-97-013/jms.eval.rep2.html.

[17] David A. Lifka. The ANL/IBM SP scheduling system. In *The IPPS'95 Workshop on Job Scheduling Strategies for Parallel Processing*, pages 187–191, April 1995.

[18] M. Litzkow, M. Livny, and M. Mutka. Condor - a hunter of idle workstations. In *Proc. 8th Intl Conf. on Distributed Computing Systems*, pages 104–111, 1988.

[19] P. Messina, S. Brunett, D. Davis, T. Gottschalk, D. Curkendall, L. Ekroot, and H. Siegel. Distributed interactive simulation for synthetic forces. In *Proceedings of the 11th International Parallel Processing Symposium*, 1997.

[20] K. Moore, G. Fagg, A. Geist, and J. Dongarra. Scalable networked information processing environment (SNIPE). In *Proceedings of Supercomputing '97*, 1997.

[21] B. C. Neuman. Prospero: A tool for organizing internet resources. *Electronic Networking: Research, Applications, and Policy*, 2(1):30–37, Spring 1992.

[22] B. C. Neuman and S. Rao. The Prospero resource manager: A scalable framework for processor allocation in distributed systems. *Concurrency: Practice & Experience*, 6(4):339–355, 1994.

[23] R. Ramamoorthi, A. Rifkin, B. Dimitrov, and K.M. Chandy. A general resource reservation framework for scientific computing. In *Scientific Computing in Object-Oriented Parallel Environments*, pages 283–290. Springer-Verlag, 1997.

[24] W. Smith, I. Foster, and V. Taylor. Predicting application run times using historical information. *Lecture Notes on Computer Science*, 1998.

[25] Amin Vahdat, Eshwar Belani, Paul Eastham, Chad Yoshikawa, Thomas Anderson, David Culler, and Michael Dahlin. WebOS: Operating system services for wide area applications. In *7th Symposium on High Performance Distributed Computing, to appear*, July 1998.

[26] J. Weissman. Gallop: The benefits of wide-area computing for parallel processing. Technical report, University of Texas at San Antonio, 1997.

[27] J. Weissman and A. Grimshaw. A federated model for scheduling in wide-area systems. In *Proc. 5th IEEE Symp. on High Performance Distributed Computing*, 1996.

[28] S. Zhou. LSF: Load sharing in large-scale heterogeneous distributed systems. In *Proc. Workshop on Cluster Computing*, 1992.

Implementing the Combination of Time Sharing and Space Sharing on AP/Linux

Kuniyasu Suzaki[1,2] and David Walsh[1]

[1] Australian National University, Canberra, ACT 0200, Australia
{suzaki, dwalsh}@cafe.anu.edu.au
http://cap.anu.edu.au/cap/projects/linux/
[2] Electrotechnical Laboratory, 1-1-4 Umezono, Tsukuba, 305, Japan

Abstract. We report the implementation of a scheduling method which combines time sharing and space sharing on AP/Linux. To run many tasks simultaneously on a parallel computer, the parallel computer system needs a partitioning algorithm that can partition processors for incoming tasks. However, a typical problem for the algorithm is a blockade situation, which causes low processor utilization and slow response. To avoid such a situation, we present a Time Sharing System(TSS) scheme that uses a partitioning algorithm. In this paper we state the implementation design of our TSS on a real parallel computer, the Fujitsu AP1000+. The design is based on the parallel operating system, AP/Linux. We report our current implementation and the performance.

Keywords: time sharing, space sharing, partitioning algorithm, AP/Linux

1   Introduction

Parallel computers are becoming more popular for many applications and many commercial parallel computers are on the market. Since every application cannot utilize all processors in a parallel computer, it is desirable to run many tasks simultaneously. To achieve this, we can use partitioning algorithms, which allocate a region of processors for an incoming task and then release the region when the task is outgoing, and do not allow the regions to overlap.

Partitioning algorithms have been proposed for many architectures. For mesh-connected parallel computers, these algorithms include the Frame Slide[1], the Two-Dimensional Buddy[2], the First Fit[3], the Best Fit[3], the Adaptive Scan[4], the Busy List[5], the Quick Allocation[6], and the non-partitioning algorithm[7,8]. However, such partitioning algorithms have a typical drawback, namely, the blockade situation.

Figure 1 illustrates the blockade situation occurring on a mesh-connected parallel computer. Since such partitioning algorithms have a first-come-first-served(FCFS) policy, their incoming tasks(1 and 2 in Figure 1) are allocated in the incoming order and can be accommodated at the same time. When task 3 is incoming, it cannot be allocated, because the allocation is prevented by tasks

Dror G. Feitelson, Larry Rudolph (Eds.): JSSPP'98, LNCS 1459, pp. 83–97, 1998.
© Springer-Verlag Berlin Heidelberg 1998

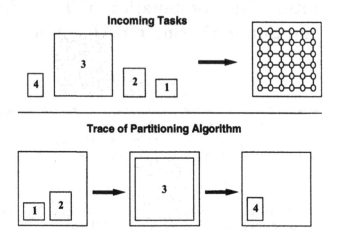

Fig. 1. Blockade situation for a mesh-connected parallel computer.

1 and 2. Task 3 is then queued until both tasks 1 and 2 are outgoing. Even if task 3 is allocated, task 4 cannot be allocated; thus, causing the blockade situation. If task 3 did not exist, tasks 1, 2, and 4 would be allocated on the parallel computer at the same time. The blockade situation causes decrease in the processor utilization and delay in response time for each task.

To avoid this blockade situation, Time Sharing System(TSS) schemes that uses a partitioning algorithm are proposed by Yoo et al.[9] and Suzaki et al.[10] as a kind of gang scheduling[11],[12]. They describe more detail of relation of space sharing and time sharing on a mesh-connected parallel computer.

The TSS provides virtual parallel computers which are activated alternately on a real parallel computer.Tasks are allocated on virtual parallel computers by a partitioning algorithm. In Figure 1, tasks 1, 2, and 4 are allocated on one virtual parallel computer and task 3 is allocated on another. TSS can avoid the blockade situation. It also achieves high processor utilization and quick response for each task.

In this paper we state the implementation design of TSS on a parallel computer, the Fujitsu AP1000+. The design is based on the parallel operating system AP/Linux[13] which is developed by the CAP group at the Australian National University(ANU). According to the design we have implemented the TSS on the AP1000+ at the ANU and at Electrotechincal Laboratory(ETL), which have 16 CPU's. We also confirmed performance of the tasks under our TSS.

In the next section, we present a number of time sharing systems which use partitioning algorithms. In Section 3, we give an overview of the Fujitsu AP1000+. In Section 4, we introduce AP/Linux, a parallel operating system for the AP1000+. In Section 5, we show the design of TSS on the AP/Linux. We report the current status of our implementation and performance in Section 6.

In Section 7, we discuss our future work. Finally, in Section 8, we state our conclusions.

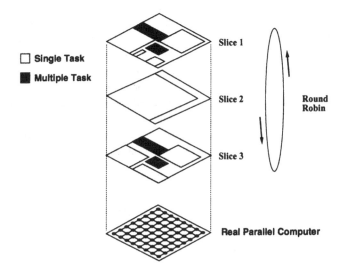

Fig. 2. TSS diagram showing single and multiple tasks.

2   Time Sharing System on Parallel Computers

On a single computer, a TSS allocates CPU time to tasks alternately, thus improving the response time of a task. This technique is also available for parallel computers. For example the CM5[14] offers TSS for users. However, there are idle processors, because not every application can utilize all the processors in a parallel computer. To decrease the number of idle processors, the use of partitioning algorithms have been proposed in the papers[9],[10]. The TSS scheme is combination of time sharing and space sharing, and is able to avoid the blockade situation, which is a typical problem in partitioning algorithms.

The TSS provides a number of virtual parallel computers that can be mapped to the structure of the target parallel computer. We call such virtual parallel computers *slices*. An incoming task is allocated on a slice. If no room is left for the incoming task on existing slices, a new slice is created and the task is allocated on this new slice. Based on round-robin scheme, each slice is alternately activated on the real parallel computer.

The TSS allows tasks to be allocated on more than one slice. If a processor region for a task on a slice is free on other slices, the task can sit on these other slices. The task is then executed as many times as the number of slices that hold that task, while all slices are activated by a round-robin scheme. We call a task that exists on more than one slices a *multiple task*, and a task that exists on only one slice a *single task*. Figure 2 illustrates multiple tasks and single tasks on slices. The idea of multiple task is resemble to multiple slot[15] and dynamic partitioning[16]. The multiple task is specialized for a mesh-connected parallel computer and is considered to searching algorithm of multiple tasks.

The tasks on slices are managed using the data structure illustrated in Figure 3. Each slice has two lists that manage the tasks, a *single task list* and a *multiple task list*. A single task list has submesh information for single tasks; namely, the x and y starting points of the submesh, the submesh width, and the submesh height. A multiple task list has the same submesh information, and also includes information for multiple tasks; namely, the slice number which links multiple tasks. The information for multiple tasks is used for the termination of tasks and reduction of slices[10].

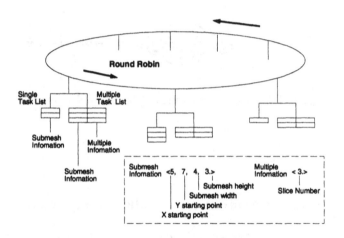

Fig. 3. Data structure for slices.

3   AP1000+

The AP1000+ is a distributed memory parallel computer, developed by Fujitsu. It has three networks; a broadcast network(B-net; 25MB/s), a torus network(T-net; 50MB/s per a link), and a synchronization network(S-net) illustrated in Figure 4. On the AP1000+ a processing unit is called a *cell*. Each cell is controlled by a host machine using the B-net and S-net. The AP1000+ offers special instructions which allow remote memory access. The remote memory access does not disturb a remote processor. Each cell can read remote memory with a *get* instruction and write with a *put* instruction.

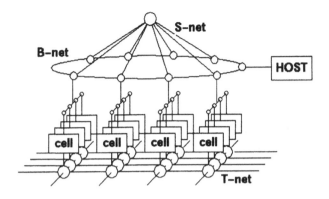

Fig. 4. AP1000+

Figure 5 shows the detail of a cell. The cell consists of a SuperSPARC processor, a memory controller(MC), a message controller(MSC+), a routing controller(RTC), and a B-net interface(BIF). The SuperSPARC offers write through cache action for memory protection due to the remote memory access. The MC has a MMU and manages address translation. The MSC+ controls messaging and remote memory accesses. The messages on the T-net are forwarded by worm hole routing. The BIF manages broadcast of messages using the B-net and synchronization using the S-net.

Fujitsu offers a simple operating system called "Cell-OS" for the AP1000+. Under Cell-OS, the machine is reset before launching each parallel program, and the kernel is loaded with the parallel program. Cell-OS offers a single-user and single-program environment and does not support all UNIX compatible functions. To improve this environment, AP/Linux has been developed by the CAP group at the Australian National University.

4   AP/Linux

AP/Linux[13] is the operating system for the Fujitsu AP1000+. It is based on the popular *Linux* operating system. It provides the facility of a parallel programming environment, as well as normal unix functionality. The Linux kernel is loaded on each cell and is long lived. It manages process scheduling, virtual memory, file systems, and system calls. Normal user logins are permitted on any cell and it behaves as a modern operating system.

AP/Linux also offers the environment to run parallel programs. We can run parallel programs on AP/Linux. To build parallel applications, AP/Linux offers APlib and MPI libraries[17]. APlib library offers a compatible Cell-OS interface. APlib and MPI libraries are able to access the MSC+ hardware directly from user space and give high throughput and low latency.

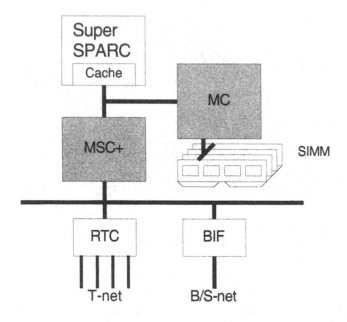

Fig. 5. Cell

The parallel programming environment is supported by the parallel run command *prun*, the parallel daemon *paralleld* which exists on each cell and manages the creation and termination of parallel processes, and special scheduling for parallel processing in the kernel(Figure 6). The normal scheduling provided by the Linux kernel can also manage parallel processes. However, performance can be poor due to the time waiting for messages, particularly when the message libraries wait by polling. The authors of AP/Linux recommend that a cooperative scheduling is used to achieve reasonable performance[13].

The procedure to run parallel programs is divided into process allocation and synchronization. We state these details.

4.1 Process Allocation

prun is the command used to launch a parallel process. It requires the number of processors and a parallel program name. For example, in Figure 6 the three *prun* commands require 2×2 processors to run *task1*, 3×3 processors for *task2*, and 1×3 for *task3*. A *prun* command can be issued on any cell and it sends a message to the *paralleld* on the primary cell. In this paper we assume that the primary cell is cell0.

The *parallelds* manage creation and termination of parallel processes and manage a standard I/O session between *prun* and the parallel process. The

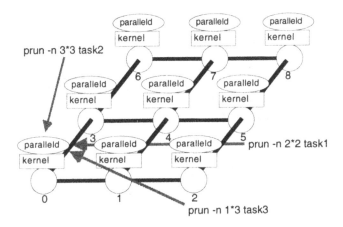

Fig. 6. AP/Linux

paralleld on cell0 reserves processors required by the *prun* and sends the parallel process image to the *paralleld*s on the reserved processors. Each *paralleld* launches the parallel process using the *clone()* system call and the parallel process enqueued to each local scheduling queue. The *clone()* system call can get the same process ID(PID) and Task ID(TID) on each cell. The IDs make it possible to identify the parallel process on all cells. On AP/Linux, high numbered PIDs are reserved for parallel processes and low numbered PIDs are reserved for single processes. The TID is attached to the header of messages and is used for posting the message to the destination process.

Figure 7 shows the process allocation required by *pruns* in Figure 6. The processors which are offered by the *paralleld* start from cell0. The scheduling queue on cell0 has all parallel processes. In the figure, cell0 has three parallel processes although cell5,6,7, and 8 have only one parallel process. This situation is caused by lack of space sharing, which results in poor load balancing over the machine.

When a parallel process is terminated, the *paralleld* catches a signal from the parallel process and cuts the standard I/O session between the parallel process and the *prun*.

4.2   Synchronization

AP/Linux provides a loose wake-up synchronization of parallel processes. It is a reasonable compromise, because it is difficult to predict the state of processes on remote processors in UNIX environments, including Linux. For example, page faults are done asynchronously.

The local scheduler on cell0 manages wake-up synchronization for each parallel process, because all parallel processes are allocated from cell0, and the local

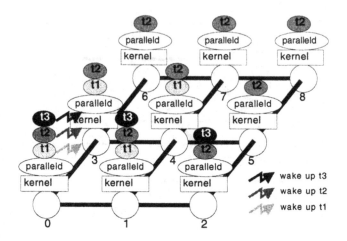

Fig. 7. Process allocation and Synchronization by AP/Linux

scheduling queue has all parallel process information. The local scheduler on cell0 is responsible for the control of wake-up synchronization for all parallel processes.

In Figure 7, three wake-up synchronizations are issued for each process. The wake-up synchronization of parallel processes is controlled by the wake-up of parallel processes on cell0. Just before a parallel process on the scheduling queue of cell0 is activated, the kernel on cell0 informs other cells that they should activate the parallel process, i.e. the kernel on cell0 sends the TID of the parallel process using B-net. The TID is used for identification of parallel process on each cells. The kernels on the cells which have the TID wake up the parallel process at the next scheduling.

The handler for identification and rescheduling of parallel process is implemented by *fast handler*, which is Linux interrupt handler. The fast handler catchs an interrupt just when an interrupt has occurred, but the main handling is done after the current process is suspended. The fast handler only handles the identification of TID just when the wake-up synchronization has occurred. If the cell has the TID, the kernel reschedules after the current process is suspended. It achieves loose synchronization.

Parallel processes can get processing time if the processor is not busy. The scheduling depends on the load on each processor. In Figure 7, while *task3* is running on cell0,1, and 2, *task1* and *task2* may be running on cell3 and 4. However, there is no guarantee of synchronization. The local scheduler decides which processes run.

The process switch sometimes cause problems with messaging on network. To solve this problem, the CM5[14] offers the *all-fall-down* mechanism on network switch. The *all-fall-down* mechanism enqueues messages to the nearest switch when a process switch has occurred. The all-fall-down mechanism clears the network. The typical overhead of a process switch on the CM5 is reported as 10 ms[18]. The AP1000+ does not offer this facility. On AP/Linux, messages can be alive on the network even after a process switch has occurred. The message header has the TID which is used for identification. Even if the process is switched on the destination cell, the message is identified by the TID and is buffered at the memory space of the process.

5   Design of Our TSS on AP/Linux

Unfortunately original AP/Linux cannot make the best use of parallel computers, because of the following reasons.

- No space sharing.
- Wake-up synchronization of parallel process depends on the scheduling queue on cell0.

Original AP/Linux does not allow space sharing. The allocations of parallel processes always start from cell0. These allocations cause concentration of load on cell0.

Wake-up synchronization is issued depending on the scheduling queue on cell0, because the scheduling queue have all PIDs of parallel processes. Only one parallel process can run synchronously at a time. At that time other parallel processes cannot run synchronously. Owing to the wake-up synchronization, space sharing is not implemented.

In order to implement our TSS, allocation of parallel processes should be allowed to start from any cells, namely the allocation must be independent form the kernel on each cell. Furthermore wake-up synchronization of parallel processes should be done by a special facility which is independent from the scheduling queue on cell0, namely, the facility does not implement in a kernel. To settle these requirements, we provide a slice daemon(*sliced*) which takes responsibility of process allocation and wake-up synchronization of parallel processes.

Our TSS design is based on the AP/Linux implementation. We use most of the facilities of the parallel execution environment provided by the original AP/Linux, as we do not want to increase special facilities, and it is easy to implement.

5.1   Process Allocation

sliced takes responsibility of space sharing. In the same manner of the original AP/Linux, *prun* requests the *paralleld* on cell0 to execute a parallel process. The new *paralleld* asks the allocation region to *sliced*. The *sliced* searches a processor region using a partitioning algorithm. If a region is decided, *sliced* supplies the region to *paralleld*. Creation of parallel processes are done in the same manner as the original AP/Linux, that is, the parallel process gets the

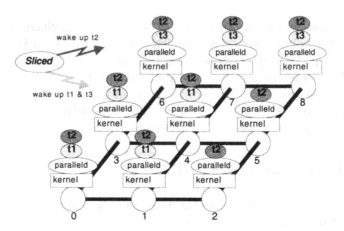

Fig. 8. Process allocation and Synchronization by our method

same PID and TID(using *clone()* system call) and is subsequently enqueued in a local scheduling queue.

The partitioning algorithm assumes slices(virtual parallel processors mentioned in Section 2.) and uses the data structure described in Figure 3. Figure 8 shows the allocation required by *pruns* in Figure 6. *task1* and *task2* are allocated on a slice and *task3* is allocated on another slice. *sliced* also manages *multiple tasks* using this data structure.

When a parallel process finishes, it sends a message to *paralleld* in the same manner as the original AP/Linux. Then *paralleld* informs *sliced* of the termination, which deletes the processor region data for the parallel process for reuse. The details of the processor region management are described in the paper[10].

5.2   Wake-Up Synchronization

The *sliced* holds the data structure which is illustrated in Figure 3, and knows the parallel processes which are on a slice. The parallel processes on a slice are activated simultaneously every certain interval, which are parameterized.

Wake-up synchronization is controlled by *sliced*. In Figure 8, synchronization is issued for *task1* and *task2* and for *task3*. This means that the wake-up of parallel processes is independent from the scheduling queue on cell0.

The synchronization request is issued using B-net, as in the original AP/Linux. The synchronization request issued by *sliced* uses PID instead of TID, because parallel processes are distinguished by PID in *sliced*. A synchronization request can send plural PIDs to achieve low overhead. In Figure 8, a synchronization request is issued to wake up *task1* and *task3*. These cells ,which have the PIDs, handle synchronization requests in the same manner as the original AP/Linux.

6   Current Status

The new *paralleld* and *sliced* are running on the 16 cell AP1000+ at Electrotech-incal Laboratory and the Australian National University. Unfortunately it does not offer 2 dimensional partitioning, as this depends on broadcast mechanism of old *paralleld* [1]. It offers 1 dimensional First Fit partitioning. The requirement of rectangular cell region is linearized. For example 2×2 cells request is translated into 4×1 cells and allocated as contiguous cells. This implementation offers multiple tasks as described in Section 2.

The *sliced* sends a wake-up synchronization every $100ms$. The Linux tick time is $16.7(1/60)ms$. Therefore A wake-up synchronization is sent once every 6 process time quantum.

6.1   Simple Performance Test

In order to evaluate the effect of our scheduling, we ran test processes and measured elapsed process time.

At first we ran 8 processes which required the similar CPU time and 2 CPUs, namely, matrix multiply. Figure 9 shows the results. The x axis indicates time and the y axis indicates the order of submitted processes, the lowest process(No.1) is submitted first and highest process(No.8) is submitted last. In this figure, lines indicate the start time and finish time of each process. The black lines indicate the results by our method and gray lines indicate the re-sults by the original AP/Linux. The number in front of the parenthesis indicates the required processors and the number in parentheses indicates the allocated processor region.

This result shows the effect of space sharing. The original scheduling allocated all processes on cell 0 and 1. Our method can distribute processes equally on all cells. The 8 processes do not overlap on any cells and run simultaneously. Therefore the theoretical improvement is $1/8.0$. However, there is the overhead of synchronization and other processes, including *paralleld* and *sliced*. The practical improvement was $1/7.1$ in this case. This result means that the overhead is insignificant, the effect of space sharing could achieve high performance.

The start time of each process(on the left side of the line) depends on the time of allocation. From Figure 9, we know that allocation time of our methods are faster than the original scheduling. The reason for this was that *paralleld* existed on cell0, and all processes were allocated on cell0 by the original scheduling policy. Cell0 had a heavier load. In our method, *paralleld* and *sliced* also exist on cell0 but only a parallel process is allocated on cell0 in this case. The load on cell0 was not high with our method. Therefore the response for allocation could be fast.

Second, we confirmed the effect of the *multiple task*. Figure 10 shows the results with 8 processes, which require random cells(2,6,6,2,2,11,4, and 3). In

---

[1] The broadcast mechanism is updated[19] and enables to get 2 dimensional regions. We are now updating our *paralleld* and *sliced*.

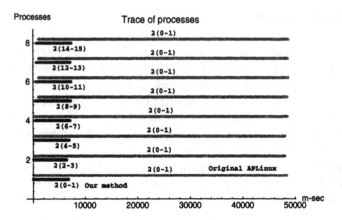

Fig. 9. Trace of parallel processes on original AP/Linux and our method

this case three slices were created. The first slice had three processes(process1,4, and 6 which occupied cell0-1, cell14-15, and cell 2-13 respectively). The second slice had 4 processes(process2,3,4, and 5 which were occupied cell2-7, cell8-13, cell14-15, and cell0-1 respectively). The third slice had 4 processes(process 3,4,7 and 8 which occupied cell8-13, cell14-15, cell0-3 and cell4-6 respectively). Process 3 and 4 could be multiple tasks. Process 3 existed on slice 2 and 3. Process 4 existed on slice 1, 2, and 3. The other tasks were single tasks. In this case process 3 was approximately 2/3 times faster than a single task. Process 4 was approximately 1/3 times faster than a single task. These results indicate that multiple tasks worked well and overhead of allocation and synchronization did not affect processes severely.

In Figure 10 the process 1,5 and 7 showed late finish times. These processes were allocated on cell0. The reason is that cell0 is busy with single processes(*paralleld* and *sliced*) as well as parallel processes. The situation caused unfairness of CPU time for parallel processes. We discuss how to settle this problem in Section 7.

7   Discussions

7.1   Parallel Process and UNIX Environment

We have implemented scheduling method which combines time sharing and space sharing. The original concepts assume that only parallel processes exist and these parallel processes can switch at the same time. Also it does not consider a process switch caused by virtual memory or I/O. However, in real implementation we must deal with these side effects.

Our implementation deals with the existence of sequential processes on each cell. Some sequential processes are standard UNIX daemons, for example *init*,

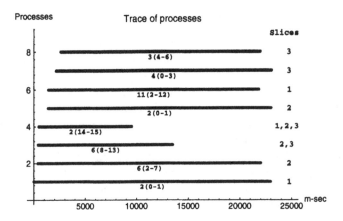

Fig. 10. Effect of multiple tasks

kswap, kflushd, and *paralleld.* Parallel processes also use virtual memory resulting in asynchronous pasing events. Both of the effects cause skew of time quantum for each process.

We use autonomous scheduling on each cell to compensate for this skew. When a parallel process on a cell causes virtual memory activity, anther process is activated to compensate for the skew while the parallel process on other cell is running. This is one solution to allow for the UNIX environment still, while running tightly scheduled parallel processes. Unfortunately the combination does not fit nicely in some cases. For example the process switch causes delay in communication with a parallel process. In the original gang scheduling algorithm, there is no process switch in a time quanta. Therefore a parallel process is supposed that there is no interference communication. However, in this implementation the problem arises. We must estimate the effect of the delay and minimize the cost.

7.2   Load Distribution

The load of parallel processes can be distributed by our TSS, which uses a partitioning algorithm. However, AP/Linux allows a mix of parallel processes and sequential processes. Unfortunately the *sliced* doesn't observe the load caused by sequential processes. The *sliced* should observe the situation and distribute the load of parallel and sequential processes on each cell. We propose it should act like NQS(Network Queuing System). NQS observes the load on each processor and allocates a job to the processor which has the smallest load. We must consider the new partitioning algorithm for this purpose.

7.3 New Partitioning Algorithm

We have proposed a new partitioning algorithm[20] which is a combination of a contiguous and a non-contiguous partitioning algorithm[7,8]. The new algorithm compensates for the weak points of contiguous and non-contiguous partitioning algorithms. It could achieve high processor utilization and quick response. We plan to implement this algorithm on a real machine.

However, there may be difficultiies implementing multiple tasks which exist on some slices, as processor regions of a task are sometimes distributed. This may invoke a significant cross-checking overhead at task load time. The multiple task is useful to decrease the number of slices as well as to increase processor utilization. If we use the non-contiguous partitioning algorithm in our TSS, we must consider the algorithm to check crossing processor regions.

8   Conclusions

In this paper we presented the design of a time sharing system on a real parallel computer, the AP1000+. The time sharing system includes space sharing by a partitioning algorithm, and can make the best use of the number of processors.

The implementation design is based on the modern operating system AP/Linux, because AP/Linux offers many facilities for parallel processing, the parallel execution command *prun*, a daemon for creating parallel processes *paralleld*, and scheduling for parallel processes. Using these facilities, we introduced space sharing on AP/Linux, and separated wake-up synchronization from the scheduling queue on the primary cell. These special facilities for space sharing and wake-up synchronization did not implemented in a kernel. We showed the improvement of the special facilities as a *sliced* daemon for process allocation and synchronization of parallel processes. Performance tests were also taken, showing the effects of space sharing. In the near future, we are planning to measure the exact performance by using some real applications. We will make clear the effect of messaging and scheduling policy.

References

1. P. Chuang and N. Tzeng. An efficient submesh allocation strategy for mesh computer systems. *Proceedings of the 11th International Conference on Distributed Computing Systems*, pages 259–263, 1991.
2. K. Li and K. Cheng. A two dimensional buddy system for dynamic resource allocation in a partitionable mesh connected system. *Journal of Parallel and Distributed Computing*, (12):79–83, 1991.
3. Y. Zhu. Efficient processor allocation strategies for mesh-connected parallel computers. *Journal of Parallel and Distributed Computing*, 16:328–337, 1992.
4. J. Ding and L. N. Bhuyan. An adaptive submesh allocation strategy for two-dimensional mesh connected systems. *Proceedings of International Conference on Parallel Processing*, pages (II)193–200, 1993.

5. D. D. Sharma and D. K. Pradhan. A fast and efficient strategy for submesh allocation in mesh-connected parallel computers. *Procedings of the 5th IEEE Symposium on Parallel and Distributed Processing*, pages 682–689, 1993.

6. S.M. Yoo and H.Y. Youn. An efficient task allocation scheme for two-dimensional mesh-connected systems. *Proceedings of the 15th International Conference on Distributed Computing Systems*, pages 501–508, 1995.

7. W. Liu, V. Lo, K. Windish, and B Nitzberg. Non-contiguous Processor Allocation Algorithms for Distributed Memory Multicomputers. *Supercomputing*, pages 227–236, 1994.

8. V. Lo, K. Windish, W. Liu, and B Nitzberg. Non-contiguous Processor Allocation Algorithms for Mesh-connected Multicomputers. *IEEE Trans. on PARALLEL AND DISTRIBUTED SYSTEMS*, 8(7):712–726, 1997.

9. B. Yoo, C. Das, and C. Yu. Processor management techniques for mesh-connected multiprocessors. *Proceedings on International Conference on Parallel Processing*, pages II–105–112, 1995.

10. K. Suzaki, H. Tanuma, S. Hirano, Y. Ichisugi, and M. Tukamoto. Time sharing systems that use a partitioning algorithm on mesh-connected parallel computers. *The Ninth International Conference on Parallel and Distributed Computing Systems*, pages 268–275, 1996.

11. J.K. Ousterout. Scheduling techniques for concurrent Systems. *Proceedings of the 3rd International Conference on Distributed Computing Systems*, pages 22–30, 1982.

12. D. Feitelson and L. Rudolph. Distributed Hierachical Control for Parallel Processing. *IEEE COMPUTER*, 23(5):65–77, 1990.

13. A. Tridgell, P. Mackerras, D. Sitsky, and D. Walsh. Ap/linux a modern os for the ap1000+. *The 6th Parallel Computing Workshop*, pages P2C1–P2C9, 1996.

14. *Connection Machine CM-5 Technical Summary*. Thinking Machines, 1992.

15. D. Feitelson. Packing Schemes for Gang Scheduling. *Lecture Notes in Computer Science 1162*, pages 89–110, 1996.

16. A. Hori, Y. Ishikawa, H. Konaka, M. Maeda, and T. Tomokiyo. A scalable time-sharing scheduling for partitionalble, distributed memory parallel machines. *Proceedings of the 28th Annual Hawaii International Conference on System Sciences*, pages 173–182, 1995.

17. D. Sitsky, P. Mackerras, A. Tridgell, and D. Walsh. Implementing MPI under AP/Linux. *Second MPI Developers Conference*, pages 32–39, 1996.

18. D. C. Burger, R. S. Hyder, B. P. Miller, and D.A. Wood. Paging Trade off in Distributed Shared-Memory Multiprocessors. *Supercomputing*, pages 590–599, 1994.

19. D. Walsh. Parallel process management on the ap1000+ under ap/linux. *The 7th Parallel Computing Workshop*, pages P1V1–P1v5, 1997.

20. K. Suzaki, H. Tanuma, S. Hirano, Y. Ichisugi, C. Connelly, and M. Tukamoto. Multi-tasking method on parallel computers which combines a contiguous and a non-contiguous processor partitioning algorithm. *Lecture Notes in Computer Science 1184*, pages 641–650, 1996.

Job Scheduling Scheme for Pure Space Sharing Among Rigid Jobs

Kento Aida[1], Hironori Kasahara[2], and Seinosuke Narita[2]

[1] Department of Mathematical and Computing Sciences,
Tokyo Institute of Technology
2-12-1, O-okayama, Meguro-ku, Tokyo, JAPAN 152
aida@noc.titech.ac.jp
http://www.noc.titech.ac.jp/~,aida
[2] Department of Electrical, Electronics and Computer Engineering,
Waseda University
3-4-1, Ohkubo, Shinjuku-ku, Tokyo, JAPAN 169
{kasahara,narita}@oscar.elec.waseda.ac.jp
http://www.oscar.elec.waseda.ac.jp/

Abstract. This paper evaluates the performance of job scheduling schemes for pure space sharing among rigid jobs. Conventional job scheduling schemes for the pure space sharing among rigid jobs have been achieved by First Come First Served (FCFS). However, FCFS has a drawback such that it can not utilize processors efficiently. This paper evaluates the performance of job scheduling schemes that are proposed to alleviate the drawback of FCFS by simulation, performance analysis and experiments on a real multiprocessor system. The results showed that Fit Processors First Served (FPFS), which searches the job queue and positively dispatches jobs that fit idle processors, was more effective and more practical than others.

1 Introduction

Parallel processing schemes such as SPMD [1] and Multigrain parallel processing scheme [2] are used on multiprocessor systems. In these schemes, a user or a compiler specifies the number of processors on which the job (program) is executed and optimizes the job (program) considering data locality. On the execution of these jobs, the job requests a certain number of processors. The number of processors that the job requests is specified by a user or a compiler. A job scheduler dispatches the job to the requested number of processors. Each job is exclusively executed until its completion on these processors. These jobs are called "rigid jobs" and this kind of scheduling is called "pure space sharing" [3].

The pure space sharing among rigid jobs has several advantages such that implementation is simple and any user can have optimal performance by executing the job on the requested number of processors exclusively. Although more complex scheduling schemes such as gang scheduling and adaptive space sharing are also discussed in the literature [4,5,6], the pure space sharing among rigid

Dror G. Feitelson, Larry Rudolph (Eds.): JSSPP'98, LNCS 1459, pp. 98–121, 1998.

jobs is adopted on most multiprocessor systems currently installed for practical use because of these advantages.

Processor allocation strategies for the pure space sharing among rigid jobs such as Frame Sliding, First Fit, Best Fit and Non-contiguous processor allocation algorithm, which allocate processors to jobs, have been proposed [7,8,9,10,11]. In these strategies, processors are allocated to the job at the head of the job queue. In other words, a job scheduling is achieved by First Come First Served (FCFS) manner. However, FCFS has a drawback such that it can not utilize processors efficiently [9]. In FCFS, when the number of idle processors is less than the number of processors requested by the job at the head of the job queue, a job scheduler does not dispatch any job to processors and causes low processor utilization.

Several schemes have been proposed to alleviate the drawback of FCFS. Queue sorting is the technique that a job scheduler sorts jobs in the job queue by the number of requested processors. Both techniques that sort jobs by non-increasing order and by non-decreasing order were discussed [12,13]. Another technique, which positively dispatches jobs that fit idle processors, was also discussed. Here, "a job that fits idle processors" means "a job that requests processors whose number is not exceeding the number of idle processors." In Fit Processors First Served (FPFS), a job scheduler searches jobs in the job queue and dispatches a job that fits idle processors to processors [14,15,16] [1]. Backfilling is a similar scheme to FPFS. In Backfilling, when the job at the head of the job queue waits for being dispatched because there are not enough idle processors for it, a job scheduler dispatches other jobs that fit idle processors without affecting the start time of the job at the head of the job queue [13,17,18].

Several job scheduling schemes described in the previous paragraph has been evaluated either by simulation or experiments on real machines [13,16,17,18]. However, none of work has compared performance of all these job scheduling schemes and has evaluated their performance by an analytical method.

This paper evaluates the performance of job scheduling schemes for pure space sharing among rigid jobs. First, this paper evaluates and compares the performance of these job scheduling schemes by simulation. Next, the performance of two job scheduling schemes that showed best performance in the simulation, FPFS and Fit Processors Most Processors First Served (FPMPFS), is analyzed using queueing model and one-dimensional bin-packing problem. The authors have implemented the FPFS and FPMPFS on a multiprocessor system NEC Cenju-3 [19]. Experimental results on the Cenju-3 are also shown.

The rest of this paper is organized as follows. Section 2 describes the job scheduling model assumed in this paper. Next, Sect. 3 describes job scheduling schemes evaluated in this paper and Sect. 4 shows simulation results. Then, Sect. 5 shows performance analysis results of FPFS and FPMPFS, and Sect. 6 shows experimental results on a multiprocessor system NEC Cenju-3.

---

[1] This scheme is referred to as FCFS-fill in [15] and as LSF-RTC in [16]. However, this paper refers to this as FPFS for convenience.

2   Job Scheduling Model

This section describes the job scheduling model assumed in this paper.

The multiprocessor system under consideration consists of a number of processors connected equally by a crossbar network or a multi-stage interconnection network. Since the execution time of a job is insensitive to the location of each processor that executes the job on this multiprocessor system, this paper assumes that a job scheduler can dispatch a job to any idle processor existing arbitrary location.

Figure 1 illustrates the model of the job scheduler. A job arrives at the job queue dynamically. Each job requests a certain number of processors. The number of processors is specified by a user or a compiler. The job scheduler obtains status of processors. Whenever a new job arrives or a job being executed on processors finishes, the job scheduler dispatches the job in the job queue to idle processors using a certain scheduling scheme. At this time, each job is dispatched to idle processors whose number is same as the number that the job requests. The job that has been dispatched to processors is executed exclusively until its completion. For an arrived job, the job scheduler has knowledge about only the number of processors that the job requests, because it is generally difficult that a job scheduler knows the execution time of an arrived job before its execution. However, this paper assumes that the execution time of the job is also known before its execution when Backfilling is applied [2].

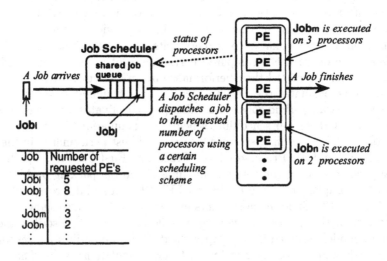

Fig. 1. The model of the job scheduler

---

[2] Backfilling requires execution time of jobs for its scheduling process.

3   Job Scheduling Schemes

This section describes job scheduling schemes evaluated in this paper. Table 1 shows the summary of scheduling schemes evaluated in this paper.

Table 1. Scheduling schemes

schemes	sorting queue	searching queue
FCFS	no	no
MPFS	yes	no
LPFS	yes	no
FPFS	no	yes
FPMPFS	yes	yes
FPLPFS	yes	yes
Backfilling	no	yes

3.1   FCFS

First Come First Served (FCFS) is a conventional scheme that is currently used on most multiprocessor systems. A job scheduler dispatches the job at the head of the job queue when the number of processors requested by the job is not exceeding the number of idle processors.

3.2   Queue Sorting

Whenever a new job arrives at the job queue, jobs in the job queue are sorted by the number of processors that jobs request. A job scheduler dispatches the job at the head of the sorted job queue when the number of processors requested by the job is not exceeding the number of idle processors. Jobs in the job queue can be sorted by non-increasing order or by non-decreasing order. This paper refers to the former as Most Processors First Served (MPFS) and refers to the latter as Least Processors First Served (LPFS).

The basic idea of MPFS is to utilize idle processors efficiently by sorting jobs by non-increasing order of the number of requested processors. It is known that sorting items by non-increasing order of items' size improves packing efficiency in bin-packing problem [20]. The basic idea of LPFS is to reduce mean response time of jobs by dispatching a large number of small jobs, jobs that request a small number of processors, preferentially.

3.3   FPFS

The basic idea of Fit Processors First Served (FPFS) is to utilize idle processors efficiently by positively dispatching jobs that fit idle processors. The scheduling algorithm of FPFS is as follows. Here, i indicates the order of jobs in the job queue and n indicates the number of jobs in the job queue. $RequestedPE_i$ denotes the number of processors requested by Job_i and $IdlePE$ denotes the number of idle processors.

1. $i = 1$.
2. Compare $RequestedPE_i$ and $IdlePE$.

    (a) if $RequestedPE_i > IdlePE$, go to 3.
    (b) if $RequestedPE_i \leq IdlePE$, dispatch Job_i to $RequestedPE_i$ of processors. Then, $IdlePE = IdlePE - RequestedPE_i$. Go to 3.

3. $i = i + 1$. if $i \leq n$ and $IdlePE > 0$, go to 2.
4. Go to 1.

The following algorithm is executed when a job being executed on processors finishes.

1. Relinquish processors on which the job has been executed.
2. $IdlePE = IdlePE + number\ of\ relinquished\ processors$

FPFS can be applied with the queue sorting technique. This paper refers to FPFS's with queue sorting as Fit Processors Most Processors First Served (FPMPFS) and Fit Processors Least Processors First Served (FPLPFS). In FPMPFS, a job scheduler sorts jobs in the job queue by non-increasing order of the number of requested processors and then dispatches jobs to processors in the same way as FPFS. In FPLPFS, a job scheduler dispatches jobs in the same way except sorting jobs in the job queue by non-decreasing order. However, FPLPFS causes same job scheduling results as LPFS because of the following reason. During searching jobs sorted by non-decreasing order of the number of requested processors, if a job scheduler finds the job that does not fit idle processors, no more job that remains in the job queue fits idle processors.

3.4   Backfilling

Backfilling is a similar scheme as FPFS except it does not affect the start time of the job at the head of the job queue. When the job at the head of the job queue, Job_{top}, waits for being dispatched because there are not enough idle processors for it, a job scheduler calculates the start time of Job_{top} from the remaining execution time of jobs that are in execution. Then, the job scheduler begins to search the job queue. When the job scheduler finds the job that fits idle processors, Job_{fit}, the job scheduler verifies if dispatching Job_{fit} delays the start time of Job_{top}. If dispatching Job_{fit} does not delay the start time of Job_{top}, the job scheduler dispatches Job_{fit} to idle processors . Otherwise, the job scheduler does not dispatch Job_{fit}. Dispatching Job_{fit} does not delay the start time of Job_{top} in the following cases.

1. Job_{fit} is going to finish and release processors before the start time of Job_{top}.

2. Job_{fit} is not going to finish before the start time of Job_{top}. However, another job is going to finish and release processors so that there are going to exist enough idle processors for Job_{top} before its start time.

Backfilling has difficulty for practical use, because it assumes that the execution time of each job is known before its execution. Generally, it is difficult that a job scheduler knows execution time of an arrived job before its execution. Therefore, this paper assumes that a job scheduler has knowledge about only the number of processors requested by the job. However, in order to compare the performance of Backfilling with others, this paper also assumes that the execution time of an arrived job is known before its execution when Backfilling is applied.

3.5   Avoiding Starvation

It is possible that starvation occurs in FPFS, FPMPFS, FPLPFS, MPFS and LPFS. In order to avoid starvation, $WaitLimit$, which is a deadline that a job continues waiting for being dispatched to processors, is given to each job.

In FPFS, FPMPFS and FPLPFS with $WaitLimit$, a job scheduler gives a priority to $Job_{overWaitLimit}$, which is a job waiting for being dispatched after its $WaitLimit$. The algorithm of FPFS, FPMPFS and FPLPFS with $WaitLimit$ can be derived by changing 2(a) of the algorithm in Sect. 3.3 as follows.

2. Compare $RequestedPE_i$ and $IdlePE$.
   (a) if $RequestedPE_i > IdlePE$,
       if Job_i is $Job_{overWaitLimit}$, go to 4, else go to 3.

In schemes that apply the queue sorting, or MPFS, LPFS, FPMPFS and FPLPFS, a job scheduler suppresses sorting jobs when there is a $Job_{overWaitLimit}$ in the job queue. In other words, a job scheduler does not enter any of newly arrived jobs at the position before $Job_{overWaitLimit}$ in the job queue.

4   Simulation

This section describes the performance evaluation of job scheduling schemes by simulation. In this simulation, the performance is measured by processor utilization, mean response time and the variance of response time.

4.1   Simulation Model

The multiprocessor system in this simulation is assumed to be as what described in Sect. 2.

The execution time of a job is exponentially distributed and the average execution time is 10[sec.]. The execution time includes overhead for loading a program and so on.

Job arrival is assumed to be Poisson and load is defined by (1).

$$load = \rho = \frac{\lambda \cdot p}{m \cdot \mu} \qquad (1)$$

Here, λ denotes the mean arrival rate of arrived jobs. μ denotes the mean service rate per processor, or $1/\mu$ denotes the mean execution time of a job. p indicates the mean number of processors requested by the job and m denotes the total number of processors on the multiprocessor system. Scheduling overhead for each job scheduling scheme is assumed to be negligible.

The number of processors on the multiprocessor system and the number of processors requested by a job are assumed to be the alternative of following two models.

1. *Uniform Dist.*

   The number of processors requested by a job is uniformly distributed on [1, 256], and the multiprocessor system has 256 processors.
2. *Real Dist.*

   The number of processors requested by a job follows the distribution on Table 2. Table 2 is obtained by recent 10027 jobs that have been executed on a real multiprocessor system NEC Cenju-3 [3] installed in the authors' laboratory. The Cenju-3 has eight processors. In the distribution, the number of jobs that request powers of two processors is larger than others, and this characteristic is consistent with previous reports [13,21]. Furthermore, the number of jobs that request eight processors is largest. It means that many users have attempted to execute their programs on all processors, or eight processors, because the Cenju-3 was a small system.

Table 2. The number of requested processors

number of requested processors	ratio
1	0.1698
2	0.1718
3	0.0464
4	0.1837
5	0.0295
6	0.0316
7	0.0357
8	0.3314

In the simulation, 5000 jobs are requested and executed in one replication and 100 replications with different jobs are practiced. All results have confidence intervals of 10% or less at a 95% confidence level. The performance of FPLPFS is represented by LPFS because these two schemes cause same results.

---

[3] See Sect. 6 for details.

4.2   Processor Utilization and Mean Response Time

Figure 2 through Fig. 6 show processor utilization and mean response time by the simulation where the number of processors requested by a job follows *Uniform Dist.*

Figure 2 and Fig. 3 show processor utilization and mean response time by the job scheduling schemes. In these results, *WaitLimit* is not given to any job. Figure 2 and Fig. 3 show that MPFS and LPFS improve processor utilization compared with FCFS. It means that the efficiency of packing jobs into idle processors is improved by queue sorting. LPFS keeps mean response time lower than MPFS and FCFS. It is caused by the reason that a large number of small jobs are dispatched prior to a small number of large jobs, which request a large number of processors, by LPFS. However performance improvement by both MPFS and LPFS is slight. On the other hand, FPFS, FPMPFS and Backfilling improve processor utilization considerably and keep mean response time much lower compared with others. It means that dispatching jobs that fit idle processors improves the efficiency of packing jobs into idle processors more considerably than MPFS and LPFS. The performance of FPFS, FPMPFS and Backfilling is almost same. However, FPMPFS shows slightly better performance than FPFS and Backfilling follows FPFS.

In MPFS, LPFS, FPFS, FPMPFS and FPLPFS, *WaitLimit* should be given to each job to avoid starvation. Figure 4 and Fig. 5 show processor utilization and mean response time where *WaitLimit*, which is equal to 600[sec.], is given to each job. Figure 4 and Fig. 5 show that processor utilization by FPFS and FPMPFS is degraded in high load while the degradation of others is slight. It is caused by the reason that searching jobs in the job queue is suppressed by *WaitLimit* in FPFS and FPMPFS. At low load, the degradation by *WaitLimit* is negligible because the number of jobs that continues waiting for being dispatched for long time is a few. However, FPFS and FPMPFS improve processor utilization compared with FCFS, MPFS and LPFS despite performance degradation by *WaitLimit*. Furthermore, the degradation for mean response time by FPFS and FPMPFS is slight. FCFS and Backfilling show no performance degradation because they did not caused starvation in the simulation. Backfilling shows the best improvement of processor utilization in this case.

Figure 6 shows processor utilization by FPFS when various *WaitLimit*'s are defined. On Fig. 6, WL denotes *WaitLimit*[sec.]. Figure 6 shows that processor utilization is degraded at high load when *WaitLimit* is given. It is clear that the scheduling result by FPFS with *WaitLimit* = 0 is same as FCFS. Therefore, processor utilization by FPFS with *WaitLimit* becomes closer to FCFS as *WaitLimit* decreases. FPMPFS with *Waitlimit* showed almost same results in the simulation.

4.3   Variance of Response Time

Table 3 shows the variance of the response time of jobs when *load* = 0.5. The number of processors requested by a job follows *Uniform Dist. WaitLimit*, which

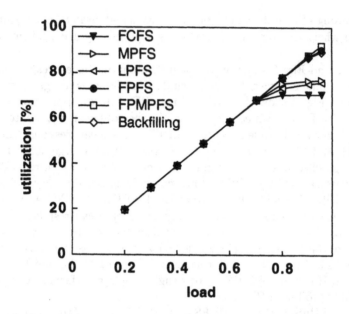

Fig. 2. Processor utilization in simulation results (*Uniform Dist.*)

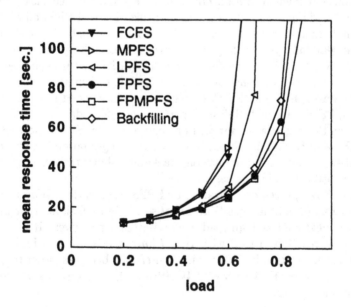

Fig. 3. Mean response time in simulation results (*Uniform Dist.*)

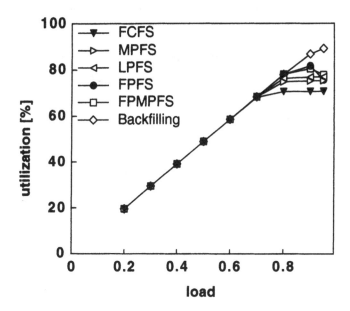

Fig. 4. Processor utilization in simulation results (*WaitLimit* = 600[sec.], *Uniform Dist.*)

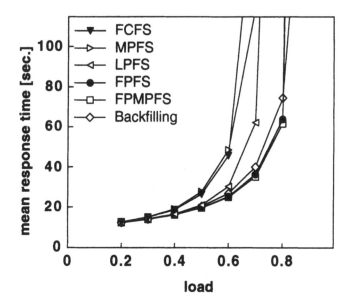

Fig. 5. Mean response time in simulation results (*WaitLimit* = 600[sec.], *Uniform Dist.*)

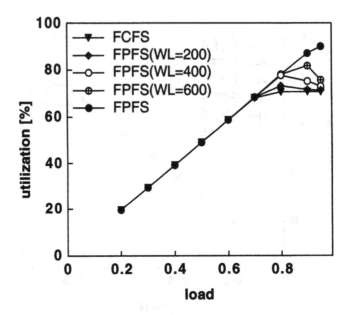

Fig. 6. Processor utilization by FPFS with various *WaitLimit* in simulation results (*Uniform Dist.*)

is equal to 600[sec.] is given to each job. MPFS and LPFS increase variance compared with FCFS. FPFS, FPMPFS and Backfilling reduce variance compared with FCFS. These results show that the technique searching the job queue and positively dispatching jobs that fit idle processors decreases the variance of the response time of jobs, however, sorting jobs in the job queue increases the variance.

Table 3. Variance of response time

schemes	variance
FCFS	639
MPFS	1765
LPFS	1058
FPFS	365
FPMPFS	498
Backfilling	370

4.4   Processor Utilization Under *Real Dist.*

Figure 7 shows processor utilization by the simulation where the number of processors requested by a job follows *Real Dist.* Figure 7 shows that FPFS, FPMPFS and Backfilling improve processor utilization considerably. However, the performance of all job scheduling schemes are improved compared with results on Fig. 2. Especially, the performance improvement of MPFS is considerable. It means that the performance is sensitive to the distribution of the number of processors requested by a job. In this case, it seems that the efficiency of packing jobs that follows *Real Dist.* is higher than that follows *Uniform Dist.*, because the number of jobs that request all processors, or eight processors, is large in *Real Dist.*

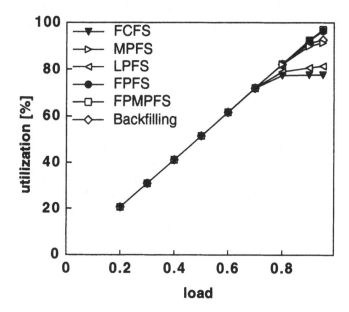

Fig. 7. Processor utilization in simulation results (*Real Dist.*)

4.5   Summary of Simulation Results

The performance of job scheduling schemes obtained by the simulation are classified into two categories.

MPFS and LPFS, which sort the job queue by the number of requested processors, showed almost same performance that is as follows.

1. Both MPFS and LPFS improved processor utilization and reduced mean response time slightly compared with FCFS.

2. The performance degradation by $WaitLimit$ of these schemes was slight.
3. These schemes increased the variance of the response time of jobs compared with FCFS.

FPFS, FPMPFS and Backfilling, which search the job queue and positively dispatch jobs that fit idle processors, showed almost same performance that is as follows.

1. FPFS, FPMPFS and Backfilling improved processor utilization and reduced mean response time considerably compared with MPFS, LPFS and FCFS.
2. Although processor utilization by FPFS and FPMPFS was degraded when $WaitLimit$ was given to each job, they maintained better performance than FCFS, MPFS and LPFS. In this case, Backfilling showed the best improvement of processor utilization. The degradation of processor utilization depended on value of $WaitLimit$.
3. These schemes decreased the variance of the response time of jobs compared with FCFS.

According to these results, it can be assumed that FPFS, FPMPFS and Backfilling caused better performance improvement than others. It shows that the effectiveness of the technique that searches the job queue and positively dispatches jobs that fit idle processors. However, Backfilling has difficulty for practical use, because it assumes that the execution time of each job is known before its execution. Therefore, this paper assumes that FPFS and FPMPFS cause best performance improvement among the job scheduling schemes discussed in this paper. Simulation results in previous work [13,15] also showed effectiveness of a part of these job scheduling schemes, LPFS and FPFS (or Backfilling). Results obtained in this section are consistent with them.

5   Performance Analysis

This section describes the performance analysis of job scheduling schemes that showed best performance in the simulation, or FPFS and FPMPFS. The performance analysis of FCFS is also described to compare the performance of FPFS and FPMPFS with FCFS. In this analysis, the performance is measured by processor utilization and stability condition.

5.1   Processor Utilization and Stability Condition

In $M/M/m$ queueing model, which assumes that the inter-arrival time and the service time of jobs are exponentially distributed and there are m servers, the stability condition is given by

$$\rho = \frac{\lambda}{m \cdot \mu} < 1 \tag{2}$$

and the utilization of servers, U, is given by

$$U \begin{cases} = \frac{\lambda}{m \cdot \mu}, \rho < 1 \\ \to 1, \quad \rho \geq 1. \end{cases} \tag{3}$$

Here, λ denotes the mean arrival rate of a job and μ denotes the mean service rate per server. The stability condition is the condition to keep the system stable. If the stability condition is satisfied, the mean response time of a job is stable[22]. In other words, if stability condition is not satisfied, the response time of a job rises suddenly.

In the job scheduling model assumed in this paper, an arrived job is executed on the requested number of processors simultaneously. Therefore, the following formula is derived from (2) where p denotes the average number of processors requested by a job.

$$\rho = \frac{\lambda \cdot p}{m \cdot \mu} < 1 \tag{4}$$

In $M/M/m$ queueing model, all of m servers are active when there are jobs waiting for being dispatched in the job queue. However, in the job scheduling model assumed in this paper, when the number of idle processors is not zero but less than the number of processors requested by any job in the job queue, idle processors remain idle. In other words, the number of active servers when there are jobs in the job queue is equal to or less than m. Therefore, the stability condition in the job scheduling model assumed in this paper is given by

$$\frac{\lambda \cdot p}{\upsilon \cdot m \cdot \mu} < 1. \tag{5}$$

Here, $\upsilon \cdot m$ denotes the mean number of active servers when there are jobs waiting for being dispatched in the job queue. In other words, υ is the ratio of active servers to all processors in the multiprocessor system when there are jobs in the job queue. Then, the following formula is derived from (4), (5).

$$\rho < \upsilon \tag{6}$$

and processor utilization, U, is given by

$$U \begin{cases} = \frac{\lambda \cdot p}{m \cdot \mu}, \rho < \upsilon \\ \to \upsilon, \quad \rho \geq \upsilon \end{cases} \tag{7}$$

from (4), (6).

The υ defines the stability condition and an upper limit of processor utilization in the job scheduling model assumed in this paper. Therefore, the processor utilization (the upper limit of processor utilization) and the stability condition can be improved by increasing the value of υ.

5.2   Derivation of υ

The value of υ can be derived from one-dimensional bin-packing problem. There are one-dimensional bins, $B_j, (j = 1, \cdots m)$, and a list of one-dimensional items,

$p_i, (i = 1, \cdots n)$. The capacity of B_j is C. The length of p_i, $s(p_i)$, is $s(p_i) \leq C$. One-dimensional bin-packing problem attempts to minimize the number of bins to pack all items in the list satisfying $\sum_{p_i \in B_j} s(p_i) \leq C$. Next Fit (NF), First Fit (FF) and First Fit Decreasing (FFD) are proposed as algorithm for one-dimensional bin-packing problem [20].

The job scheduling model assumed in this paper can be considered as one-dimensional bin-packing problem in which a job scheduler attempts to pack jobs into the idle processors. Here, the job corresponds to the item and "the number of processors requested by the job" is $s(p_i)$. Similarly, the idle processors correspond to the bin and "the number of idle processors" is C. Then, it can be assumed that the value of v is same as the utilization of B_j in one-dimensional bin-packing problem. In several previous works, two-dimensional bin-packing problem has been used for the job scheduling model in which the job has two-dimensional quantity, the number of requested processors and the execution time [23]. However, one-dimensional bin-packing is suitable for the job scheduling model assumed in this paper because this paper assumes that the execution time of a job is unknown.

Worst Case Analysis. The performance of NF, FF and FFD in the worst case is given as follows [20]. Here, $h_{wc}(A)$ denotes the number of bins to pack n items by algorithm A in the worst case and $h(opt)$ denotes the number of bins to pack n items in the optimal case.

$$\frac{h_{wc}(NF)}{h(opt)} = 2.0, \, n \to \infty \tag{8}$$

$$\frac{h_{wc}(FF)}{h(opt)} = \frac{17}{10}, \, n \to \infty \tag{9}$$

$$\frac{h_{wc}(FFD)}{h(opt)} = \frac{11}{9}, \, n \to \infty \tag{10}$$

Since it is safe to say that there is no fragmentation in bins in the optimal case, utilization by NF, FF and FFD is the reciprocal of (8), (9) and (10) respectively. Therefore, values of v by FCFS, FPFS and FPMPFS in the worst case, $v_{wc}(FCFS)$, $v_{wc}(FPFS)$ and $v_{wc}(FPMPFS)$ are given as follows respectively.

$$v_{wc}(FCFS) = \frac{1}{2} = 0.5 \tag{11}$$

$$v_{wc}(FPFS) = \frac{10}{17} = 0.588 \tag{12}$$

$$v_{wc}(FPMPFS) = \frac{9}{11} = 0.818 \tag{13}$$

These results show that FPFS and FPMPFS improve processor utilization and stability condition in the worst case as compared with FCFS. These results also show that FPMPFS improves performance more than FPFS.

Average Case Analysis. The performance of NF in the average case where $s(p_i)$ is uniformly distributed on $(0,1]$ is given as follows [24]. Here, $h_{ac}(A)$ denotes the number of bins to pack n items by algorithm A in the average case and $h(opt)$ denotes the number of bins to pack n items in the optimal case.

$$\frac{h_{ac}(NF)}{h(opt)} = \frac{4}{3}, \; n \to \infty \tag{14}$$

Next, the performance of FF in the average case is given by

$$h_{ac}(FF) = h(opt) + \theta(n^{\frac{2}{3}}) \tag{15}$$

[24,25]. Since $s(p_i)$ is uniformly distributed on $(0,1]$, $h(opt) = n/2$. Then,

$$\frac{h_{ac}(FF)}{h(opt)} = 1 + \frac{\theta(n^{\frac{2}{3}})}{n/2} = 1 + \theta(n^{-\frac{1}{3}}) \tag{16}$$

is derived from (15) and then,

$$\frac{h_{ac}(FF)}{h(opt)} = 1, \; n \to \infty. \tag{17}$$

In the same way, the performance of FFD in the average case is given by

$$h_{ac}(FFD) = h(opt) + \theta(n^{\frac{1}{2}}) \tag{18}$$

[24]. Then,

$$\frac{h_{ac}(FFD)}{h(opt)} = 1, \; n \to \infty. \tag{19}$$

From (14), (17) and (19), values of v by FCFS, FPFS and FPMPFS in the average case, $v_{ac}(FCFS)$, $v_{ac}(FPFS)$ and $v_{ac}(FPMPFS)$ are given as follows respectively.

$$v_{ac}(FCFS) = \frac{3}{4} = 0.75 \tag{20}$$

$$v_{ac}(FPFS) = 1 \tag{21}$$

$$v_{ac}(FPMPFS) = 1 \tag{22}$$

These results show that FPFS and FPMPFS improve processor utilization and stability condition in the average case as compared with FCFS.

5.3   Comparison with Simulation Results

Figure 8 shows processor utilization obtained by the simulation (on Fig. 2) and results of average case analysis. On Fig. 8, solid lines indicate processor utilization in the simulation and dotted lines indicate results of the average case analysis. Figure 8 shows that processor utilization by FCFS is saturated at nearby $load = 0.75$ or more, while processor utilization by FPFS and FPMPFS maintain to improve at high load.

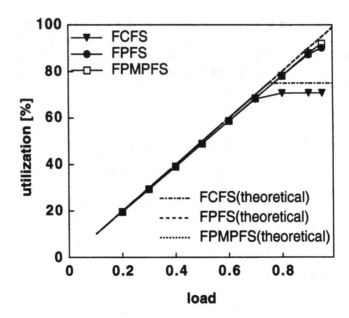

Fig. 8. Processor utilization in simulation results and average case analysis

Furthermore, on Fig. 3, mean response time by FCFS rises suddenly when load is less than 0.75, because the stability condition is not satisfied at $load \geq$ 0.75. On the other hand, FPFS and FPMPFS keep mean response time lower than FCFS, because FPFS and FPMPFS improve the stability condition compared with FCFS. These results show that the performance of FCFS, FPFS and FPMPFS in the simulation follows results in the average case analysis.

6   Experiments on a Cenju-3

This section describes experimental results of FPFS and FPMPFS on a multi-processor system NEC Cenju-3.

6.1   Architecture of a Cenju-3

Cenju-3 is composed of up to 256 processor elements (PE's) connected by a multi-stage interconnection network like baseline network. The system is connected to the workstation, which acts as a host computer. Each PE has a microprocessor VR4400 and up to 64 ,MB local memory. The multi-stage interconnection network is composed of 4 × 4 switches, and its maximum throughput is 40 ,MB/s [19].

Figure 9 illustrates architecture of a multiprocessor system NEC Cenju-3 Model 8S that is used for the experiments. Cenju-3 Model 8S has eight PE's.

The peak performance of a single PE is 33.3 MFlops and each PE has 32 ,MB local memory in the system. The host computer, NEC EWS4800/330 EX, is connected to the system.

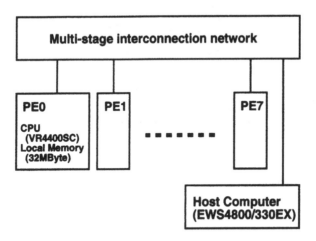

Fig. 9. Architecture of a Cenju-3 Model 8S

6.2   Job Scheduling Mechanism on a Cenju-3

The job scheduling mechanism on a Cenju-3 is achieved by two processes executed on a host computer, Job Scheduler and Maser. Job Scheduler decides the scheduling of arrived jobs and sends the scheduling result to MASER. MASER watches information about PE's, sends the information to Job Scheduler and executes the job on PE's following the scheduling result sent by Job Scheduler [26].

The authors have developed the new job scheduler based on the original Job Scheduler to evaluate performance of FPFS and FPMPFS. Figure 10 shows basic scheduling routines on the new job scheduler. On Fig. 10, FCFS_Scheduler or FPFS_Scheduler dispatches jobs to processors by FCFS or FPFS respectively. A job scheduler executes one of these routines repeatedly. FPMPFS_job_spooler registers arrived jobs into the job queue and sorts jobs by non-increasing order of the number of requested processors. FPFS_Scheduler is also used for FPMPFS. Processor_relinquishment relinquishes processors on which the job finishes execution.

6.3   Results on a Cenju-3

In the experiment, the authors executed 500 jobs composed of three application programs, Electro-magnetic field analysis [27], 3D multigrid [28] and Sparse matrix solver by Gauss-Seidel method. Arrival of these jobs are Poisson. All PE's

```
queue[QUEUEMAX];        /* job queue */
queue[i].job;           /* a job at i th position in a job queue */
queue[i].job.penum;     /* number of demanded PE's by queue[i].job */
queue[i].job.wl;        /* WaitLimit of queue[i].job */
QueueLength;            /* number of jobs in a job queue */
IdlePeNumber;           /* number of idle processors */
ArrivalJob;             /* arrival job */
ArrivalJob.penum;       /* number of requested PE's by ArrivalJob */
FinishJob;              /* job which finished its execution */
FinishJob.penum;        /* number of demanded PE's by FinishJob */


FCFS_Scheduler()
{
  while (){
    if(queue[1].job.penum <= IdlePeNumber){
      Dispatch_queue[1].job_to_Processors;
      IdlePeNumber - = queue[1].job.penum;
    }
}


FPFS_Scheduler()
{
  while (){
    i = 1;
    while(i <= QueueLength && IdlePeNumber > 0){
      if(queue[i].job.penum <= IdlePeNumber){
        Dispatch_queue[i].job_to_Processors;
        IdlePeNumber - = queue[i].job.penum;
        i++;
      } else {
        if(queue[i].job.wl <= waiting_time_of_queue[i].job )
          break;
        else
          i++;
      }
    }
  }
}


FPMPFS_job_spooler()
{
  i = QueueLength;
  while(i > 0){
    if(queue[i].job.wl <= waiting_time_of_queue[i].job )
      break;
    if(queue[i].job.penum < Arrivaljob.penum)
      i - -;
    else
      break;
  }
  Insert_Arrivaljob_into_(i+1 )th_position_in_a_job_queue;
}


Processor_relinquishment()
{
  Release_processors_which_executed_Finishjob;
  IdlePeNumber += FinishJob.penum;
}
```

Fig. 10. Basic structure of job scheduling routines on a Cenju-3

on the Cenju-3 are dedicated to the experiment. Among these 500 jobs, the number of processors requested by a job is uniformly distributed on [1,8] and the average execution time of a job including time for loading a program and so on is 32[sec.]. Each job is given $WaitLimit$, which is equal to 600[sec.], for FPFS and FPMPFS.

Figure 11 and Fig. 12 show processor utilization and mean response time in the experiment. FCFS(native) denotes the native version of FCFS implemented on a Cenju-3 generally and FCFS(improved) denotes the improved version of FCFS that the authors have developed newly. Difference between FCFS(native) and FCFS(improved) is scheduling overhead. In FCFS(native), Job Scheduler inquires MASER periodically to obtain the number of idle processors and this process requires large overhead. In FCFS(improved), Job Scheduler has a local data, or table, to watch the number of idle processors.

Figure 11 and Fig. 12 show that FPFS and FPMPFS improve processor utilization and keep mean response time lower compared with FCFS. FPFS improves processor utilization by 9[%] compared with FCFS(improved) and by 19[%] compared with FCFS(native) at $load = 0.9$. Mean response time by FCFS(native) and FCFS(improved) rises suddenly at $load = 0.7$ and $load = 0.8$ respectively, however, FPFS and FPMPFS keep mean response time below 116[sec.] at $load = 0.8$.

Processor utilization by FPFS and FPMPFS is degraded to 81[%] at $load = 0.95$ because of the influence by $WaitLimit$. Processor utilization by FPMPFS is degraded by 3[%] compared with FPFS at $load = 0.9$, because searching jobs in the job queue in FPMPFS was suppressed 12 times more than FPFS. In other words, FPMPFS suffered the influence by $WaitLimit$ more than FPFS. FCFS(improved) shows much better performance than FCFS(native), because FCFS(native) requires larger overhead to watch the number of idle processors than FCFS(improved).

These experimental results on a Cenju-3 show that FPFS and FPMPFS improve processor utilization and keep mean response time lower, or improve stability condition, compared with FCFS as results in the simulation and the performance analysis.

7   Conclusions

This paper evaluated the performance of job scheduling schemes for pure space sharing among rigid jobs. More complex scheduling schemes such as gang scheduling and adaptive space sharing are discussed in the literature. However, the discussion of job scheduling schemes for pure space sharing among rigid jobs is still important, because these schemes are adopted on most multiprocessor systems currently installed for practical use. The performance of these job scheduling schemes has been discussed in the literature. In most of the previous work, the performance has been evaluated by either simulation, performance analysis or experiments. However, this paper evaluated performance of the job scheduling

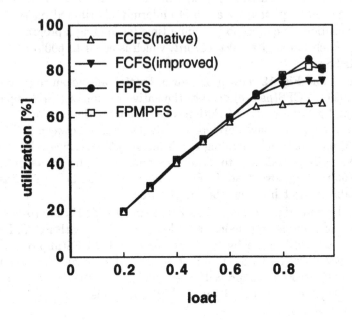

Fig. 11. Processor utilization on a Cenju-3

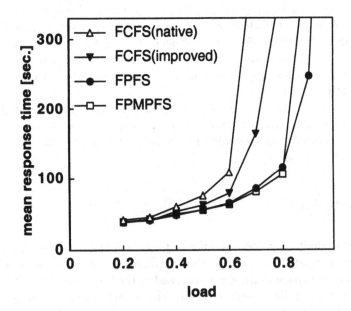

Fig. 12. Mean response time on a Cenju-3

schemes by combination of simulation, performance analysis and experiments to verify the effectiveness and the practicality of these schemes.

Simulation results showed that FPFS, FPMPFS and Backfilling caused considerable performance improvement compared with others. This result means that searching the job queue and positively dispatching jobs that fit idle processors can utilize processors more efficiently and keep mean response time lower than others. However, Backfilling has difficulty for practical use, because it assumes that the execution time of each job is known before its execution. Performance analysis of job scheduling schemes that showed best performance in the simulation, or FPFS and FPMPFS, showed that these schemes improved processor utilization and stability condition compared with FCFS in both worst case and average case. The comparison of results in the simulation and those in the average case analysis showed that simulation results followed the analysis. Experimental results on a multiprocessor system NEC Cenju-3 also showed the advantage of FPFS and FPMPFS as the simulation and the performance analysis.

According to these results, this paper concludes that,

1. FPFS and FPMPFS, which search the job queue and positively dispatch jobs that fit idle processors, are more effective and more practical than other job scheduling schemes discussed in this paper. Although Backfilling can also improve performance, it has difficulty for practical use because it requires knowledge about the execution time of an arrived job before its execution.
2. Performance improvement by FPFS and FPMPFS is almost same. Therefore, FPFS is more practical than FPMPFS because the algorithm of FPFS is simpler than FPMPFS in average case.

Results in Sect. 4.4 showed that the performance of job scheduling schemes was sensitive to the distribution of the number of processors requested by a job. Further investigation on the sensitivity is required as future work.

References

1. High Performance Fortran Forum. High Performance Fortran Language Specification Version 1.0, 1993.
2. H. Kasahara, H. Honda, K. Aida, M. Okamoto, and S. Narita. OSCAR Fortran Compiler. In *Proc. Workshop on Compilation of Languages for Parallel Computers*, pages 30–37, 1991.
3. D. G. Feitelson and L. Rudolph. Toward Convergence in Job Schedulers for Parallel Supercomputers. In *Job Scheduling Strategies for Parallel Processing, Lecture Notes in Computer Science 1162*, pages 1–26. Springer-Verlag, 1996.
4. S. T. Leutenegger and M. K. Vernon. The Performance of Multiprogrammed Multiprocessor Scheduling Policies. In *Proc. of 1990 ACM SIGMETRICS Conference on Measurement and Modeling of Computer Systems*, pages 226–236, 1990.
5. A. Gupta, A. Tucker, and S. Urushibara. The Impact of Operating System Scheduling Policies and Synchronization Methods on the Performance of Parallel Applications. In *Proc. of 1991 ACM SIGMETRICS Conference on Measurement and Modeling of Computer Systems*, pages 120–132, 1991.

6. C. McCann, R. Vaswani, and J. Zahorjan. A Dynamic Processor Allocation Policy for Multiprogrammed Shared-Memory Multiprocessors. *ACM Trans. on Computer Systems*, 11(2):146–178, 1993.
7. K. Li and K. Cheng. A Two-Dimensional Buddy System for Dynamic Resource Allocation in a Partitionable Mesh Connected System. *J. Parallel and Distributed Computing*, 12:79–83, 1991.
8. P. Chuang and N. Tzeng. An Efficient Submesh Allocation Strategy for Mesh Computer Systems. In *Proc. of International Conference on Distributed Computing Systems*, pages 256–263, 1991.
9. Y. Zhu. Efficient Processor Allocation Strategies for Mesh-Connected parallel Computers. *J. Parallel and Distributed Computing*, 16:328–337, 1992.
10. V. Lo, K. J. Windisch, W. Liu, and B. Nitzberg. Noncontiguous Processor Allocation Algorithms for Mesh-Connected Multicomputers. *IEEE Trans. on Parallel and Distributed Systems*, 8(7):712–726, 1997.
11. D. G. Feitelson and L. Rudolph. Parallel Job Scheduling: Issues and Approaches. In *Job Scheduling Strategies for Parallel Processing, Lecture Notes in Computer Science 949*, pages 1–18. Springer-Verlag, 1995.
12. K. Li and K. Cheng. Job Scheduling in a Partitionable Mesh Using a Two-Dimensional Buddy System Partitioning Scheme. *IEEE Trans. on Parallel and Distributed Systems*, 2(4):413–422, 1991.
13. J. Subhlok, T. Gross, and T Suzuoka. Impact of Job Mix on Optimizations for Space Sharing Scheduler. In *Proc. of Supercomputing '96*, 1996.
14. K. Aida, H. Kasahara, and S. Narita. A Scheduling Scheme of Parallel Jobs to Processor Groups on a Multiprocessor System. *Trans. of IEICE*, J80-D-I(6):463–473, 1997, (in Japanese).
15. R. Gibbons. A Historical Application Profiler for Use by Parallel Schedulers. In *Job Scheduling Strategies for Parallel Processing, Lecture Notes in Computer Science 1291*, pages 58–77. Springer-Verlag, 1997.
16. E. W. Parsons and K. C. Sevcik. Implementing Multiprocessor Scheduling Disciplines. In *Job Scheduling Strategies for Parallel Processing, Lecture Notes in Computer Science 1291*, pages 166–192. Springer-Verlag, 1997.
17. D. A. Lifka. The ANL/IBM SP Scheduling System. In *Job Scheduling Strategies for Parallel Processing, Lecture Notes in Computer Science 949*, pages 295–303. Springer-Verlag, 1995.
18. J. S. Skovira, W. Chan, and H. Zhou. The EASY - LoadLeveler API Project. In *Job Scheduling Strategies for Parallel Processing, Lecture Notes in Computer Science 1162*, pages 41–47. Springer-Verlag, 1996.
19. T. Maruyama, Y. Kanoh, T. Hirose, T. Nakata, K. Muramatsu, Y. Asano, and Y Inamura. Architecture of a Parallel Machine: Cenju-3. *IEICE Trans. The Institute of Electronics, Information and Communication Engineers*, J78-D-I(2):59–67, 1995, (in Japanese).
20. E. G. Coffman, M. R. Garey, and D. S. Johnson. Approximation Algorithms for Bin-packing - An Updated Survey. In *Algorithm Design for Computer System Design*, pages 49–106. Springer-Verlag, 1984.
21. S. Hotovy. Workload Evolution on the Cornell Theory Center IBM SP2. In *Job Scheduling Strategies for Parallel Processing, Lecture Notes in Computer Science 1162*, pages 27–40. Springer-Verlag, 1996.
22. R. Jain. *The Art of Computer Systems Performance Analysis*. Wiley, 1991.
23. Y. Zhu and M. Ahuja. On Job Scheduling on a Hypercube. *IEEE Trans. on Parallel and Distributed Systems*, 4(1):62–69, 1993.

24. E. G. Coffman and G. S. Lueker. *Probabilistic Analysis of Packing and Partitioning Algorithms.* Wiley, 1991.
25. P. W. Shor. The Average-case Analysis of Some On-line Algorithms for Bin Packing. *Combinatorica*, 6(2):179–200, 1986.
26. NEC. *NEC Parallel Computer Cenju-3 User's Manual*, 1994, (in Japanese).
27. T. Sakamoto, Y. Maekawa, S. Wakao, T. Onuki, and H. Kasahara. Parallelization of the Electro-magnetic Field Analysis Application Using Hybrid Finite Element and Boundary Element Method. In *Proc. 52th Annual Convention IPSJ*, pages 4L–8, 1996, (in Japanese).
28. D. Bailey, E. Barszcz, J. Barton, D. Browningand R. Carter, L. Dagum, R. Fatoohi, S. Fineberg, P. Frederickson, T. Lasinski, R. Schreiber, H. Simon, V. Venkatakrishnan, and S. Weeratunga. The NAS Parallel Benchmarks. Technical Report BNR-94-007, NASA Ames Research Center, 1994.

Predicting Application Run Times Using Historical Information

Warren Smith[1][2], Ian Foster[1], and Valerie Taylor[2]

[1] Mathematics and Computer Science Division
Argonne National Laboratory
Argonne, IL 60439
{wsmith, foster}@mcs.anl.gov
http://www.mcs.anl.gov
[2] Electrical and Computer Engineering Department
Northwestern University
Evanston, IL 60208
taylor@ece.nwu.edu
http://www.ece.nwu.edu

Abstract. We present a technique for deriving predictions for the run times of parallel applications from the run times of "similar" applications that have executed in the past. The novel aspect of our work is the use of search techniques to determine those application characteristics that yield the best definition of similarity for the purpose of making predictions. We use four workloads recorded from parallel computers at Argonne National Laboratory, the Cornell Theory Center, and the San Diego Supercomputer Center to evaluate the effectiveness of our approach. We show that on these workloads our techniques achieve predictions that are between 14 and 60 percent better than those achieved by other researchers; our approach achieves mean prediction errors that are between 40 and 59 percent of mean application run times.

1 Introduction

Predictions of application run time can be used to improve the performance of scheduling algorithms [8] and to predict how long a request will wait for resources [4]. We believe that run-time predictions can also be useful in meta-computing environments in several different ways. First, they are useful as a means of estimating queue times and hence guiding selections from among various resources. Second, they are useful when attempting to gain simultaneous access to resources from multiple scheduling systems [2].

The problem of how to generate run time estimates has been examined by Downey [4] and Gibbons [8]. Both adopt the approach of making predictions for future jobs by applying a "template" of job characteristics to identify "similar" jobs that have executed in the past. Unfortunately, their techniques are not very accurate, with errors frequently exceeding execution times.

Dror G. Feitelson, Larry Rudolph (Eds.): JSSPP'98, LNCS 1459, pp. 122–142, 1998.
© Springer-Verlag Berlin Heidelberg 1998

We believe that the key to making more accurate predictions is to be more careful about which past jobs are used to make predictions. Accordingly, we apply greedy and genetic algorithm search techniques to identify templates that perform well when partitioning jobs into categories within which jobs are judged to be similar. We also examine and evaluate a number of variants of our basic prediction strategy. We look at whether it is useful to use linear regression techniques to exploit node count information when jobs in a category have different node counts. We also look at the effect of varying the amount of past information used to make predictions, and we consider the impact of using user-supplied maximum run times on prediction accuracy.

We evaluate our techniques using four workloads recorded from supercomputer centers. This study shows that the use of search techniques makes a significant difference to prediction accuracy: our prediction algorithm achieves prediction errors that are 14 to 49 percent lower than those achieved by Gibbons, depending on the workload, and 27 to 60 percent lower than those achieved by Downey. The genetic algorithm search performs better than greedy search.

The rest of the paper is structured as follows. Section 2 describes how we define application similarity, perform predictions, and use search techniques to identify good templates. Section 3 describes the results when our algorithm is applied to supercomputer workloads. Section 4 compares our techniques and results with those of other researchers. Section 5 presents our conclusions and notes directions for further work. An appendix provides details of the statistical methods used in our work.

2   Prediction Techniques

Both intuition and previous work [6, 4, 8] indicate that "similar" applications are more likely to have similar run times than applications that have nothing in common. This observation is the basis for our approach to the prediction problem, which is to derive run-time predictions from historical information of previous similar runs.

In order to translate this general approach into a specific prediction method, we need to answer two questions:

1. *How do we define "similar"?* Jobs may be judged similar because they are submitted by the same user, at the same time, on the same computer, with the same arguments, on the same number of nodes, and so on. We require techniques for answering the question: Are these two jobs similar?
2. *How do we generate predictions?* A definition of similarity allows us to partition a set of previously executed jobs into buckets or categories within which all are similar. We can then generate predictions by, for example, computing a simple mean of the run times in a category.

We structure the description of our approach in terms of these two issues.

2.1 Defining Similarity

In previous work, Downey [4] and Gibbons [8] demonstrated the value of using historical run-time information for "similar" jobs to predict run times for the purpose of improving scheduling performance and predicting wait times in queues. However, both Downey and Gibbons restricted themselves to relatively simple definitions of similarity. A major contribution of the present work is to show that more sophisticated definitions of similarity can lead to significant improvements in prediction accuracy.

A difficulty in developing prediction techniques based on similarity is that two jobs can be compared in many ways. For example, we can compare the application name, submitting user name, executable arguments, submission time, and number of nodes requested. We can conceivably also consider more esoteric parameters such as home directory, files staged, executable size, and account to which the run is charged. We are restricted to those values recorded in workload traces obtained from various supercomputer centers. However, because the techniques that we propose are based on the automatic discovery of efficient similarity criteria, we believe that they will apply even if quite different information is available.

Table 1. Characteristics of the workloads used in our studies. Because of an error when the trace was recorded, the ANL trace does not include one-third of the requests actually made to the system.

Workload Name	System	Number of Nodes	Location	Number of Requests	Mean Run Time (minutes)
ANL	IBM SP2	120	ANL	7994	97.40
CTC	IBM SP2	512	CTC	79302	182.18
SDSC95	Intel Paragon	400	SDSC	22885	107.76
SDSC96	Intel Paragon	400	SDSC	22337	166.48

The workload traces that we consider are described in Table 1; they originate from Argonne National Laboratory (ANL), the Cornell Theory Center (CTC), and the San Diego Supercomputer Center (SDSC). Table 2 summarizes the information provided in these traces: text in a field indicates that a particular trace contains the information in question; in the case of "Type," "Queue," or "Class" the text specifies the categories in question. The characteristics described in rows 1–9 are physical characteristics of the job itself. Characteristic 10, "maximum run time," is information provided by the user and is used by the ANL and CTC schedulers to improve scheduling performance. Rows 11 and 12 are temporal information, which we have not used in our work to date; we hope to evaluate the utility of this information in future work. Characteristic 13 is the run time that we seek to predict.

Table 2. Characteristics recorded in workloads. The column "Abbr" indicates abbreviations used in subsequent discussion.

	Abbr	Characteristic	Argonne	Cornell	SDSC
1	t	Type	batch, interactive	serial, parallel, pvm3	
2	q	Queue			29 to 35 queues
3	c	Class		DSI/PIOFS	
4	u	User	Y	Y	Y
5	s	Loadleveler script		Y	
6	e	Executable	Y		
7	a	Arguments	Y		
8	na	Network adaptor		Y	
9	n	Number of nodes	Y	Y	Y
10		Maximum run time	Y	Y	
11		Submission time	Y	Y	Y
12		Start time	Y	Y	Y
13		Run time	Y	Y	Y

The general approach to defining similarity taken by ourselves, Downey, and Gibbons is to use characteristics such as those presented in Table 2 to define *templates* that identify a set of *categories* to which jobs can be assigned. For example, the template (q, u) specifies that jobs are to be partitioned by *queue* and *user*; on the SDSC Paragon, this template generates categories such as (q16m,wsmith), (q64l,wsmith), and (q16m,foster).

We find that using discrete characteristics 1–8 in the manner just described works reasonably well. On the other hand, the number of nodes is an essentially continuous parameter, and so we prefer to introduce an additional parameter into our templates, namely a "node range size" that defines what ranges of requested number of nodes are used to decide whether applications are similar. For example, the template (u, n=4) specifies a node range size of 4 and generates categories (wsmith, 1-4 nodes) and (wsmith, 5-8 nodes).

Once a set of templates has been defined (see Section 2.4) we can categorize a set of jobs (e.g., the workloads of Table 1) by assigning each job to those categories that match its characteristics. Categories need not be disjoint, and hence the same job can occur in several categories. If two jobs fall into the same category, they are judged similar; those that do not coincide in any category are judged dissimilar.

2.2 Generating Predictions

We now consider the question of how we generate run-time predictions. The input to this process is a set of templates T and a workload W for which runtime predictions are required. In addition to the characteristics described in the preceding section, a maximum history, type of data, and prediction type are also defined for each template. The maximum history indicates the maximum number of data points to store in each category generated from a template. The type of data is either an actual run time, denoted by act, or a relative run time, denoted by rel. A relative run-time incorporates information about user-supplied run time estimates by storing the ratio of the actual run time to the user-supplied estimate (as described in Section 2.3). The prediction type determines how a run-time prediction is made from the data in each category generated from a template. We use a mean, denoted by mean, or a linear regression, denoted by lr, to compute estimates.

The output from this process is a set of run-time predictions and associated confidence intervals. (As discussed in the appendix, a confidence interval is an interval centered on the run-time prediction within which the actual run time is expected to appear some specified percentage of the time.) The basic algorithm comprises three phases: initialization, prediction, and incorporation of historical information:

1. Define T, the set of templates to be used, and initialize C, the (initially empty) set of categories.
2. At the time each application a begins to execute:
   (a) Apply the templates in T to the characteristics of a to identify the categories C_a into which the application may fall.
   (b) Eliminate from C_a all categories that are not in C or that cannot provide a valid prediction, as described in the appendix.
   (c) For each category remaining in C_a, compute a run-time estimate and a confidence interval for the estimate.
   (d) If C_a is not empty, select the estimate with the smallest confidence interval as the run-time prediction for the application.
3. At the time each application a completes execution:
   (a) Identify the set C_a of categories into which the application falls. These categories may or may not exist in C.
   (b) For each category $c_i \in C_a$
       i. If $c_i \notin C$, then create c_i in C.
       ii. If $|c_i| = $ maximum history(c_i), remove the oldest point in c_i.
       iii. Insert a into c_i.

Note that steps 2 and 3 operate asynchronously, since historical information for a job cannot be incorporated until the job finishes. Hence, our algorithm suffers from an initial ramp-up phase during which there is insufficient information in C to make predictions. This deficiency could be corrected by using a training set to initialize C.

We now discuss how a prediction is generated from the contents of a category in step 2(c) of our algorithm. We consider two techniques in this paper. The first simply computes the mean of the run times contained in the category. The second attempts to exploit the additional information provided by the node counts associated with previous run times by performing a linear regression to compute coefficients a and b for the equation $R = aN + b$, where N is node count and R is run time. This equation is then used to make the prediction. The techniques used to compute confidence intervals in these two cases, which we term *mean* and *linear regression* predictors, respectively, are described in the appendix.

The use of maximum histories in step 3(b) of our algorithm allows us to control the amount of historical information used when making predictions and the amount of storage space needed to store historical information. A small maximum history means that less historical information is stored, and hence only more recent events are used to make predictions.

2.3 User Guidance

Another approach to obtaining accurate run-time predictions is to ask users for this information at the time of job submission. This approach may be viewed as complementary to the prediction techniques discussed previously, since historical information presumably can be used to evaluate the accuracy of user predictions.

Unfortunately, none of the systems for which we have workload traces ask users to explicitly provide information about expected run times. However, all of the workloads provide implicit user estimates. The ANL and CTC workloads include user-supplied maximum run times. This information is interesting because users have some incentive to provide accurate estimates. The ANL and CTC systems both kill a job after its maximum run time has elapsed, so users have incentive not to underestimate this value. Both systems also use the maximum run time to determine when a job can be fit into a free slot, so users also have incentive not to overestimate this value.

Users also provide implicit estimates of run times in the SDSC workloads. The scheduler for the SDSC Paragon has many different queues with different priorities and different limits on application resource use. When users pick a queue to submit a request to, they are providing a prediction of the resource use of their application. Queues that have lower resource limits tend to have higher priority, and applications in these queues tend to begin executing quickly, so users are motivated to submit to queues with low resource limits. Also, the scheduler will kill applications that go over their resource limits, so users are motivated not to submit to queues with resource limits that are too low.

A simple approach to exploiting user guidance is to base predictions not on the run times of previous applications, but on the relationship between application run times and user predictions. For example, a prediction for the ratio of actual run time to user-predicted run time can be used along with the user-predicted run time of a particular application to predict the run time of the application. We use this technique for the ANL and CTC workloads by storing relative run times, the run times divided by the user-specified maximum run times, as data points in categories instead of the actual run times.

2.4   Template Definition and Search

We have not yet addressed the question of how we define an appropriate set of templates. This is a nontrivial problem. If too few categories are defined, we group too many unrelated jobs together, and obtain poor predictions. On the other hand, if too many categories are defined, we have too few jobs in a category to make accurate predictions.

Downey and Gibbons both selected a fixed set of templates to use for all of their predictions. Downey uses only a single template containing only the queue name; prediction is based on a conditional probability function. Gibbons uses the six templates/predictor combinations listed in Table 3. The age characteristic indicates how long an application has been executing when a prediction is made. Section 4 discusses further details of their approaches and a comparison with our work.

Table 3. Templates used by Gibbons for run-time prediction.

Number	Template	Predictor
1	(u,e,n,age)	mean
2	(u,e)	linear regression
3	(e,n,age)	mean
4	(e)	linear regression
5	(n,age)	mean
6	()	linear regression

We use search techniques to identify good templates for a particular workload. While the number of application characteristics included in our traces is relatively small, the fact that effective template sets may contain many templates means that an exhaustive search is impractical. Hence, we consider alternative search techniques. Results for greedy and genetic algorithm search are presented in this paper.

The greedy and genetic algorithms both take as input a workload W from Table 1 and produce as output a template set; they differ in the techniques used to explore different template sets. Both algorithms evaluate the effectiveness of a template set T by applying the algorithm of Section 2.2 to workload W. Predicted and actual values are compared to determine for W and T both the mean error and the percentage of predictions that fall within the 90 percent confidence interval.

Greedy Algorithm The greedy algorithm proceeds iteratively to construct a template set $T = \{t_i\}$ with each t_i of the form

$$\{ \; () \; (h_{1,1}) \; (h_{2,1}, h_{2,2}), \ldots, (h_{i,1}, h_{i,2}, \ldots, h_{i,i}) \; \},$$

where every $h_{j,k}$ is one of the n characteristics $h_1, h_2 \ldots, h_n$ from which templates can be constructed for the workload in question. The search over workload W is performed with the following algorithm:

1. Set the template set $T = \{()\}$
2. For $i = 1$ to n
   (a) Set T_c to contain the $\binom{n}{i}$ different templates that contain i characteristics.
   (b) For each template t_c in T_c
        i. Create a candidate template set $X_c = T \cup \{t_c\}$
        ii. Apply the algorithm of Section 2.2 to W and X_c, and determine mean error
   (c) Select the X_c with the lowest mean error, and add the associated template t_c to T

Our greedy algorithm can search over any set of characteristics. Here, however, because of time constraints we do not present searches over maximum history sizes. This restriction reduces the size of the search space, but potentially also results in less effective templates.

Genetic Algorithm Search The second search algorithm that we consider uses genetic algorithm techniques to achieve a more detailed exploration of the search space. Genetic algorithms are a probabilistic technique for exploring large search spaces, in which the concept of cross-over from biology is used to improve efficiency relative to purely random search [10]. A genetic algorithm evolves individuals over a series of generations. The processing for each generation consists of evaluating the fitness of each individual in the population, selecting which individuals will be mated to produce the next generation, mating the individuals, and mutating the resulting individuals to produce the next generation. The process then repeats until a stopping condition is met. The stopping condition we use is that a fixed number of generations have been processed. There are many different variations to this process, and we will next describe the variations we used.

Our individuals represent template sets. Each template set consists of between 1 and 10 templates, and we encode the following information in binary form for each template:

1. Whether a mean or linear regression prediction is performed
2. Whether absolute or relative run times are used
3. Whether each of the binary characteristics associated with the workload in question is enabled
4. Whether node information should be used and, if so, the range size from 1 to 512 in powers of 2

A fitness function is used to compute the fitness of each individual and therefore its chance to reproduce. The fitness function should be selected so that the most desirable individuals have higher fitness and therefore have more offspring, but the diversity of the population must be maintained by not giving the best individuals overwhelming representation in succeeding generations. In our genetic algorithm, we wish to minimize the prediction error and maintain a range of individual fitnesses regardless of whether the range in errors is large or small. The fitness function we use to accomplish this goal is

$$F_{min} + \frac{E_{max}-E}{E_{max}-E_{min}} \cdot (F_{max} - F_{min}),$$

where E is the error of the individual E_{min} and E_{max} are the minimum and maximum errors of individuals in the generation and F_{min} and F_{max} are the desired minimum and maximum fitnesses desired. We chose $F_{max} = 4 \cdot F_{min}$.

We use a common technique called stochiastic sampling without replacement to select which individuals will mate to produce the next generation. In this technique, each individual is selected $\lfloor \frac{F}{F_{avg}} \rfloor$ times to be a parent. The rest of the parents are selected by Bernoulli trials where each individual is selected, in order, with a probability of $F - F_{avg}\lfloor \frac{F}{F_{avg}} \rfloor$ until all parents are selected.

The mating or crossover process is accomplished by randomly selecting pairs of individuals to mate and replacing each pair by their children in the new population. The crossover of two individuals proceeds in a slightly nonstandard way because our chromosomes are not fixed length but a multiple of the number of bits used to represent each template. Two children are produced from each crossover by randomly selecting a template i and a position in the template p from the first individual $T_1 = t_{1,1}, \ldots, t_{1,n}$ and randomly selecting a template j in the second individual $T_2 = t_{2,1}, \ldots, t_{2,m}$ so that the resulting individuals will not have more than 10 templates. The new individuals are then $T_1 = t_{1,1}, \ldots, t_{1,i-1}, n_1, t_{2,j+1}, \ldots, t_{2,m}$ and $T_2 = t_{2,1} \ldots t_{2,j-1}, n_2, t_{1,i+1}, \ldots, t_{i,n}$. If there are b bits used to represent each template, n_1 is the first p bits of $t_{1,i}$ concatenated with the last $b - p$ bits of $t_{2,j}$. and n_2 is the first p bits of $t_{2,j}$ concatenated with the last $b - p$ bits of $t_{1,i}$.

In addition to using crossover to produce the individuals of the next generation, we also use a process called elitism whereby the best individuals in each generation survive unmutated to the next generation. We use crossover to produce all but 2 individuals for each new generation and use elitism to select the last 2 individuals for each new generation. The individuals resulting from the crossover process are mutated to help maintain a diversity in the population. Each bit representing the individuals is flipped with a probability of 0.001.

3   Experimental Results

In the preceding section we described our basic approach to run-time prediction. We introduced the concept of *template search* as a means of identifying efficient criteria for selecting "similar" jobs in historical workloads. We also noted potential refinements to this basic technique, including the use of alternative search methods (greedy vs. genetic), the introduction of node count information via linear regression, support for user guidance, and the potential for varying the amount of historical information used. In the rest of this paper, we discuss experimental studies that we have performed to evaluate the effectiveness of our techniques and the significant of the refinements just noted.

Our experiments used the workload traces summarized in Table 1 and are intended to answer the following questions:

- How effectively do our greedy and genetic search algorithms perform?
- What is the relative effectiveness of mean and linear regression predictors?
- What is the impact of user guidance as represented by the maximum run times provided on the ANL and CTC SPs?
- What is the impact of varying the number of nodes in each category on prediction performance?
- What are the trends for the best templates in the workloads?
- How do our techniques compare with those of Downey and Gibbons?

3.1 Greedy Search

Figure 1 and Figure 2 showy the results of performing a greedy search for the best category templates for all four workloads. Several trends can be observed from this data. First, adding a second template with a single characteristic results in the most dramatic improvement in performance. The addition of this template has the least effect for the CTC workload where performance is improved between 5 and 25 percent and has the greatest effect for the SDSC workloads which improve between 34 and 48 percent. The addition of templates using up to all possible characteristics results in less improvement than the addition of the template containing a single characteristic. The improvements range from an additional 1 to 20 percent improvement with the ANL workload seeing the most benefit and the SDSC96 workload seeing the least.

Second, the graphs show that the mean is a better predictor than linear regression except when a single template is used with the SDSC workloads. The final predictors obtained by using means are between 2 and 48 percent more accurate than those based on linear regressions. The impact of the choice of predictor on accuracy is greatest in the ANL and least in the SDSC96 workload.

A third trend, evident in the ANL and CTC results, is that using the relative run times gives a significant improvement in performance. When this information is incorporated, prediction accuracy increases between 23 and 48 percent with the ANL workload benefiting most.

Table 4 lists for each workload the accuracy of the best category templates found by the greedy search. In the last column, the mean error is expressed as a fraction of mean run time. Mean errors of between 42 and 70 percent of mean run times may appear high; however, as we will see later, these figures are comparable to those achieved by other techniques, and genetic search performs significantly better.

Looking at the templates listed in Table 4, we observe that for the ANL and CTC workloads, the executable and user name are both important characteristics to use when deciding whether applications are similar. Examination of other data

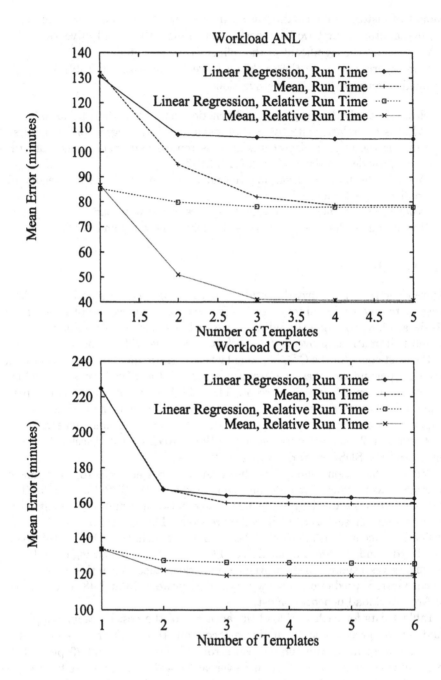

Fig. 1. Mean errors of ANL and CTC greedy searches

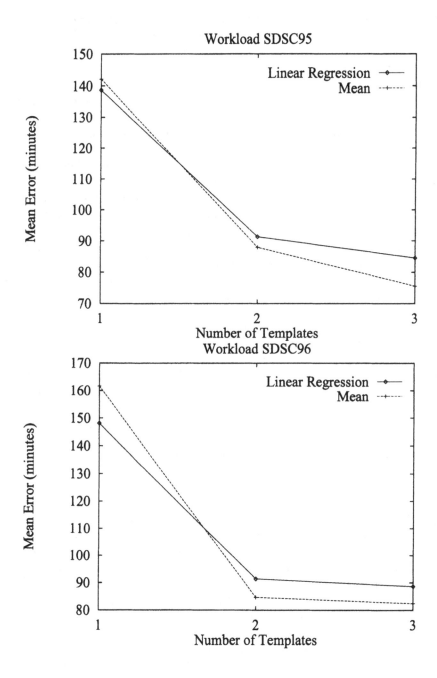

Fig. 2. Mean errors of SDSC greedy searches

gathered during the experiments shows that these two characteristics are highly correlated: substituting u for e or s or vice versa in templates results in similar performance in many experiments. This observation may imply that users tend to run a single application on these parallel computers.

The templates selected for the SDSC workloads indicate that the user who submits an application is more important in determining application similarity than the queue to which an application is submitted. Furthermore, Figure 2 shows that adding the third template results in performance improvements of only 2 to 12 percent on the SDSC95 and SDSC96 workloads. Comparing this result with the greater improvements obtained when relative run times are used in the ANL and CTC workloads suggests that SDSC queue classes are not good user-specified run-time estimates. It would be interesting to use the resource limits associated with queues as maximum run times. However, this information was not available to us when this paper was being written.

We next perform a second series of greedy searches to identify the impact of using node information when defining categories. We use node ranges when defining categories as described in Section 2.1. The results of these searches are shown in Table 5. Because of time constraints, no results are available for the CTC workload.

The table shows that using node information improves prediction performance by 2 and 10 percent with the largest improvement for the San Diego workloads. This information and the fact that characteristics such as executable, user name, and arguments are selected before nodes when searching for templates indicates that the importance of node information to prediction accuracy is only moderate.

Further, the greedy search selects relatively small node range sizes coupled with user name or executable. This fact indicates, as expected, that an application executes for similar times on similar numbers of nodes.

3.2   Genetic Algorithm Search

Figure 3 shows the progress of the genetic algorithm search of the ANL workload. While the average and maximum errors tend to decrease significantly as evolution proceeds, the minimum error decreases only slightly. This behavior suggests that the genetic algorithm is working correctly but that it is not difficult to find individual templates with low prediction errors.

As shown in Table 6, the best templates found during the genetic algorithm search provide mean errors that are 2 to 12 percent less than the best templates found during the greedy search. The largest improvements are obtained on the CTC and SDSC95 workloads. These results indicate that the genetic search performs slightly better than the greedy search. This difference in performance may increase if the search space becomes larger by, for example, including the maximum history characteristic while searching.

The template sets identified by the genetic search procedure are listed in Table 7. Studying these and other template sets produced by genetic search, we see that the mean is not uniformly used as a predictor. From the results

Table 4. Best predictions found during greedy first search.

Workload	Predictor	Data Point	Template Set	Mean Error (minutes)	Percentage of Mean Run Time
ANL	mean	relative	(), (e), (u,a),	40.68	41.77
		run time	(t,u,a), (t,u,e,a)		
CTC	mean	relative	(), (u), (u,s), (t,c,s),	118.89	65.25
		run time	(t,u,s,ni), (t,c,u,s,ni)		
SDSC95	mean	run time	(), (u), (q,u)	75.56	70.12
SDSC96	mean	run time	(), (u), (q,u)	82.40	49.50

Table 5. Best predictions found during second greedy search.

Workload	Predictor	Data Point	Template Set	Mean Error (minutes)	Percentage of Mean Run Time
ANL	mean	relative	(), (e), (u,a), (t,u,n=2),	39.87	40.93
		run time	(t,e,a,n=16), (t,u,e,a,n=32),		
SDSC95	mean	run time	(), (u), (u,n=1), (q,u,n=1)	67.63	62.76
SDSC96	mean	run time	(), (u), (u,n=4), (q,u,n=8)	76.20	45.77

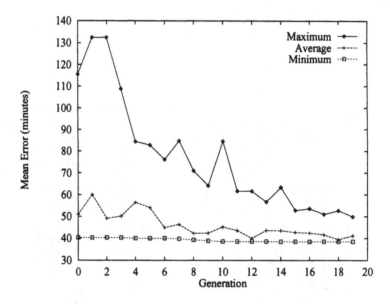

Fig. 3. Errors during genetic algorithm search of workload ANL

of the greedy searches, the mean is clearly a better predictor in general but these results indicate that combining mean and linear regression predictors does provide a performance benefit. Similarly to the greedy searches of the ANL and CTC workloads, using relative run times as data points provides the best performance.

Table 6. Performance of the best templates found during genetic algorithm search. Results for greedy search are also presented, for comparison.

Workload	Genetic Algorithm		Greedy	
	Mean Error (minutes)	Percentage of Mean Run Time	Mean Error (minutes)	Percentage of Mean Run Time
ANL	38.48	39.51	39.87	40.93
CTC	106.73	58.58	118.89	65.25
SDSC95	59.65	55.35	67.63	62.76
SDSC96	74.56	44.79	76.20	45.77

A third observation is that node information is used in the templates of Table 7 and throughout the best templates found during the genetic search. This confirms the observation made during the greedy search that using node information when defining templates results in improved prediction performance.

Table 7. The best templates found during genetic algorithm search

Workload	Best Template Set
ANL	(t,u,a,n=4,mean,rel), (u,e,n=16,lr,rel), (t,u,e,a,lr,rel), (t,u,e,a,n=16,lr,rel), (t,u,e,a,mean,rel)
CTC	(u,n=512,mean,rel), (c,e,a,ni,n=4,mean,rel)
SDSC95	(q,u,n=1,mean,act), (q,n=16,lr,act) (q,u,n=16,lr,act), (q,u,n=4,lr,act)
SDSC96	(u,n=1,mean,act), (q,n=4,lr,act), (q,u,n=4,lr,act), (q,u,n=128,mean,act), (q,u,n=16,mean,act), (q,u,n=2,mean,act), (q,u,n=4,mean,act)

4 Related Work

Gibbons [8, 9] also uses historical information to predict the run times of parallel applications. His technique differs from ours principally in that he uses a fixed set of templates and different characteristics to define templates.

Gibbons produces predictions by examining categories derived from the templates listed in Table 3, in the order listed, until a category that can provide a valid prediction is found. This prediction is then used as the run time prediction.

The set of templates listed in Table 3 results because Gibbons uses templates of (u,e), (e), and () with subtemplates in each template. The subtemplates use the characteristics n and age (how long an application has executed). In our work we have used the user, executable, and nodes characteristics. We do not use the age of applications in this discussion, although this characteristic has value [4, 3]. Gibbons also uses the requested number of nodes slightly differently from the way we do: rather than having equal-sized ranges specified by a parameter, as we do, he defines the fixed set of exponential ranges 1, 2-3, 4-7, 8-15, and so on.

Another difference between Gibbons's technique and ours is how he performs a linear regression on the data in the categories (u,e), (e), and (). These categories are used only if one of their subcategories cannot provide a valid prediction. A weighted linear regression is performed on the mean number of nodes and the mean run time of each subcategory that contains data, with each pair weighted by the inverse of the variance of the run times in their subcategory.

Table 8 compares the performance of Gibbons's technique with our technique. Using code supplied by Gibbons, we applied his technique to our workloads. We see that our greedy search results in templates that perform between 4 and 46 percent better than Gibbons's technique and our genetic algorithm search finds template sets that have between 14 and 49 percent lower mean error than the template sets Gibbons selected.

In his original work, Gibbons did not have access to workloads that contained the maximum run time of applications, so he could not use this information to refine his technique. In order to study the potential benefit of this data on his

Table 8. Comparison of our prediction technique with that of Gibbons

Workload	Gibbons's Mean Error (minutes)	Our Mean Error Greedy Search (minutes)	Genetic Algorithm (minutes)
ANL	75.26	39.87	38.48
CTC	124.06	118.89	106.73
SDSC95	74.05	67.63	59.65
SDSC96	122.55	76.20	74.56

approach, we reran his predictor while using application run time divided by the user-specified maximum run time. Table 9 shows our results. Using maximum run times improves the performance of Gibbons's prediction technique on both workloads, although not to the level of the predictions found during our genetic algorithm search.

Table 9. Comparison of our prediction technique to that of Gibbons, when Gibbons's technique is modified to use run times divided by maximum run times as data points

Workload	Gibbons's Mean Error (minutes)	Our Mean Error Greedy Search (minutes)	Genetic Algorithm (minutes)
ANL	49.47	39.87	38.48
CTC	107.41	118.89	106.73

Downey [4] uses a different technique to predict the execution time of parallel applications. His technique is to model the applications in a workload and then use these models to predict application run times. His procedure is to categorize all applications in the workload, then model the cumulative distribution functions of the run times in each category, and finally use these functions to predict application run times. Downey categorizes applications using the queues that applications are submitted to, although he does state that other characteristics can be used in this categorization.

Downey observed that the cumulative distributions can be modeled by using a logarithmic function: $\beta_0 + \beta_1 \ln t$, although this function is not completely accurate for all distributions he observed. Once the distribution functions are calculated, he uses two different techniques to produce a run-time prediction. The first technique uses the median lifetime given that an application has executed for a time units. Assuming the logarithmic model for the cumulative distribution, this equation is

$$\sqrt{ae^{\frac{1.0-\beta_0}{\beta_1}}} \, .$$

The second technique uses the conditional average lifetime

$$\frac{t_{max} - a}{\log t_{max} - \log a}$$

with $t_{max} = e^{(1.0 - \beta_0)/\beta_1}$.

The performance of both of these techniques are shown in Table 10. We have reimplemented Downey's technique as described in [4] and used his technique on our workloads. The predictions are made assuming that the application being predicted has executed for one second. The data shows that of Downey's two techniques, using the median has better performance in general and the template sets found by our genetic algorithm perform 27 to 60 percent better than the Downey's best predictors. There are two reasons for this performance difference. First, our techniques use more characteristics than just the queue name to determine which applications are similar. Second, calculating a regression to the cumulative distribution functions minimizes the error for jobs of all ages while we concentrate on accurately predicting jobs of age 0.

Table 10. Comparison of our prediction technique with that of Downey

	Downey's Mean Error		Our Mean Error	
Workload	Conditional Median Lifetime (minutes)	Conditional Average Lifetime (minutes)	Greedy Search (minutes)	Genetic Algorithm (minutes)
ANL	97.01	106.80	39.87	38.48
CTC	179.46	201.34	118.89	106.73
SDSC95	82.44	171.00	67.63	59.65
SDSC96	102.04	168.24	76.20	74.56

5 Conclusions

We have described a novel technique for using historical information to predict the run times of parallel applications. Our technique is to derive a prediction for a job from the run times of previous jobs judged similar by a template of key job characteristics. The novelty of our approach lies in the use of search techniques to find the best templates. We experimented with the use of both a greedy search and a genetic algorithm search for this purpose, and we found that the genetic search performs better for every workload and finds templates that result in prediction errors of 40 to 59 percent of mean run times in four supercomputer center workloads. The greedy search finds templates that result in prediction errors of 41 to 65 percent of mean run times. Furthermore, these templates provide more accurate run-time estimates than the techniques of other researchers: we achieve mean errors that are 14 to 49 percent lower error than those obtained by Gibbons and 27 to 60 percent lower error than Downey.

We find that using user guidance in the form of user-specified maximum run times when performing predictions results in a significant 23 percent to 48 percent improvement in performance for the Argonne and Cornell workloads. We used both means and linear regressions to produce run-time estimates from similar past applications and found that means provide more accurate predictions in general. For the best templates found in the greedy search, using the mean for predictions resulted in between 2 percent and 48 percent smaller errors. The genetic search shows that combining templates that use both mean and linear regression improves performance.

Our work also provides insights into the job characteristics that are most useful for identifying similar jobs. We find that the names of the submitting user and the application are the most useful and that the number of nodes is also valuable.

In future work, we hope to use search techniques to explore yet more sophisticated prediction techniques. For example, we are interested in understanding whether it is useful to constrain the amount of history information used to make predictions. We are also interested in understanding the potential benefit of using submission time, start time, and application age when making predictions. We may also consider more sophisticated search techniques and more flexible definitions of similarity. For example, instead of applications being either similar or disimilar, there could be a range of similarities. A second direction for future work is to apply our techniques to the problem of selecting and co-allocating resources in metacomputing systems [1, 7, 2]

Acknowledgments

We thank the Mathematics and Computer Science Division of Argonne National Laboratory, the Cornell Theory Center, and the San Diego Supercomputer Center for providing us with the trace data used in this work. We also thank Gene Rackow for helping to record the ANL trace, Allen Downey for providing the SDSC workloads, Jerry Gerner for providing the CTC workload, and Richard Gibbons for providing us with the code used for the comparative analysis.

This work was supported by the Mathematical, Information, and Computational Sciences Division subprogram of the Office of Computational and Technology Research, U.S. Department of Energy, under Contract W-31-109-Eng-38 and a NSF Young Investigator award under Grant CCR-9215482.

Appendix: Statistical Methods

We use statistical methods [11, 5] to calculate run-time estimates and confidence intervals from categories. A category contains a set of data points called a *sample*, which are a subset of all data points that will be placed in the category, the *population*. We use a sample to produce an estimate using either a mean or a linear regression. This estimate includes a confidence interval that is useful as a measure of the expected accuracy of this prediction. If the $X\%$ confidence interval is of size c, a new data point will be within c units of the prediction $X\%$ of the time. A smaller confidence interval indicates a more accurate prediction.

A mean is simply the sum of the data points divided by the number of data points. A confidence interval is computed for a mean by assuming that the data points in our sample S are an accurate representation of all data points in the population P of data points that will ever be placed in a category. The sample is an accurate representation if they are taken randomly from the population and the sample is large enough. We assume that the sample is random, even though it consists of the run times of a series of applications that have completed in the recent past. If the sample is not large enough, the sample mean $\bar{x}$ will not be nearly equal to the population mean μ, and the sample standard deviation s will not be near to the population standard deviation σ. The prediction and confidence interval we compute will not be accurate in this case. In fact, the central limit theorem states that a sample size of at least 30 is needed for $\bar{x}$ to approximate μ, although the exact sample size needed is dependent on σ and the standard deviation desired for $\bar{x}$ [11].

We used a minimum sample size of 2 when making our predictions in practice. This is because while a small sample size may result in $\bar{x}$ not being nearly equal to μ, we find that an estimate from a category that uses many characteristics but has a small sample is more accurate than an estimate from a category that uses few characteristics but has a larger sample size.

The $X\%$ confidence interval can be computed when using the sample mean as a predictor by applying Chebychev's theorem. This theorem states that the portion of data that lies within k standard deviations to either side of the mean is at least $1 - \frac{1}{k^2}$ for any data set. We need only compute the sample standard deviation and k such that $1 - \frac{1}{k^2} = \frac{X}{100}$.

Our second technique for producing a prediction is to perform a linear regression to a sample using the equation

$$t = b_0 + b_1 n,$$

where n is the number of nodes requested and t is the run time. This type of prediction attempts to use information about the number of nodes requested. A confidence interval can be constructed by observing how close the data points are to this line. The confidence interval is computed by the equation

$$t_{\frac{\alpha}{2}} \sqrt{MSE} \sqrt{1 + \frac{1}{N} + \frac{(n_0 - \bar{n})^2}{\sum n^2 - \frac{\left(\sum n\right)^2}{N}}},$$

where N is the sample size, MSE is the mean squared error of the sample, n_0 is the number of nodes requested for the application being predicted, and $\bar{n}$ is the mean number of nodes in the sample. Alpha is computed with the equation

$$\alpha = 1 - \frac{X\%}{100}$$

if the $X\%$ confidence interval is desired and $t_{\frac{\alpha}{2}}$ is the Student's t-distribution with $N - 2$ degrees of freedom [11, 5].

References

[1] C. Catlett and L. Smarr. Metacomputing. *Communications of the ACM*, 35(6):44–52, 1992.

[2] K. Czajkowski, I. Foster, C. Kesselman, S. Martin, W. Smith, and S. Tuecke. A Resource Management Architecture for Metasystems. *Lecture Notes on Computer Science*, 1998.

[3] Murthy Devarakonda and Ravishankar Iyer. Predictability of Process Resource Usage: A Measurement-Based Study on UNIX. *IEEE Transactions on Software Engineering*, 15(12):1579–1586, December 1989.

[4] Allen Downey. Predicting Queue Times on Space-Sharing Parallel Computers. In *International Parallel Processing Symposium*, 1997.

[5] N. R. Draper and H. Smith. *Applied Regression Analysis, 2nd Edition*. John Wiley and Sons, 1981.

[6] Dror Feitelson and Bill Nitzberg. Job Characteristics of a Production Parallel Scientific Workload on the NASA Ames iPSC/860. *Lecture Nodes on Computer Science*, 949, 1995.

[7] Ian Foster and Carl Kesselman. Globus: A Metacomputing Infrastructure Toolkit. *International Journal of Supercomputing Applications*, 11(2):115–128, 1997.

[8] Richard Gibbons. A Historical Application Profiler for Use by Parallel Scheculers. *Lecture Notes on Computer Science*, pages 58–75, 1997.

[9] Richard Gibbons. A Historical Profiler for Use by Parallel Schedulers. Master's thesis, University of Toronto, 1997.

[10] David E. Goldberg. *Genetic Algorithms in Search, Optimization, and Machine Learning*. Addison-Wesley, 1989.

[11] Neil Weiss and Matthew Hassett. *Introductory Statistics*. Addison-Wesley, 1982.

Job Scheduling Strategies for Networks of Workstations

B. B. Zhou[1], R. P. Brent[1], D. Walsh[2], and K. Suzaki[3]

[1] Computer Sciences Laboratory, Australian National University,
Canberra, ACT 0200, Australia
[2] CAP Research Program, Australian National University,
Canberra, ACT 0200, Australia
[3] Electrotechnical Laboratory, 1-1-4 Umezono,
sukuba, Ibaraki 305, Japan

Abstract. In this paper we first introduce the concepts of utilisation ratio and effective speedup and their relations to the system performance. We then describe a two-level scheduling scheme which can be used to achieve good performance for parallel jobs and good response for interactive sequential jobs and also to balance both parallel and sequential workloads. The two-level scheduling can be implemented by introducing on each processor a registration office. We also introduce a loose gang scheduling scheme. This scheme is scalable and has many advantages over existing explicit and implicit coscheduling schemes for scheduling parallel jobs under a time sharing environment.

1 Introduction

The trend of parallel computer developments is toward *networks of workstations* [3], or *scalable parallel systems* [1]. In this type of system each processor, having a high-speed processing element, a large memory space and full functionality of a standard operating system, can operate as a stand-alone workstation for sequential computing. Interconnected by high-bandwidth and low-latency networks, the processors can also be used for parallel computing. To establish a truly general-purpose and user-friendly system, one of the main problems is to provide users with a *single system image*. By adopting the technique of *distributed shared memory* [12], for example, we can provide a single addressing space for the whole system so that communication for transferring data between processors is completely transparent to the client programs. In this paper we discuss another very important issue relating to the provision of single system image, that is, effective *job scheduling strategies* for both *sequential and parallel processing* on networks of workstations.

Many job scheduling schemes have been introduced in the literature and some of them implemented on commercial parallel systems. These scheduling schemes for parallel systems can be classified into either *space sharing*, or *time sharing*, or a combination of both. With space sharing a system is partitioned into subsystems, each containing a subset of processors. There are boundary

Dror G. Feitelson, Larry Rudolph (Eds.): JSSPP'98, LNCS 1459, pp. 143–157, 1998.
© Springer-Verlag Berlin Heidelberg 1998

lines laid between subsystems and so only processors of the same subsystem can be coordinated to solve problems assigned to that subsystem. During the computation each subsystem is allocated only for a single job at a time.

The space partition can be either *static*, or *adaptive*. With static partitioning the system configuration is determined before the system starts operating. The whole system has to be stopped when the system needs to be reconfigured. With adaptive partitioning processors in the system are not divided before the computation. When a new job arrives, a job manager in the system first locates idle processors and then allocates certain number of those idle processors to that job according to some processor allocation policies, e.g., those described in [2,10,14,15,17,18,20]. Therefore, the boundary lines are drawn during the computation and will disappear after the job is terminated. Normally the static partitioning is used for very large systems, while the adaptive partitioning is adopted in systems, or subsystems of small to medium size. One disadvantage of space partitioning is that short jobs can easily be blocked by long ones for a long time before being executed. However, in practice short jobs usually demand a short turnaround time. To alleviate this problem jobs can be grouped into classes and a special treatment will be given to the class of short jobs [15]. However, it can only partially solve the problem. Thus *time sharing* needs to be considered.

Many scheduling schemes for time-sharing of a parallel system have been proposed in the literature. They may be classified into two basic types. The first one is *local scheduling*. With local scheduling there is only a single queue on each processor. Except for higher (or lower) priorities being given, processes associated with parallel jobs are not distinguished from those associated with sequential jobs. The method simply relies on existing local schedulers on each processor to schedule parallel jobs. Thus there is no guarantee that the processes belonging to the same parallel job can be executed at the same time across the processors. When many parallel programs are simultaneously running on a system, processes belonging to different jobs will compete for resources with each other and then some processes have to be blocked when communicating or synchronising with non-scheduled processes on other processors. This effect can lead to a great degradation in overall system performance [4,6,9,11,13]. One method to alleviate this problem is to use *two-phase* blocking [8,22] which is also called *implicit coscheduling* in [8]. In this method a process waiting for communication spins for some time in the hope that the process to be communicated with on the other processor is also scheduled, and then blocks if a response has not been received. The reported experimental results show that for parallel workloads this scheduling scheme performs better than the simple local scheduling. However, the problem is that the scheduling policy is based on communication requirements. Then it tends to give special treatment to jobs with a high frequency of communication demands. The policy is also independent of service times. The performance of parallel computation is thus unpredictable.

The second type of scheduling schemes for time sharing is *coscheduling* [16] (or *gang scheduling* [9]), which may be a better scheme in adopting *short-job-first* policy. Using this method a number of parallel programs is allowed to enter a *service* queue (as long as the system has enough memory space). The processes of the same job will run simultaneously across the processors for only certain amount of time which is called *scheduling slot*. When a scheduling slot is ended, the processors will context-switch at the same time to give the service to processes of another job. All programs in the service queue take turns to receive the service in a coordinated manner across the processors. Thus programs never interfere with each other and short jobs are likely to be completed more quickly. There are also certain drawbacks associated with coscheduling. A significant one is that it is designed only for parallel workloads. For networks of workstations we need an effective scheduling strategy for both sequential and parallel processing. The simple coscheduling technique is not a suitable solution.

The future networks of workstations should provide a *programming-free* environment to general users. By providing a variety of high-performance computing libraries for a wide range of applications plus user-friendly interfaces for the access to those libraries, parallel computing will no longer be considered just as client's special requests, but become a *natural and common phenomenon* in the system. Along with many other critical issues, therefore, highly effective job management strategies are required for the system to meet various client's requirements and to achieve high efficiency of resource utilisation. Because of the lack of efficient job scheduling strategies, most networks of workstations are currently used exclusively either as an MPP for processing parallel batch jobs, or as a group of separate processors for interactive sequential jobs. The potential power of this type of system are not exploited effectively and the system resources are not utilised efficiently under these circumstances.

In this paper we discuss some new ideas for effectively scheduling both sequential and parallel workloads on networks of workstations. To achieve a desired performance for a parallel job on a network of workstations with a variety of competitive background workloads, it is essential to provide a sustained ratio of CPU utilisation to the associated processes on each processor, to allocate more processors to the job if the assigned utilisation ratio is small and then to coordinate the execution across the processors. We first introduce the concepts of *utilisation ratio* and *effective speedup* and their relations to the system performance in Section 2. In this section we also argue that, because the resources in a system are limited, one cannot guarantee every parallel job to have a sustained CPU utilisation ratio in a time sharing environment. One way to solve the problem is that we give short jobs sustained utilisation ratios to ensure a short turnaround time, while to each large job we allocate a large number of processors and assign a utilisation ratio which can vary in a large range according to the current system workload so that small jobs will not be blocked and the resource utilisation can be kept high. we then present in Section 3 a *two-level scheduling* scheme which can be used to achieve good performance for parallel jobs and good response for interactive sequential jobs and also to balance both parallel and sequential workloads. The two-level scheduling can be implemented by introducing on each processor a *registration office* which is described in Section 4. We discuss a scalable coscheduling scheme – *loose gang scheduling* in Section 5. This scheme requires both global and local job managers. It is scalable because the coscheduling is mainly controlled by local job managers on each processor so that frequent signal-broadcasting for simultaneous context switch across the processors is avoided. Using a global job manager we believe that the system can work more efficiently than those using only local schedulers. With a local job manager on each processor the system will become more flexible and more effective in handling more complicated situations than those adopting only the conventional gang scheduling policy. Finally the conclusions are given in Section 6.

2   Utilisation Ratio and Effective Speedup

Assuming that the overall computational time for a parallel job on p *dedicated* processors is $T_d(p)$, the *conventionally defined speedup* is then obtained as

$$S_d(p) = \frac{T_d(1)}{T_d(p)}. \tag{1}$$

This speedup can only be achieved by using dedicated processors. It may be impossible to achieve on a network of workstations because there a parallel job usually has to time-share resources with other sequential/parallel jobs. If we provide a *sustained ratio of CPU utilisation* for a job on each processor and use *more processors*, however, we can still achieve the desired performance in terms of time.

Define utilisation ratio β for $0 \le \beta \le 1$ as the ratio of CPU utilisation for a given job on each processor. By a given β the job on a processor can on the average obtain a service time $\beta \Delta T$ in each unit of time ΔT. In our scheduling strategy each parallel job will be assigned a utilisation ratio which is usually determined based on the current system working conditions. Different ratios can also be given on different processors for naturally unbalanced parallel jobs to achieve better system load-balancing.

Assume that the same utilisation ratio β is assigned to a parallel job across all the associated processors and that the job's processes are gang scheduled. The *turnaround time* $T_e(p)$ for that job can then be calculated as

$$T_e(p) = \frac{T_d(p)}{\beta} \tag{2}$$

where $T_d(p)$ is the computational time obtained on p dedicated processors.

Defining effective speedup $S_e(p)$ as the ratio of $T_d(1)$ and $T_e(p)$, then

$$S_e(p) = \frac{T_d(1)}{T_e(p)} = \beta \frac{T_d(1)}{T_d(p)} = \beta S_d(p). \tag{3}$$

where $S_d(p)$ is the conventional speedup obtained on p dedicated processors.

To achieve a desired performance, we may set a performance target γ and require

$$T_d(1) \geq \gamma T_e(p), \tag{4}$$

or

$$S_e(p) \geq \gamma. \tag{5}$$

If the effective speedup for a given job is lower than that target, the performance will be considered unacceptable.

¿From equations in (3) and (5) we can obtain

$$S_d(p) \geq \frac{\gamma}{\beta}. \tag{6}$$

Using the above inequality we can easily determine how many processors should be allocated to a given job in order to achieve a desired performance when a particular β is given. Assuming $\gamma = 2$ and $\beta = 0.5$, for example, $S_d(p)$ must be greater than, or equal to 4. Allocating 5 processors or more to that job can then achieve a desired performance if $S_d(5) \geq 4$. When the current system workload is not heavy, we may need to use less number of processors to achieve the same performance. If there are several idle processors, we may set $\beta = 1$ in the above example. Then only 3 processors may be required if $S_d(3) \geq 2$.

In practice the exact speedup $S_d(p)$ may not be known except for those programs in standard general-purpose parallel computing libraries. Thus the values can only be approximate in those cases. However, good approximations can often be obtained. For example, the results of the Linpack Benchmark [7] can be used as a good approximation for problems of matrix computation.

The utilisation ratios of the existing jobs may be decreased whenever a new job enters the system to time-share the resources. The problem is how to ensure a sustained ratio of CPU utilisation for each job so that the performance can be predictable in a time sharing environment. Since the resources in a system are really limited, the answer to this question is simply that we cannot guarantee every job to have a sustained ratio when the system workload is heavy.

One way to solve the above problem is to adopt the following scheme. First we set a limit to the length of each *scheduling round ΔT* (or a limit to the number of jobs in the system). A common misunderstanding about time-sharing for parallel jobs is that good performance will be obtained as long as parallel jobs can enter the system and start operation quickly. As we mentioned previously that the resources in a system are limited, however, good performance just cannot be guaranteed if the length of scheduling round is unbounded. Consider a simple example when several large jobs are time-sharing the resources in a round robin manner. In this case the conventional gang scheduling simply fail to produce good performance in terms of turnaround time.

Because of the limit to the length of each scheduling round short jobs still can be blocked for a long time. We then adopt a scheduling policy, that is, small jobs should have sustained utilisation ratios to ensure a short turnaround time, while each large job should be assigned a large number of processors, but given a utilisation ratio which can vary in a large range according to the current system workload. In this way we think that small jobs will not be blocked, the resource utilisation can be kept high and reasonably good performance for large jobs may also be obtained.

Based on the above ideas a *multi-class time/space sharing system* is designed. A detailed description of this system is beyond the scope of this paper. Interested readers may refer [24] for more details.

3   Two-Level Scheduling

It can be seen from the previous section that our scheduling strategy is based on the utilisation ratios assigned to parallel jobs. In this section we introduce a *two-level scheduling* scheme for balancing the workloads for both sequential and parallel processing,

At the top level, or *global level* the *gang scheduling*, or a *loose gang scheduling* scheme to be discussed in the next section, is adopted to coordinate parallel computing. Each *scheduling round* ΔT is divided into *time slots*. An example of the time distribution for different processes on each processor is shown in Fig. 1. In the figure time slot $\Delta t_s^{(i)}$ is allocated only to *sequential processes* associated with sequential jobs, while slot $\Delta t_p^{(i)}$ is assigned to a single *parallel process* associated with a parallel job. A parallel process may share its time slots with sequential processes through the scheduling at the bottom level, or *local level*. However, no parallel processes will share the same time slots. This is to avoid many different types of parallel jobs competing for resources at the same time and then to guarantee that each parallel process can obtain its proper share of resources. The relation between a scheduling round and those time slots satisfies the following equation

$$\Delta T = \Delta T_s + \sum_{i=1}^{n} \Delta t_p^{(i)} \tag{7}$$

where $\Delta T_s = \sum_{i=1}^{m} \Delta t_s^{(i)}$ is the total time dedicated for sequential jobs in a scheduling round and is distributed to gain good response to interactive clients.

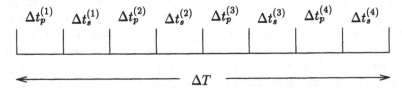

$$\Delta t_p^{(1)} \quad \Delta t_s^{(1)} \quad \Delta t_p^{(2)} \quad \Delta t_s^{(2)} \quad \Delta t_p^{(3)} \quad \Delta t_s^{(3)} \quad \Delta t_p^{(4)} \quad \Delta t_s^{(4)}$$

$$\longleftarrow \text{—————— } \Delta T \text{ ——————} \longrightarrow$$

Fig. 1. The time distribution in a scheduling round.

The width of each time slot is determined by the corresponding utilisation ratio $\beta_p^{(i)}$, or $\beta_s^{(i)}$. We can then calculate the width of each time slot as

$$\Delta t_p^{(i)} = \beta_p^{(i)} \Delta T \tag{8}$$

and

$$\Delta T_s = \beta_s \Delta T \tag{9}$$

where $\beta_s = \sum_{i=1}^{m} \beta_s^{(i)}$.

There are many ways to distribute ΔT_s. For example, each slot for a parallel process can be followed by a small slot for sequential processes and ΔT_s is *uniformly* distributed across the whole scheduling round. Then

$$\Delta t_s^{(i)} = \frac{\Delta T_s}{n}. \tag{10}$$

We can also distribute ΔT_s *proportionally* to the width of each time slot for parallel processes, that is,

$$\Delta t_s^{(i)} = \frac{\beta_p^{(i)}}{\sum_{j=1}^{n} \beta_p^{(j)}} \Delta T_s. \tag{11}$$

The calculation for *proportional distribution* is a bit more complicated than that for *uniform distribution*. However it is useful when a *proper-share* policy, which will be described later in the section, is applied at the local level.

Different local policies can be adopted to schedule processes within each time slot. In those time slots dedicated for sequential processing conventional local scheduling schemes of any standard operating system will be good enough. In the following we discuss how to schedule processes in each time slot $\Delta t_p^{(i)}$ in which parallel processing is involved.

To ensure that a parallel process can obtain its assinged share of CPU utilisation, the whole slot $\Delta t_p^{(i)}$ may be dedicated just to the associated parallel process. In that case a very high priority will be given and the process simply does *busy-waiting*, or *spins* during communication/synchronisation so that no other processes can disturb its execution within each associated time slot. One problem associated with this policy is that the performance of sequential jobs, especially of those which demand good interactive response, may significantly be affected. Therefore, its use will be treated as special cases under the environment of networks of workstations to achieve certain client's special requests .

To prevent great performance degradation of sequential interactive jobs, *implicit coscheduling* scheme can be adopted. However, a potential problem is that the execution of a parallel process may be disturbed by several sequential processes and then it is possible that certain parallel processes may not receive their proper shares in their associated time slots.

The above problem may be alleviated by adopting a *proper-share* policy. In this policy we do not consider individual shares allocated for each sequential job. Except for special ones, e.g., multimedia workloads, which may be treated in the same way as parallel jobs to achieve constant-rate services, only a combined share of sequential processes $\Delta t_s^{(i)}$ is considered. Each distributed time slot for sequential processes $\Delta t_s^{(i)}$ is also integrated with its associated time slot $\Delta t_p^{(i)}$ to form a single time slot of width $\Delta t^{(i)}$, that is,

$$\Delta t^{(i)} = \Delta t_p^{(i)} + \Delta t_s^{(i)}. \tag{12}$$

In each integrated time slot implicit coscheduling is applied to support both parallel and sequential processing. When its allocated share is not used up in time $\Delta t_p^{(i)}$, a parallel process can still obtain services till the end of the integrated time slot $\Delta t^{(i)}$ though $\Delta t^{(i)}$ is longer than $\Delta t_p^{(i)}$. When a parallel process has consumed its share before the end of an integrated time slot, however, it will be blocked and the services in the remaining time slot then dedicated to sequential processes. With this policy parallel processes and sequential processes as a whole may be guaranteed to obtain their proper shares during the computation.

Similar to the one described in [5], the policy may be realised by applying the *proportional-share* technique which are originally used for *real-time* applications [19,21]. However, our scheduling scheme is much simpler and easier to implement because only the proper share of a *single* parallel process is considered against a *combined* share of sequential processes in each time slot.

Now the problem is how to distribute the total time ΔT_s allocated for processing sequential jobs. The uniform distribution using the equation in (10) is easy to calculate. However, the resulting $\Delta t_s^{(i)}$ may be too small to compensate the lost share of parallel processes which have large $\beta_p^{(i)}$s. Therefore, the proportional distribution using (11) may be a more proper one.

Normalising ΔT, that is, setting $\Delta T = 1$, the equation in (7) will become

$$1 = \beta_s + \sum_{i=1}^{n} \beta_p^{(i)}. \tag{13}$$

Using equations in (8), (9), (11) and (13), we obtain

$$\Delta t^{(i)} = \Delta t_s^{(i)} + \Delta t_p^{(i)} = \frac{\beta_p^{(i)}}{\sum_{j=1}^{n} \beta_p^{(j)}} \Delta T. \tag{14}$$

The width of an integrated time slot $\Delta t^{(i)}$ can directly be obtained by using the equation in (14) and thus there is no need to explicitly calculate $\Delta t_s^{(i)}$s.

4   Registration Office

When a parallel process has used up its time slot, it will be *preempted* at the global level and another parallel process be *dispatched*. After being dispatched, parallel processes may time-share resources with sequential processes on each processor. Just like sequential processes, parallel processes will then be either in *running* state, or *ready* and *blocked* states, which is controlled by a local scheduler. Because in our two-level scheduling the execution of parallel processes are controlled at both global and local levels, special care has to be taken to avoid potential scheduling conflicts. For example, the global scheduler wants to preempt a parallel process which is currently not in running state. To solve this problem we introduce a *registration office* on each processor.

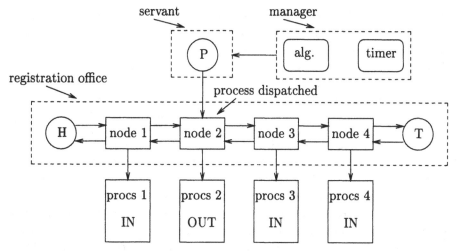

Fig. 2. The organisation of a registration office.

The registration office is constructed by using a linked list as shown in Fig. 2. When a parallel job is initiated, each associated process will enter the local sequential queueing system the same way as sequential processes on the corresponding processor. Just like sequential processes, parallel processes can be either in running state, or in ready state requesting for service, or in blocked state during communication/synchronisation. However, every parallel process has to be *registered* in the registration office, that is, on each processor the linked list will be extended with a new node which has a pointer pointing to the process just being initiated. Similarly, when a parallel job is terminated, it has to *check out* from the office, that is, the corresponding node on each processor will be deleted from the linked list.

As we discussed in the previous section, certain parallel processes may be assigned a very high priority so that they can occupy the whole time slots allocated to them. In that case the execution of sequential workloads can be seriously deteriorated. To alleviate this problem we may introduce certain time slots $\Delta t_s^{(i)}$ which are dedicated to sequential jobs only. This can be done by introducing *dummy nodes* in the linked list. A dummy node is the same type of nodes in a linked list except its pointer points to NULL, the *constant zero*, instead of a real parallel process. It seems that there is a *dummy parallel process* associated with that node. When a service is given to that dummy parallel process, the whole time slot will be dedicated to sequential processes.

There is a *servant* working in the office. When the servant comes to a place, or a node in the linked list, the process associated with that node can receive services, or *be dispatched*. When a process is dispatched, it will be marked *out*. Other processes which are not dispatched will be marked *in*. In practice a process may be *blocked* if it is marked *in*. Therefore, a parallel process can come out of the blocked status only if it is *ready* for service (controlled by the local scheduler) and the event *out* occurs (controlled by the top level scheduler). By letting only one parallel process be marked *out* on each processor at any time, we can guarantee that only one parallel process time-shares resources with sequential processes in each time slot.

When a time slot is ended for the current parallel process, the servant will move to a new node. The parallel process associated with that node can then be serviced next. However, the movement of the servant is totally controlled by an *office manager* which has a *timer* to determine when the servant is to move and an *algorithm* to determine which node the servant is to move to. The algorithm can be simple ones such as the conventional round-robin. (To obtain a high system throughput, however, other more sophisticated scheduling schemes may also be considered.) The timer is to ensure that processes can obtain their allocated service times, that is, $\Delta t_p^{(i)}$'s, or $\Delta t_s^{(i)}$'s in each scheduling round.

The use of registration offices is similar to that of the two-dimensional matrix adopted in the conventional coscheduling. Each column of the matrix corresponds to a time slot and each row to a processor. The coscheduling is then controlled based on that matrix. It is easy to see that the linked list on each processor plays the same role as a row of that matrix in coscheduling parallel processes. However, the key difference is that our two-level scheduling scheme allows both parallel and sequential jobs to be executed simultaneously.

5   Loose Gang Scheduling

The conventional gang scheduler is centralised. The system has a central controller. At the end of each time slot the controller broadcasts a message to all processors. The message contains the information about which parallel workload will receive a service next. The centralised system is easy to implement, especially when the scheduling algorithm is simple. However, frequent signal-broadcasting for simultaneous context switch across the processors may degrade the overall system performance on machines such as networks of workstations and space-sharing policies may not easily be adopted to enhance the efficiency of resource utilisation. Because in our system there is a registration office on each processor, we can adopt a *loose gang scheduling* policy to alleviate these problems.

In our system there is a *global job manager*. It is used to monitor the working conditions of each processor, to locate and allocate processors and to assign utilisation ratios to parallel jobs, and to balance parallel and sequential workloads. We believe that resources in networks of workstations cannot efficiently be utilised without an effective global job manager. This global job manager is also able to broadcast signals for the purpose of synchronisation to coordinate the execution of parallel jobs. However, the signals need not be frequently broadcast for simultaneous context switch between time slots across the processors. They are sent only once after each scheduling round, or even many scheduling rounds to adjust the potential skew of the corresponding time slots (or simply *time skew*) across the processors caused by using *local job managers* on each processor.

There is a local job manager on each processor. It is used to monitor and report to the global job manager the working conditions on that processor. It also takes orders from the global job manager to properly set up its registration office and to coordinate the execution of parallel jobs with other processors. With help of the global job manager the effective coscheduling is guaranteed by using local job managers on each processor.

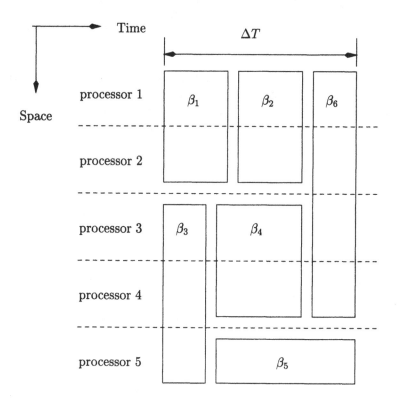

Fig. 3. The time/space allocation for six jobs on five processors.

In the following we give a simple example which demonstrates more clearly the effectiveness of using the loose gang scheduling scheme and which also presents another way of deriving the registration office for the scheme.

Our simple example considers the execution of six jobs on five processors. We assume that the time/space allocation has already been done, that is, the number of processor and the utilisation ratio have been assigned for each job, as depicted in Fig. 3. For various reasons such as described in the previous sections the shapes of time/space allocation may not be the same for each job as indicated in the figure. This will make it very difficult for a centralised controller to coschedule jobs. However, the problem can easily be solved by adopting our loose gang scheduling.

On each processor we run a local job manager and we also set up a *scheduling table* which is given by the global job manager. Parallel processes are then scheduled according to this scheduling table. In our example there are three different scheduling tables, as shown in Fig. 4(a). The processes and the lengths of their allocated time slots in a scheduling round are listed in each table in an ordered manner. It is easy to see that, if the processors are synchronised at the beginning of each scheduling round (It is also possible that the processors can be synchronised once many scheduling rounds.) and local job managers schedule parallel processes according to the given scheduling tables, the correct coscheduling across the processors is then guaranteed.

Because both content and size of each table vary from time to time during the computation, it is quite natural to implement the scheduling tables using linked lists, which results in our registration office. A registration office on processor 1 is depicted in Fig. 4(b). Note each node in the linked list has a pointer which points at the corresponding process so that any unnecessary search for parallel processes can be avoided.

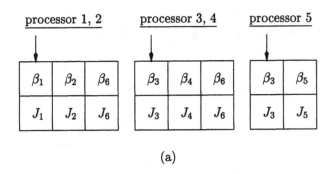

(a)

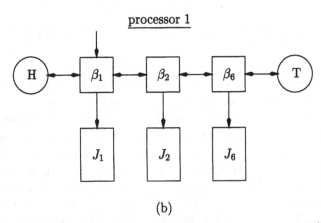

(b)

Fig. 4. (a) The scheduling tables assigned for each processor and (b) The registration office on processor 1.

With the collaboration of the global and local job managers the system can work correctly and effectively. A potential disadvantage of the loose gang scheduling is that there is an additional cost for executing the coscheduling algorithm on each processor. However, in practice time slots $\Delta t_p^{(i)}$, or $\Delta t^{(i)}$ are usually in order of seconds. This extra cost for running a process for coscheduling will be relatively very small.

6   Conclusions

In this paper we discussed some new ideas for effectively scheduling both parallel and sequential workloads on networks of workstations.

To achieve a desired performance in a system with a variety of competitive background workloads, the key is to assign a sustained CPU utilisation ratio on each processor to a parallel job so that the performance becomes predictable. Because the resources in a system are limited, however, we cannot guarantee that every job will be given a sustained utilisation ratio. One way to solve this problem is that small parallel jobs are assigned a sustained ratio of resource utilisation, while each large parallel job is allocated a large number of processors and assigned a utilisation ratio which can vary in a wide range according to the current system workload. Thus small jobs are not blocked by larger ones and a short turnaround time is guaranteed, high efficiency of resource utilisation can be achieved and reasonably good performance for large jobs may also be obtained.

To balance the workloads for both sequential and parallel processing, we introduced a two-level scheduling scheme. At the global level parallel jobs are coscheduled so that they can obtain their proper shares without interfering with each other and they can also be coordinated across the processors to achieve high efficiency in parallel computation. At the local level many different policies, e.g., the busy-waiting (or spinning) and the implicit coscheduling (or two-phase blocking), can be considered to schedule both parallel and sequential processes. We introduced a proper-share policy for effectively scheduling processes at the local level. By adopting this policy we can obtain good performance for each parallel job and also maintain good response for interactive sequential jobs. The two-level scheduling can be implemented by adopting a registration office on each processor. The organisation of the registration office (which is also described in [23]) is simple and the main purpose is to effectively schedule parallel processes at both global and local levels.

We also introduced a loose gang scheduling scheme to coschedule parallel jobs across the processors. This scheme requires both global and local job managers. The coscheduling is mainly controlled by local job managers on each processor, so frequent signal-broadcasting for simultaneous context switch across the processors is avoided. There is only a bit extra work for global job manager to adjust potential time skew. The name *loose gang* has two meanings. First the coscheduling is achieved by mainly using local job managers but not just a central controller and second parallel processes may time-share their allocated time slots with sequential processes. Since both global and local job managers play effective roles in job scheduling, we think this may lead a way for us to find good strategies for efficiently scheduling both parallel and sequential workloads on networks of workstations.

A new system based on these ideas is currently under construction on a distributed memory parallel machine, the Fujitsu AP1000+, at the Australian National University.

References

1. T. Agerwala, J. L. Martin, J. H. Mirza, D. C. Sadler, D. M. Dias and M. Snir, SP2 system architecture, *IBM Systems Journal*, 34(2), 1995.
2. S. V. Anastasiadis and K. C. Sevcik, Parallel application scheduling on networks of workstations, *Journal of Parallel and Distributed Computing*, 43, 1997, pp.109-124.
3. T. E. Anderson, D. E. Culler, D. A. Patterson and the NOW team, A case for NOW (networks of workstations), *IEEE Micro*, 15(1), Feb. 1995, pp.54-64.
4. R. H. Arpaci, A. C. Dusseau, A. M. Vahdat, L. T. Liu, T. E. Anderson and D. A. Patterson, The interaction of parallel and sequential workloads on a network of workstations, *Proceedings of ACM SIGMETRICS'95/PERFORMANCE'95 Joint International Conference on Measurement and Modeling of Computer Systems*, May 1995, pp.267-278.
5. A. C. Arpaci-Dusseau and D. E. Culler, Extending proportional-share scheduling to a network of workstations, *Proceedings of International Conference on Parallel and Distributed Processing Techniques and Applications*, Las Vegas, Nevada, June 1997.
6. M. Crovella, P. Das, C. Dubnicki, T. LeBlanc and E. Markatos, Multiprogramming on multiprocessors, *Proceedings of the Third IEEE Symposium on Parallel and Distributed Processing*, Dec. 1991, pp.590-597.
7. J. J. Dongarra, Performance of various computers using standard linear equations software, Technical Report CS-89-95, Computer Science Department, University of Tennessee, Nov. 1997.
8. A. C. Dusseau, R. H. Arpaci and D. E. Culler, Effective distributed scheduling of parallel workloads, *Proceedings of ACM SIGMETRICS'96 International Conference*, 1996.
9. D. G. Feitelson and L. Rudolph, Gang scheduling performance benefits for fine-grained synchronisation, *Journal of Parallel and Distributed Computing*, 16(4), Dec. 1992, pp.306-318.
10. D. Ghosal, G. Serazzi and S. K. Tripathi, The processor working set and its use in scheduling multiprocessor systems, *IEEE Transactions on Software Engineering*, 17(5), May 1991, pp.443-453.
11. A. Gupta, A. Tucker and S. Urushibara, The impact of operating system scheduling policies and synchronisation methods on the performance of parallel applications. *Proceedings of the 1991 ACM SIGMETRICS Conference on Measurement and Modeling of Computer Systems*, May 1991, pp.120-131.
12. K. Li, IVY: A shared virtual memory system for parallel computing, *Proceedings of International Conference on Parallel Processing*, 1988, pp.94-101.
13. S.-P. Lo and V. D. Gligor, A comparative analysis of multiprocessor scheduling algorithms, *Proceedings of the 7th International Conference on Distributed Computing Systems*, Sept. 1987, pp.205-222.

14. V. K. Naik, S. K. Setia and M. S. Squillante, Performance analysis of job scheduling policies in parallel supercomputing environments, *Proceedings of Supercomputing '93*, Nov. 1993, pp.824-833.

15. V. K. Naik, S. K. Setia and M. S. Squillante, Processor allocation in multiprogrammed distributed-memory parallel computer systems, IBM Research Report RC 20239, 1995.

16. J. K. Ousterhout, Scheduling techniques for concurrent systems, *Proceedings of Third International Conference on Distributed Computing Systems*, May 1982, pp.20-30.

17. E. Rosti, E. Smirni, L. Dowdy, G. Serazzi and B. M. Carlson, Robust partitioning policies of multiprocessor systems, *Performance Evaluation*, 19(2-3), 1994, pp.141-165.

18. S. K. Setia, M. S. Squillante and S. K. Tripathi, Analysis of processor allocation in multiprogrammed, distributed-memory parallel processing systems, *IEEE Transactions on Parallel and Distributed Systems*, 5(4), April 1994, pp.401-420.

19. I. Stoica, H. Abdel-wahab, K, Jeffay, S. Baruah, J. Gehrke and C. G. Plaxton, A Proportional share resource allocation algorithm for real-time, time-shared systems, *IEEE Real-Time Systems Symposium*, Dec. 1996.

20. K. Suzaki, H. Tanuma, S. and Y. Ichisugi, Design of combination of time sharing and space sharing for parallel task scheduling, *Proceedings of the International Conference on Parallel and Distributed Processing Techniques and Applications*, Las Vegas, Nevada, Nov. 1997.

21. C. A. Waldspurger and W. E. Weihl, Stride scheduling: deterministic proportional-share resource management, Technical Report MIT/LCS/TM-528, MIT Laboratory for Computer Science, MIT, June 1995.

22. J. Zahorjan and E. D. Lazowska, Spinning versus blocking in parallel systems with uncertainty, *Proceedings of the IFIP International Seminar on Performance of Distributed and Parallel Systems*, Dec. 1988, pp.455-472.

23. B. B. Zhou, X. Qu and R. P. Brent, Effective scheduling in a mixed parallel and sequential computing environment, *Proceedings of the 6th Euromicro Workshop on Parallel and Distributed Processing*, Madrid, Jan 1998.

24. B. B. Zhou, R. P. Brent, D. Walsh and K. Suzaki, A multi-class time/space sharing system, Tech. Rep., DCS and CSLab, Australian National University, 1998, in process.

Probabilistic Loop Scheduling Considering Communication Overhead*

Sissades Tongsima, Chantana Chantrapornchai, and Edwin H.-M. Sha

University of Notre Dame, Notre Dame IN 46556, USA

Abstract. This paper presents a new methodology for statically scheduling a cyclic data-flow graph whose node computation times can be represented by random variables. A communication cost issue is also considered as another uncertain factor in which each node from the graph can produce different amount of data depending on the probability of its computation time. Since such communication costs rely on the amount of transfered data, this overhead becomes uncertain as well. We propose an algorithm to take advantage of the parallelism across a loop iteration while hiding the communication overhead. The resulting schedule will be evaluated in terms of confidence probability—the probability of having a schedule completed before a certain time. Experimental results show that the proposed framework performs better than a traditional algorithm running on an input which assumes fixed average timing information.

1 Introduction

In many practical applications such as interface systems, fuzzy systems, and artificial intelligence systems and others, the required tasks normally have uncertain computation times (called *uncertain* or *probabilistic* tasks for brevity). Such tasks normally contain conditional instructions and/or operations that could take different computation times for different inputs. Traditional scheduling methods assume either the worst-case or the average-case computation time. However, the resulting schedule may be inefficient in the real operating situation. To improve the productivity, the probabilistic nature of such tasks needs to be properly considered during the scheduling phase. Furthermore, for a parallel system, which is a common platform for these computation-intensive applications, the communications between two processors should not be neglected. According to the current routing technology in parallel architectures, e.g. wormhole routing [6], an amount of data being sent among different processors constitutes a significant part of the underlying communication overhead. Therefore, such communications can directly affect the total execution time of an application. Since the amount of data created by a task may depend on varying task computation, these communication overheads can be varied. For instance, if a probabilistic task represents a group of statements from a conditional block, the computation

---

* This research was supported in part by the Royal Thai Government Scholarship and the NSF grant MIP 95-01006

Dror G. Feitelson, Larry Rudolph (Eds.): JSSPP'98, LNCS 1459, pp. 158–179, 1998.

times of this task depend on the probabilities inherited from the branching statement. This probability also implies the different amount of data produced from different branches in the conditional block. In order to realistically capture the random nature of task computation and communication times, a probabilistic model must be used. Therefore, to maximize scheduling results, scheduling techniques which properly consider such probabilistic data should be investigated.

Considerable research has been conducted in the area of scheduling of a directed-acyclic graphs (DAG) on multiple processing systems. (Note that DAGs are obtained from data-flow graphs, DFGs, by ignoring edges of a DFG containing one or more delays.) Many heuristics have been proposed to schedule DAGs, e.g., list scheduling, graph decomposition [9, 7] etc. These methods, however, do not explore the parallelism across iterations nor do they address the problems of probabilistic tasks. Loop transformations are also common techniques used to restructure loops from the repetitive code segment in order to reduce the total execution time of the schedule [24, 23, 16, 1]. These techniques, however, do not consider that the target systems have limited number of processors or that task computation times are uncertain. For global scheduling, software pipelining [13] is used to overlap instructions, whereby the parallelism is exposed across iterations. This technique, however, expands the graph by unfolding it. Furthermore, such an approach is limited to solving the problem without considering uncertain computation times for operations [5, 13].

Some research considers the uncertainty inherit in the computation time of nodes. Ku and De Micheli [11, 12] proposed a relative scheduling method which handles tasks with unbounded delays. Nevertheless, their approach considers a DAG as an input and does not explore the parallelism across iterations. Furthermore, even if the statistics of the computation time of uncertain nodes is collected, their method will not exploit this information. A framework that is able to handle imprecise propagation delays is proposed by Karkowski and Otten [8]. In their approach, fuzzy set theory [25] was employed to model the imprecise computation time. Although their approach is equivalent to scheduling imprecise tasks to non-resource constrained system, their model is restricted to a simple triangular fuzzy distribution and does not consider probability values.

For scheduling under resource constraints, the *rotation scheduling* technique was proposed by Chao, LaPaugh and Sha [2, 3] and extended to handle multidimensional applications by Passos, Sha and Bass [19]. Rotation scheduling schedules loops by assigning nodes from the loop to the system with limited number of functional units. It implicitly explores retiming [15] in order to reduce the total computation time of the nodes along the longest paths, (also called the critical paths) in the DFG. In other words, the graph is transformed in such a way that the parallelism is exposed but the behavior of the graph is preserved. The idea of using loop pipelining to schedule DFGs while considering communication costs is presented in [22]. This method, called cyclo-compaction scheduling also consider the message collision scenario when wormhole routing is applied. Nevertheless, this approach assumes computation time of a node to be a fixed value.

In this paper, we propose an algorithm which considers the probabilistic behavior in both computation times and communication overhead. A new graph model which is a generalized version of a regular DFG, called probabilistic extended data-flow graph (PEG) is introduced to represent an application with uncertain computation times as well as data volume. If this graph represents a repeated loop, a weighted-edge will be added between any two nodes that have inter-iteration dependencies ($A[i]$ depends on $B[i-1]$) where the weight on each edge represents the dependency distance. We assume that the data volume is initiated from a sender and will render the communication cost when both sender and receiver nodes are executed in different processors. The communication cost model is based on wormhole routing assumption where a data packet is broken down to small sub-packets, called flits, and they can be transmitted uninterruptedly from source to destination processors. When the size of data is large comparing with the distance between processors, the communication cost will be dominated by the packet length. XY-routing model is assumed in order to determine a route of the message being sent through the system. This assumption helps us determine if there exist the message collisions.

Since the timing information is uncertain, the scheduling result will have no control steps. Moreover, the resulting schedule represents only one iteration of the input graph where the rest of the iterations are assumed to be identical and the synchronization must exist at the end of each iteration. Our approach produces a static schedule for an application and this schedule is believed that if the system follows its order, the application will finish within a particular time. In other words, with some confidence probability our schedule guarantees to finish within a certain time constraint. Again, we used a DAG, called a probabilistic communication&task graph (PT&C-G) to model the scheduling order where each node can take varying computation time. Furthermore, a communication node will be added to the graph whenever data is transmitted from source to destination processors and message contentions will be handled by serializing these communication nodes.

As an example, if a target system architecture comprises of 4 processing elements connected as a 2D-mesh, a processor assignment and a possible schedule (order to execute nodes, namely a PT&C-G) can be presented as in Figures 2(a) and 2(b) respectively. Note that this schedule must satisfy the dependency constraint depicted in the PEG shown in Figure 1(a). Figure 1(b) lists possible computation time of a node associated with probability, as well as its corresponding data volume. Nodes x_i in the PT&C-G represent communication nodes which are added when their corresponding source and sink nodes are scheduled in different processors, e.g., node 3 depends on data from node 1 but both nodes are assigned to different processors. The communication node x_3 is appended to the PT&C-G since node 0 depends on this message (x_3) but gets scheduled to the different processor from its parent (node 3). By using our technique, the order in Figure 2(b) can be improved by overlapping the current iteration with node 0 from the next iterations resulting in Figures 2(c) and 2(d). According to Figure 2(c), node 0 can be executed simultaneously with nodes 1, 2, and 4 which results in an ability to hide the communication latency x_0. In other words, this communication node can be computed while the other nodes are executing.

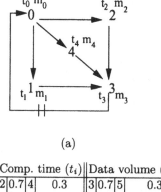

(a)

Node n_i	Comp. time (t_i)				Data volume (m_i)			
0	2	0.7	4	0.3	3	0.7	5	0.3
1	3	0.5	4	0.5	1	0.5	3	0.5
2	1	0.2	4	0.8	1	0.2	4	0.8
3	3	0.5	4	0.5	1	0.5	3	0.5
4	2	0.4	5	0.6	2	0.4	4	0.6

(b)

Fig. 1. Example of the PEG

If we use the traditional scheduling approach, which approximates all uncertain timing information with the node average computation times, to minimize the modified input graph, the order given by such scheduling, however, may not be a good static schedule in practice. For instance, rather than placing node 0 at PE_2 (as shown in Figure 2(c)), the traditional algorithm may assign node 0 to PE_1 since it can eliminate x_3 but when this schedule is employed in practice the performance of this system might be worse than we expected due to the timing variations. By using a simulator to simulate how a parallel computer computes tasks in a schedule, this paper shows the comparison between the results obtained from the proposed approach with the ones given by traditional scheduling [22]. The contributions of this paper can be listed as follows: First, the probabilistic model is used in this work to make a static schedule more realistic. Second, this paper also considers and minimizes the underlying communication costs which can degrade the performance of running an application on the parallel system. Third, the results obtained from our approach can tell designers with a confidence probability what to be expected in practice when applying our resulting static schedule. Finally, this paper compares the effectiveness of the proposed approach with traditional scheduling and shows the benefit of using our algorithm by realistically simulating an execution of a resulting schedule in a parallel system.

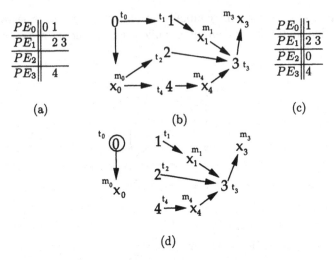

(a)

(b)

(c)

(d)

Fig. 2. Result from scheduling the graph in Figure 1

The outline of this paper is as follows. The following section discusses some background and the graph model of this work. Then Section 3 presents how to construct a schedule as a graph and also shows an algorithm to probabilistically evaluate such a schedule. The proposed loop scheduling is also discussed in this section. Section 4 shows the experimental results from our algorithm and compare them with the results given by the traditional method. Finally, the conclusions are drawn in Section 5.

2   Background

In this paper, we generalize traditional DFGs in such a way that each node may have uncertain computation time. Furthermore, the amount of data produced by each node can be varied depending on the probability of the node computation time. The following presents the definition of this graph called a probabilistic extended data-flow graph (PEG).

Definition 1. *A probabilistic extended data-flow graph (PEG) is a node-weighted, edge-weighted, directed graph $G = \langle V, E, \delta, m, t \rangle$ where V is a set of nodes, E is a set of edges representing node precedence relations. The tuple δ is a function from E to positive integers representing a number of dependence distance between two nodes on the corresponding edge. The tuples m and t represent random variables of uncertain amount of data sent out from each node and random variables of uncertain computation time of each node respectively.*

As an example, Figure 1(a) depicts the PEG where all the random variables, associated with each node in the graph, are presented in Figure 1(b). Each entry of the table presents two timing information of a node which are possible computation times and possible data volume. A probability corresponding to each timing value is presented next to its possible value in each entry. For instance, node 0 has possible computation times of 1 with probability of 0.5 and 2 with the same probability. In this example, both computation time of a node and its corresponding data volume are *dependent*. This is because a node could represent a group of operations in a conditional block. This representation causes a node to have varying computation times and varying amount of data produced at one instance. These timing and data volume, however, are related in their probabilities. For example, if node 0 takes 2 time units with 0.7 probability, then with the same probability there must also exist the amount of data produced when the node computation time is 2. In this paper, we assume that the probability distributions of both m and t are discrete, i.e., a single possible node computation time and data volume produced by this node are integer. The notation $P(rv = x)$ is read "the probability that random variable rv assumes value x".

A notation $n_u \xrightarrow{\delta} n_v$ conveys a precedence relation between nodes u (n_u) and v (n_v) where δ represents number of delays on this edge (short bar-lines in the graph). For example, the edge between nodes 3 and 0 can be shown as $n_3 \xrightarrow{2} n_0$. Note that in this graph, $n_3 \xrightarrow{2} n_0$ represents a loop carried dependence (also called delays in this paper) where two short bar lines are used to denote two dependency distance between n_3 and n_0 in the graph. In other words, for any iteration j, an edge e from n_u to n_v with delay $\delta(e)$ conveys that the computation of node v at iteration j depends on the execution of node u at iteration $j - \delta(e)$. An edge with no delays represents a data dependency within the same iteration.

With the advent of worm-hole routing and parallel processing, we may assume that a distance between source and destination processors can be negligible when comparing with a packet length. Consider the following: given a packet length Pl (bits), a channel bandwidth Bw (bits/sec.), length of subdivided packet (flit) Fl, and number of processors D which are traversed when sending the packet from source to destination. The communication latency for transferring data from source processor to destination processor can be summarized as $T_{wh} = \frac{Pl}{Bw} + \frac{Fl}{Bw} \times D$. If Pl is much greater than D, the underlying communication costs are directly proportional to the amount of data (Pl) being transfered between two processors [6]. Note that the wormhole routing model is assumed in all the experiments conducted in this paper.

Since the computation time of a node and the corresponding data volume are random variables, manipulating the computation time of two vertices involves a function of two random variables, namely $Z = f(X, Y)$ [4, 18]. In this study, function f can be, for instance, addition and maximum operations. Assume that X and Y are random variables representing the computation time of two vertices. The outcome of this function f is also a random variable. As an example, suppose that we would like to add computation times of n_0 with that of n_2 (timing information is shown in Figure 1(b)). The addition result is depicted in Figure 3. Likewise, the maximum operation can be done in the same fashion.

$$+ \quad \begin{array}{c|cc} & 0.7 & 0.3 \\ \hline t_0 & 2 & 4 \\ t_2 & 1 & 4 \\ \hline & 0.2 & 0.8 \end{array} \qquad \Rightarrow \quad \begin{array}{c|c|c|c} 3 & 5 & 6 & 8 \\ \hline 0.14 & 0.06 & 0.56 & 0.24 \end{array}$$

Fig. 3. Adding two random variables $T = t_0 + t_2$

The *retiming* operation rearrange delays in a data-flow graph so as to reduce the longest path of the graph [15,14,17]. Retiming of n_u ($r(n_u) = 1$) is equivalent to deleting one delay from *each* incoming edge of n_u and adding one delay on *each* outgoing edge of this node. A value of a retiming function reflects a number of delay moved through the retimed node. The example of this operation is shown in Figure 4 where $r(n_0) = r(n_1) = 1$. Originally $n_3 \xrightarrow{2} n_0$ has 2 delays and with $r(n_0) = r(n_1) = 1$, one delay from $n_3 \xrightarrow{2} n_0$ is moved from this edge to each of n_0 outgoing edges. The function $r(n_1) = 1$ then removes one delay from $n_0 \xrightarrow{1} n_1$ and places it on $n_1 \xrightarrow{1} n_3$ (see Figure 4(b)). After retiming, some operations (nodes in the graph) called prologue must be computed before entering the loop body—the original data-flow graph represents the whole entity of this loop. The number of prologue operations is directly related to values from the retiming functions [2]. On the other hand, some operations called epilogue must also be computed after the loop due to the reshaping of the loop body indices. To show how the retiming goal can be achieved on a graph in Figure 4(a), let each nodes in the graph have a unit computation time. After retiming the graph the longest path—a path comprises of edges with no delays and has the largest value of summation of the node computation times on this path, is shorter in the retimed graph. In a literature, such a path is also referred to the *clock period* of a graph.

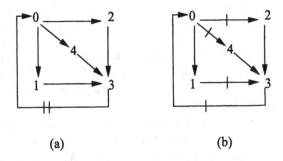

(a)   (b)

Fig. 4. Retiming example where $r(n_0) = r(n_1) = 1$

Rotation scheduling employs the idea of reshaping a loop body [2]. It implicitly uses retiming to explore the parallelism across iterations. Given a legal schedule—a schedule where all precedence relations are satisfied, and a corresponding data-flow graph, rotation scheduling incrementally retimes nodes from the first row of the table and reschedules them so as to reduce the schedule length. The idea behind this technique is that the dependency distance associated with all the parents and children of the rotated nodes will change due to the retiming property. Rotating a node introduces an opportunity to parallelize it with others in the graph. This process is equivalent to taking nodes from the first row of the next iteration to be rescheduled with the others. As an example, considering the scheduling problem when a limited number of target processors is accounted. Given a schedule table (see Figure 5(b)) which complies with all precedence relations the data-flow graph (see Figure 5(a)), rotation scheduling reshapes this repetitive loop body by including n_0' from the next adjacent iteration and puts n_0 at the first iteration as a prologue operation (see Figure 5(c)). This action can be described by a retimed graph in Figure 5(d) where n_0 in Figure 5(a) is retimed by one. This node (n_0') is then rescheduled to a new position such that the total computation time of the iteration is reduced. In this example, after performing rotation once, the schedule length or the time to finish executing one iteration, is reduced by one time step. Note that performing rotation can be done repeatedly until there will be no more reduction.

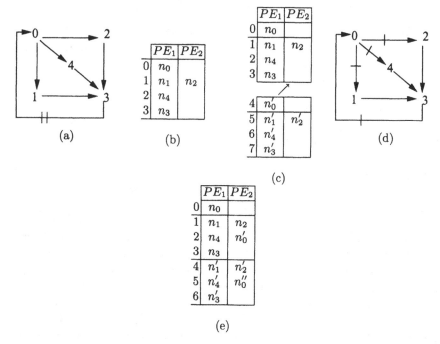

Fig. 5. Rotation scheduling example

3   Loop Scheduling & Communication

Our scheduling problem on parallel processing system where node computation times and communication costs can be varied has not yet been addressed in the previous work. Due to these uncertainties, a scheduler should also produce a schedule with uncertain schedule length. When considering communication, the message collision issue arises and complicates the scheduling problem. Therefore, to obtain a good static schedule which allows the corresponding application to have a shorter completion time in most cases becomes difficult. This section discusses these issues in more detail.

3.1   Probabilistic Task&Communication Graph

Since this paper deals with scheduling uncertain tasks to a parallel system, the concept of control step (synchronization time used to initiate operations in an application) is no longer valid. Rather, the resulting static schedule is concerned with the *order* of nodes to be executed in a processor and how to bind each node to which processor. Furthermore, when it comes to the case that two dependent nodes, e.g., $n_u \longrightarrow n_v$, are bound to different processors, this order should be able to explicitly express this situation. In order to cope with this scenario, a graph called *probabilistic task&communication* is introduced.

Definition 2. *A probabilistic task&communication graph (PT&C-G) is a directed weighted acyclic graph $G = \langle V, E, w \rangle$ where v is a set of nodes, E is a set of precedence relations between any two nodes, and w is a function from V to random variables.*

An *execution order* represented by the PT&C-G is the precedence relations defined by the graph. This graph implies the execution of one *iteration* of a loop body in the corresponding application. Each node in one iteration will be computed exactly once according to the dependency order in the graph. The synchronization will be applied at the end of each iteration. In other words, all the nodes including the communication latencies, which may occur across an iteration due to loop carried dependences, must finish before starting the next iteration. All nodes from the PEG plus extra communication nodes—which are added to the graph when scheduling any two dependent nodes to different processors (assuming there is no communication costs when they are scheduled in the same processor)—will be included in this graph. Recall that the timing of a communication node can be derived from the data volume information in the PEG. Hence, a computation node n_i in a PTC-G is associated with x_i because its communication latency is computed from the amount of data volume of n_i. In the following graph examples, we put m_i next to each x_i to indicate this relationship. Edges between two computational nodes are defined according to the precedence relations in a PEG and/or the order of nodes executed in the same processor. Furthermore, extra edges between a computation node and its communication node, as well as between the communication node and the computation node which the data is sent to are inserted. Edges between two communication nodes may be added to serialize a channel usage and avoid message collision if these nodes require the same channel to send data.

Unlike a probabilistic extended data-flow graph, a PT&C-G cannot have any cycle since it represents only one static schedule. If the target system applies wormhole routing, the communication cost can be calculated by the communication latency function presented in the previous section. It is worth noting that the PT&C-G model presented here is independent of any routing or architecture topology assumption. In other words, given different system architecture configuration, one can independently calculate the communication costs for this graph.

As an example, given a system with 4 processing elements connected as a mesh by 4 bidirectional links (channels), a PEG, and a processor assignment (see Figure 6). Let us assume that XY-routing technique [6] is employed to govern the pattern of sending data from one processor to the other. Suppose that Figure 6(c) is a processor assignment of this graph. A corresponding PT&C-G can be constructed as shown in Figure 6(d). Nodes from the original PEG $(n_0, n_1, n_2, n_3, n_4)$ are included in the PT&C-G where the weights w for these node are their computation times. Since n_1 is scheduled to the same processor as n_0, its parent, there is no communication node needed. Therefore an edge from n_0 to n_1 is presented in the graph. As for n_2 and n_4, a communication node x_0 is inserted in between their parent n_0 and each of them. Here we also assume that there is no message collision occurred when multicasting a message (sending a message from n_0 to both n_2 and n_4). Considering n_3, an edge from n_2 is added between them. Due to XY-routing behavior where a message is routed in X direction first and then in Y direction, sending a message from both n_1 and n_4 to n_3 uses different routes. Consequently, x_1 and x_4 are added to the graph just before n_3. Finally, since $n_3 \xrightarrow{2} n_0$ from the PEG and n_3 is scheduled PE_3 while n_0 is in different processor, this communication must be completed before the next iteration begins. The communication node x_3 is appended to the PT&C-G.

Let us consider a message collision scenario where communication nodes may be serialized due to the limited usage of a physical channel. For demonstrating the contention scenario, assume that no virtual channel [6] is employed. Therefore, if more than two messages are requesting for the same channel, e.g., the channel is still in used while there is another request for the channel, these two requests will have a message contention. As an example, consider Figures 6(a) and 6(b). If the processor assignment in Figure 7(a) is used in place of the one in Figure 6(c), the resulting PT&C-G will be constructed as presented in Figure 7(b). In this case, n_3 is scheduled to PE_2 where none of its parents are assigned to. Communication nodes are then required for the message sending to n_3. By observing Figure 7(b), there is a possible contention on channel between PE_0 and PE_2, because n_1 in PE_0 and n_2 in PE_1 use the same channel to send their data to n_3 in PE_3. Therefore, the communication nodes x_1 and x_2 may need to be serialized. Assume that x_1 gets to use this channel first, then x_2 has

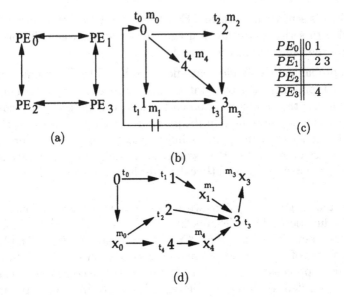

(a)

(b)

(c)

(d)

Fig. 6. Example of how to construct a PT&C-G from a PEG and its processor assignment

to wait for x_1 to finish and that explains the edge from x_1 to x_2. Since there is no possible contention with a message sending from n_4, no serialization is done for its communication node (x_4). The serialization order of such communication nodes, e.g., either x_1 before x_2 or vice versa, is important when evaluating how good this schedule order will be. If routing channels are allocated by hardware in a first come first serve fashion, this order may be changed due to varying node computation times. Hence, it results in different completion time of the PT&C-G. The following subsection discusses how this graph can be probabilistically evaluated.

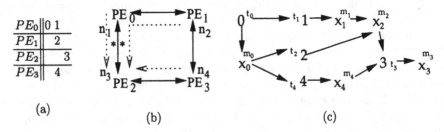

(a)

(b)

(c)

Fig. 7. Example of a PT&C-G where there exists a contention

3.2   Evaluating Probabilistic Schedule Length of PT&C-G

Suppose a PT&C-G has only two nodes, e.g., $n_u \longrightarrow n_v$ where t_u and t_v are independent of each other. The schedule length of this graph can be computed by probabilistically adding these two random variables. On the other hand, if these two nodes do not connect to each other, the max operation can be used to compute the length as presented in Figure 8. Both "add" and "max" operations are two fundamental functions for evaluating the schedule length of the graph. Not all the node timing information (random variables) in PT&C-G are, however, independent of one another. Nevertheless, thoroughly checking the dependency of these random variables and efficiently calculating a probabilistic schedule length considering both dependent and independent cases are difficult. Since these communication nodes also cause the dependence of random variables when performing those basic probabilistic operations, here we dependently add the computation time of the node and its communication time, to be more realistic in estimating probabilistic schedule length.

Considering that n_v depends on data produced by n_u but these nodes are scheduled to different processors. According to our assumption, x_u, a communication node of n_u, must be inserted in between $n_u \longrightarrow n_v$. If $(t_u = 2, m_u = 1)$ with 0.3 probability and $(t_u = 5, m_u = 3)$ with 0.7 probability, one property that must be held is that if n_u takes 2 time units, this node must also produce 1 volume of data. Therefore, adding t_u and x_u could be done by adding outcomes which are associated with the same probability together, e.g., $t_u + m_u = 2 + 1$ with 0.3 probability and $t_u + m_u = 5 + 3$ with 0.7 probability. In our case we call this operation *adding two dependent random variables*.

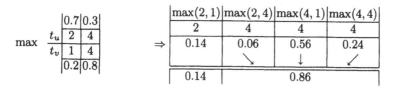

Fig. 8. Maximizing two random variables $M = \max(t_u, t_v)$

It becomes more complex when the serialization of the communication nodes occurs in the graph. Consider a typical segment of a PT&C-G in Figure 9(a). The probabilistic value associated with these nodes are presented in Figure 9(b). If x_0 was any computation node, says n_y for example, we would have probabilistically maximized t_0 with m_1 and added this result to t_y. However, the probability distribution of m_0 is dependent upon that of t_0, and therefore, some combination will not occur when adding $\max(t_0, m_1)$ to m_0.

One possible way of getting around this problem is to separate the result from probabilistic max operation based on the probability distributions of t_0 or m_0, e.g., a group of possible timing whose probability is 0.7 and the reciprocal (0.3)

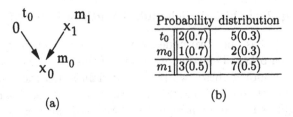

Fig. 9. Example of serialized communication nodes

group. When it comes to the adding, pick a value from m_0 that is associated with each group to be added with the max result. As an example, Figure 10 depicts this calculation. Value 1 from m_0 is added with $\max(2,3)$ and $\max(2,7)$ where they all are associated with 0.7 probability. Likewise, value 2 is added with the rest of the combination. Each of the addition result inherits the probability from the maximum result (boxed numbers in the figure). Given a PT&C-G, Algorithm 1 summarizes how we evaluate a schedule length from this graph.

	0.7		0.3	
	0.35	0.35	0.15	0.15
$\max(t_0, m_1)$	$(2,3)$	$(2,7)$	$(5,3)$	$(5,7)$
	+		+	
m_0	1		2	
$m_0 + \max(t_0, m_1)$	4	8	7	9

Fig. 10. Maximizing and adding dependent random variables

In this algorithm, $weight(u), start\_time(u)$, and $finish\_time(u)$ are data structure that hold their corresponding random variables. The probabilistic timing information (computation or communication time) of n_u can be retrieved by calling $weight(u)$. Either dependently or independently adding $start\_time(u)$ and $weight(u)$ to establish $finish\_time(u)$, a finishing time of n_u which will then be propagated to all n_u's successors. The starting time of a node comes from probabilistically maximizing finishing time of all the node's predecessors. Note that if n_u is a communication node and when adding its starting time to its weight, the operation discussed in Figure 10 may be applied. As an example, consider a PT&C-G in Figure 11.

The algorithm starts off with n_0 where its computation time t_0 gets propagated to n_1 and x_0. Since n_1 and x_0 have no other parents, t_0 is then added to t_1 and m_0, providing the starting time for x_1 and n_2 respectively. At this point the $finish\_time(x_1)$ is holding a random variable $[4(0.15), 5(0.15), 7(0.35), 8(0.35)]$ and $finish\_time(n_2)$ has $[5(0.25), 7(0.5), 9(0.25)]$. Using the strategy described in Figure 10, $finish\_time(x_2)$ becomes $[6(0.075), 8(0.25), 9(0.175), 11(.1625),$

12(0.0875), 13(0.25)] which will then be added to t_3 to complete the calculation for the probabilistic schedule length. Since the computation time of n_3 is fixed, this value is then added to each of the previous possible outcome resulting in [8(0.075), 10(0.25), 11(0.175), 13(.1625), 14(0.0875), 15(0.25)]. According to this result, one can conclude that approximately 75% of the time, this graph will have its schedule length (sl) less than or equal to 14, or $P(sl \leq 14) = 0.75$.

Algorithm 1 Calculate probabilistic schedule length of a PT&C-G

Input: PT&C-G $G = \langle V, E, w \rangle$
Output: Probabilistic schedule length
 1: $start\_time(u) = 0$, and $finish\_time(u) = weight(u), \forall u \in V$
 2: $Q \leftarrow get\_root(G)$;
 3: **while** $Q \neq \emptyset$ **do**
 4:     $u = dequeue(Q)$ and mark node u visited
 5:     **if** u is a communication node **then**
 6:         $finish\_time(u) \leftarrow$ dependently add $weight(u)$ and $start\_time(u)$
 7:     **else**
 8:         $finish\_time(u) \leftarrow$ add two independent random variable, $weight(u)$ and $start\_time(u)$
 9:     **end if**
10:     **for all** children v of u **do**
11:         $start\_time(v) \leftarrow$ maximize $finish\_time(u)$ and $start\_time(v)$
12:         $indegree(v) = indegree(v) - 1$
13:         **if** $indegree(v) = 0$ **then**
14:             $Q = enqueue(v)$
15:         **end if**
16:     **end for**
17: **end while**

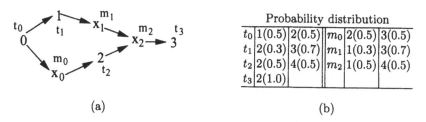

Probability distribution						
t_0	1(0.5)	2(0.5)		m_0	2(0.5)	3(0.5)
t_1	2(0.3)	3(0.7)		m_1	1(0.3)	3(0.7)
t_2	2(0.5)	4(0.5)		m_2	1(0.5)	4(0.5)
t_3	2(1.0)					

(a)   (b)

Fig. 11. PT&C-G for computing probabilistic schedule length

3.3   Loop Scheduling Algorithm

In order to get a good static schedule where the total completion time of the schedule is minimized, the rotation scheduling concept presented in Section 2 is employed. Traditional rotation scheduling, however, does not consider communications between nodes. Furthermore, it has no concept of how to deal with uncertain timing information. Therefore, this algorithm needs to be extended to consider these problems while computing a schedule. Algorithm 2 presents the framework which handle the above considerations. Based on this framework, some detailed modifications are required in each routine. First, an algorithm for producing the initial schedule such as list scheduling [9, 7] needs to be modified so as to consider probabilistic computation and communication timing information. The variation of list scheduling algorithms differ from one another by how each algorithm prioritized the list. Note that this list keeps nodes (called ready nodes) whose all their parents have been scheduled. The scheduler will select a node with the highest priority to be scheduled to a processor so that a resulting intermediate schedule is in the most compact form of the current schedule length. New ready nodes may be inserted into the list during this time. The above sequence is repeated until the ready list is empty and no more nodes to be added to the list. Having discussed the list scheduling process, it is clear that if a graph contains uncertain timing information, the fundamental question here is how to compare two random variables. In addition, if the communication issue is taken into account, the scheduler must be able to handle the message collision case.

Algorithm 2 Rotation scheduling framework

Input: PEG $G = \langle V, E, \delta, m, t \rangle$, number of processors and their connections
Output: PT&C-G G_s, processor assignment *proc*, and retiming function r
1: $(G_{s\_cur}, proc\_cur) \leftarrow$ initial schedule /* produce an initial order and processor assignment */
2: $G_s \leftarrow G_{s\_cur}$, $proc \leftarrow proc\_cur$
3: **for** $i = 1$ to $2|V|$ **do**
4:     $u \leftarrow$ pick rotated node from G_{cur}
5:     $r(u) = r(u) + 1$ /* retime node u */
6:     $proc\_cur \leftarrow$ find available processor for u
7:     $G_{s\_cur} \leftarrow$ reschedule u to G_{s_cur}
8:     **if** $better(G_s, proc_s, G_{s\_cur}, proc\_cur)$ **then**
9:         $G_s \leftarrow G_{s\_cur}$, $proc \leftarrow proc\_cur$ /* store the best schedule and processor assignment */
10:    **end if**
11: **end for**

To compare two random variables, considering the example in Figure 12. If t_u and t_v are to be compared in this case, one can set up a probability value to help decide if one is bigger or smaller than the other. As in the example, we obtain that t_v is smaller than t_u with a 0.56 probability. If a probability constraint is set to 50%, then t_v is really smaller than t_u according to this constraint. This approach can be used to prioritize the list in list scheduling. For deciding where to schedule a node, one can tentatively schedule the node to different possible positions and select the one which contributes the smallest length among all of its intermediate probabilistic schedule lengths. Not only does this comparison technique apply to list scheduling, but also is used in Algorithm 2 where rotation scheduling stores its best resulting schedule and processor assignment.

	0.2	0.8
t_u	1	4
t_v	3	7
	0.7	0.3

$\Rightarrow$

$t_u < t_v$	$(1 < 3)$	$(1 < 7)$	$(4 < 7)$	
	0.14	0.06	0.24	0.44
$t_u > t_v$	$(4 > 3)$			
	0.56			0.56

Fig. 12. Comparing which random variable is greater

Regarding to the communication issue, communication channel usage information must be kept so that the scheduler knows if there exists a contention [22]. The communication node concept presented in the previous subsection can be applied to acknowledge when a channel is released. When the contention occurs, serializing communication nodes helps us approximate the real situation. One can use the above comparison method to suggest where possible contentions can happen. Once the contention is detected, the communication nodes are serialized. Note that possible serialization of the communication nodes may be generated, and the above technique may be used as a tool to select a sequence of communication nodes which yields the shortest possible intermediate schedule length. As an example consider the segment of the PT&C-G from Figure 7(c) again in Figure 13. Suppose that the contention occurs when n_1 and n_2 send data to their children. If t_1 is much larger than t_2, the segment in Figure 13(b) should be smaller than the previous one because the time consuming portion has been changed from (t_1, m_1, m_2) to (t_1, m_1). Communication node x_1 does not need to wait for the available channel, previously occupied by x_2, since by the time n_1 finishes, n_2 and x_2 will be done. On the other hand, in Figure 13(a), x_2 needs to be idle, waiting for x_1 to finish using channel before it can send the message.

By incorporating those aforementioned techniques, we can construct an initial schedule which is represented by a PT&C-G and a processor assignment. Recall that if an input graph has cycles which imply inter-iteration dependences (delays), list scheduling will ignore these cycles and consider only edges with no delays. After a PT&C-G is derived, corresponding nodes from the PEG to which non-zero delay edges are connected, will be checked with their processor assignment if the communication nodes should be added to the PT&C-G (source and sink nodes are scheduled to different processors). At this point the modified rotation scheduling algorithm is able to perform loop pipelining. Nodes at the

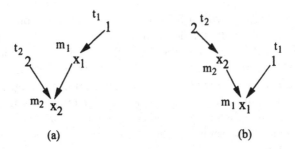

Fig. 13. Comparison between two serializations

top of a schedule—nodes which are ready to be executed first in this schedule, will be selected to be rotated. (Recall that these rotated nodes will be retimed and dependency distance on the edges connected to these nodes will be changed accordingly.) For the rescheduling part, the algorithm will again search for a position to reschedule these nodes one by one so that the resulting PT&C-G is smallest among all other positions. The comparison technique discussed earlier can be used here to help select a good PT&C-G. Since, the order of the nodes in this graph may be different depending on the processor assignment, the message collision and communication channel usage should be carefully investigated at each step. The new intermediate PT&C-G and processor assignment will be created for every rescheduling process. This allows the algorithm to evaluate how good each schedule is and select the best PT&C-G and its processor assignment as its final result.

4 Experiment

In this section, we perform experiments using our algorithm on several benchmarks. These benchmarks were obtained from examples used in [10] and from a fuzzy rule-based system which assumes 5 rules, 3 linguistic variables whose fuzzy sets contain 64 elements, and 50% overlap, centroid as a defuzzification method, and max-min inference [21]. These inputs were modified to serve the purpose of the experiment in this paper. Nodes from two mutual exclusive branches are grouped together to create a node in a PEG. A probabilistic computation time of a node in the PEG is then obtained from putting a node computation time and its probability (inherited from the probability of taking a branch) together with the one from the reciprocal branch. All arithmetic operations are assumed to take 2 time units except the multiplication and the division which take 3 time units. In this experiment, the probability of taking each branch was arbitrarily given. Note that in practice these probability values can be obtained by an analysis of the program structures or a profiling methodology [20]. The size of data volume associated with each new node is assumed to be a number of outgoing edges of each grouped node. All target architectures in these experiments are 2-D mesh. The XY-routing approach is assumed in each target system for determine how a message is delivered to a destination. In order to compute a communication overhead for each message, we assume that wormhole routing with no virtual channel technique is applied in all systems. The algorithm used the data volume information in the PEG to create the communication cost (wormhole routing latency) used in constructing a PT&C-G when a message is transfered from one processor to the other. The result of these experiments are compared with the technique presented in [22] where each uncertain timing information in those input graphs assume their average values.

Table 1. Results from list scheduling v.s. probabilistic version, tested for 4 processors

Ben.	#nds	Average case		Probabilistic case	
		range	$P(sl<?){\approx}0.9$	range	$P(sl<?){\approx}0.9$
liu1-uf-2	22	(17,42)	34	(14,31)	26
liu2	16	(29,51)	48	(29,51)	48
liu2-uf-2	32	(45,85)	76	(41,72)	65
liu2-uf-4	48	(57,96)	87	(52,91)	83

Table 2. Results from rotation scheduling v.s. probabilistic version, tested for 4 processors

Ben.	#nds	Average case		Probabilistic case	
		range	$P(sl<?){\approx}0.9$	range	$P(sl<?){\approx}0.9$
liu1-uf-2	22	(17,39)	33	(13,29)	21
liu2	16	(23,44)	41	(25,40)	38
liu2-uf-2	32	(45,85)	76	(40,68)	62
liu2-uf-4	48	(52,91)	82	(50,89)	80

Table 1 shows results obtained from running a modified version of list scheduling (probabilistic list scheduling). The target architecture of this table is four processors connected as a mesh. Column *ben.* presents the list of selected benchmarks while its adjacent column presents the number of nodes in each benchmark. Most of them are obtained from [10]. The benchmarks with suffix "uf-x" are unfolded graph where "x" represents the unfolding factor. Column *average case* presents results given by running traditional list scheduling with the benchmark graphs assuming average node computation and communication times. The results in this column are compared with the results in Column *probabilistic case* where results from running the modified list scheduling algorithm (considering probabilistic timing information) are presented. Inside each of these two columns, there are two sub-columns called range and $P(sl <?) \approx 0.9$. The for-

mer one shows spanning range (minimum and maximum values) of the resulting schedule lengths. The latter shows how long the schedule length (sl) can be expected if a confidence probability is given (in this experiment this confidence is approximately 90 percent, i.e., $P(sl <?) \approx 0.9$. Note that for Column *average case*, in order to compare both average and probabilistic approaches, the probabilistic timing information were substituted back to the resulting PT&C-G and then Algorithm 1 was used to evaluate the schedule lengths.

Table 3. Simulation results for tested benchmarks: 4 processors

Ben.	#nds	Average case		Probabilistic case	
		list	rot.	list	rot.
liu1-uf-2	22	25.78	23.71	22.76	17.40
liu2	16	42.77	39.32	42.77	31.55
liu2-uf-2	32	62.45	62.45	57.91	54.91
liu2-uf-4	48	72.31	69.91	69.52	69.11

Table 2 presents the comparison between results obtained by running the algorithm presented in [22] with the proposed algorithm's. The definition for each column is the same as that of Table 1. Tables 4 and 5 discuss the same issue but with eight processors as the target system. Since those results shown in previous tables were all evaluated from the PT&C-G model where we used our heuristic to decide how to serialize communication nodes when the message collision occurs, such a serialization pattern that we assumed might not happen every time in practice. Therefore, in order to show the effectiveness of the proposed approach, the simulation on each experiment was performed. The simulation takes the following as its inputs: the processor assignment, the order of nodes within each processor, and the benchmark graph (for list scheduling) or retimed graph (for rotation scheduling). A fixed timing information for each node will be randomly selected from the range of uncertain time according to its probability. The simulator then performs the simulation regardless of where

Table 4. Results from list scheduling v.s. probabilistic version, tested for 8 processors

Ben.	#nds	Average case		Probabilistic case	
		range	$P(sl<?)\approx0.9$	range	$P(sl<?)\approx0.9$
liu1-uf-2	22	(18,41)	34	(14,31)	26
liu2	16	(29,51)	48	(29,51)	48
liu2-uf-2	32	(45,85)	76	(41,72)	65
liu2-uf-4	48	(57,96)	87	(52,91)	83
liu3	79	(50, 198)	124	(69,165)	95
fuzzy	88	(75,904)	792	(75,645)	541

Table 5. Result from rotation scheduling v.s. probabilistic version, tested for 8 processors

Ben.	#nds	Average case		Probabilistic case	
		range	$P(sl<?)\approx0.9$	range	$P(sl<?)\approx0.9$
liu1-uf-2	22	(17,31)	28	(13,29)	21
liu2	16	(23,43)	38	(31,38)	35
liu2-uf-2	32	(44,74)	67	(42,58)	58
liu2-uf-4	48	(50,89)	70	(47,73)	67
liu3	79	(69,165)	94	(38,135)	92
fuzzy	88	(63,557)	466	(63,362)	312

communication nodes are put in the PT&C-G. The results from the simulator operating on each schedule were collected for a thousand times and only average values of these results are presented in the Tables 3 and 6. First Table 3 presents the simulation of the results from Tables 1 and 2 while Table 6 presents the simulation of those results shown in Tables 4 and 5. In these simulations, Column *average case* presents results obtained from running the simulator on those processor assignments generated by traditional list and rotation scheduling while column *probabilistic case* presents the simulation results given by the proposed scheduling algorithms.

Table 6. Simulation results for tested benchmarks: 8 processors

Ben.	#nds	Average case		Probabilistic case	
		list	rot.	list	rot.
liu1-uf-2	22	25.87	19.23	21.42	17.34
liu2	16	42.77	33.77	39.32	30.77
liu2-uf-2	32	62.45	59.39	57.91	50.61
liu2-uf-4	48	64.67	65.82	62.23	58.48
liu3	79	73.36	67.94	71.30	51.63
fuzzy	88	690.41	321.96	448.77	292.12

5   Conclusion

We have presented a loop pipelining algorithm for scheduling nodes with varying computation times for parallel systems while considering the communication costs. These communication costs can be uncertain since they are associated with the amount of data generated by those uncertain computation nodes. Moreover, such costs only occur when data is transferred between two processors. The proposed algorithm reflects the message collision issue by introducing a graph model called the probabilistic task&communication graph. Communication nodes are separated from the computation nodes and can be serialized if the contention occurs. We also proposed a method for evaluating the underlying probabilistic schedule length. The result obtained from this evaluation can help designer decide how long in practice a probabilistic schedule will take. Experimental results show the effectiveness of our algorithm. By comparing the results obtained from the schedule produced by our method and the traditional approach which assumes the average computation time, the resulting schedule length obtained from our schedule is shorter than using that obtained by the traditional approach on average.

References

[1] U. Banerjee. Unimodular transformations of double loops. In *Proceedings of the Workshop on Advances in Languages and Compilers for Parallel Processing*, pages 192–219. IEEE, August 1990.

[2] L. Chao, A. LaPaugh, and E. Sha. Rotation scheduling: A loop pipelining algorithm. In *Proceedings of the 30th Design Automation Conference*, pages 566–572, Dallas, TX, June 1993.

[3] L.-F. Chao and E. H.-M. Sha. Static scheduling for synthesis of DSP algorithms on various models. *Journal of VLSI Signal Processing*, 10:207–223, 1995.

[4] W. Feller. *An introduction to probability theory and its applications*. John Wiley & Sons, New York, 1968.

[5] E. M. Girczyc. Loop winding—a data flow approach to functional pipeline. In *Proceedings of the International Symposium on Circuits and Systems*, pages 382–385, May 1987.

[6] K. Hwang. *Advanced Computer Architecture: Parallelism, Scalability, Programmability*. McGraw-Hill Series in Computer Science, New York, NY, 1993.

[7] R. A. Kamin, G. B. Adams, and P. K. Dubey. Dynamic list-scheduling with finite resources. In *Proceedings of the 1994 International Conference on Computer Design*, pages 140–144, Cambridge, MA, October 1994.

[8] I. Karkowski and R. H. J. M. Otten. Retiming synchronous circuitry with imprecise delays. In *Proceedings of the 32nd Design Automation Conference*, pages 322–326, San Francisco, CA, 1995.

[9] A. A. Khan, C. L. McCreary, and M. S. Jones. A comparison of multiprocessor scheduling heuristics. In *Proceedings of the 1994 International Conference on Parallel Processing*, volume II, pages 243–250, 1994.

[10] T. Kim, N. Yonezawa, J. W. S. Liu, and C. L. Liu. A scheduling algorithm for conditional resource sharing—a hierachical reduction approach. *IEEE Transactions on Computer-Aided Design of Integrated Circuits and Systems*, 13(4):425–438, April 1994.

[11] D. Ku and G. De Micheli. *High-Level synthesis of ASICS under Timing and Synchronization constraints*. Kluwer Academic, 1992.

[12] D. Ku and G. De Micheli. Relative scheduling under timing constraints: Algorithm for high-level synthesis. *IEEE transactions on CAD/ICAS*, pages 697–718, June 1992.

[13] M. Lam. Software pipelining. In *Proceedings of the ACM SIGPLAN'88 Conference on Programming Language Design and Implementation*, pages 318–328, Atlanta, GA, June 1988.

[14] C. E. Leiserson and J. B. Saxe. Optimizing synchronous systems. *Journal of VLSI and Computer Systems*, 1(1):41–67, 1983.

[15] C. E. Leiserson and J. B. Saxe. Retiming synchronous circuitry. *Algorithmica*, 6:5–35, 1991.

[16] W. Li and K. Pingali. A singular loop transformation framework based on non-singular matrices. Technical Report TR 92-1294, Cornell University, Ithaca, NY, July 1992.

[17] B. Lockyear and C. Ebeling. Optimal retiming of multi-phase, level-clocked circuits. In T. Knight and J. Savage, editors, *Advanced Research in VLSI and Parallel Systems: Proceedings of the 1992 Brown/MIT Conference*, pages 265–280, Cambridge, MA, 1992.

[18] P. L. Meyer. *Introductory Probability and Statistical Applications*. Addison-Wesley, Reading, MA, 2nd edition, 1979.

[19] N. L. Passos, E. Sha, and S. C. Bass. Loop pipelining for scheduling multi-dimensional systems via rotation. In *Proceedings of the 31st Design Automation Conference*, pages 485–490, June 1994.

[20] D. A. Patterson and J. L. Hennessy. *Computer architecture: A Quantitative approach*. Morgan-Kaufman, 1996.

[21] T. J. Ross. *Fuzzy Logic with Engineering Applications*. MC-Graw Hill, 1995.

[22] S. Tongsima, E.-H. Sha, and N. L. Passos. Communcation-sensitive loop scheduling for DSP applications. *IEEE Transactions on Signal Processing*, 45(5):1309–1322, May 1997.

[23] M. E. Wolfe. *High Performance Compilers for Parallel Computing*, chapter 9. Addison-Wesley, Redwood City, CA, 1996.

[24] M. E. Wolfe and M. S. Lam. A loop transformation theory and an algorithm to maximize parallelism. *IEEE Transactions on Parallel and Distributed Systems*, 2(4):452–471, October 1991.

[25] L. A. Zadeh. Fuzzy sets as a basis for a theory of possibility. *Fuzzy Sets and Systems*, 1:3–28, 1978.

Improving First-Come-First-Serve Job Scheduling by Gang Scheduling *

Uwe Schwiegelshohn and Ramin Yahyapour

Computer Engineering Institute, University Dortmund
44221 Dortmund, Germany
uwe@ds.e-technik.uni-dortmund.de
yahya@ds.e-technik.uni-dortmund.de

Abstract. We present a new scheduling method for batch jobs on massively parallel processor architectures. This method is based on the First-come–first–serve strategy and emphasizes the notion of fairness. Severe fragmentation is prevented by using gang scheduling which is only initiated by highly parallel jobs. Good worst–case behavior of the scheduling approach has already been proven by theoretical analysis. In this paper we show by simulation with real workload data that the algorithm is also suitable to be applied in real parallel computers. This holds for several different scheduling criteria like makespan or sum of the flow times. Simulation is also used for determination of the best parameter set for the new method.

1 Introduction

The job scheduling strategy is one of the key elements in the resource management of a massively parallel processor (MPP). It is therefore of interest to both, the manufacturer and the owner of such a machine. For the manufacturer a better management system may be used as an additional marketing argument while also requiring more development effort to implement the necessary system components. On the other hand, the owner would like to see a flexible system which can be fine tuned to his specific environment. Unfortunately, this usually requires significant effort from the system administrator to select the correct parameter setting. In both cases the performance evaluation of a strategy together with a parameter set is a necessity.

Unfortunately, such a performance evaluation is a difficult task. Theoretical worst case analysis is only of limited help as typical workloads on production machines never exhibit the specific structure that will create a really bad case. Further, there is no random distribution of job parameter values, see e.g. Feitelson and Nitzberg [4]. Hence, a theoretical analysis of random workloads will not provide the desired information either. A trial and error approach on a commercial machine will be tedious and may affect system performance in a significant

---

* Supported by the NRW Metacomputing grant

fashion. Therefore, most users will probably object to such an approach except for the final fine tuning. This just leaves simulation for all other cases.

Simulation may either be based on real trace data or on a workload model. While workload models, see e.g. Jann et al. [14] or Feitelson and Nitzberg [4], enable a wide range of simulations by allowing job modifications, like a varying amount of assigned processor resources, the concurrency with real workloads is not always guaranteed. This is especially true in the case of workloads whose characteristics change over time. On the other hand, trace data restrict the freedom to select different allocation and scheduling strategies as the performance of a specific job is only known under the given circumstances. For instance, trace data specifying the execution time of a batch job do not provide similar information, if the job would be assigned to a different subset of processors. Therefore, the selection of the base data for the simulation depends on the circumstances determined by the scheduling strategy and the MPP architecture. There are already a variety of examples for simulation based on a workload model, see e.g. Feitelson [2], Feitelson and Jette [3] or on trace data, see e.g. Wang et al. [21]. Here, we describe the use of trace data for the evaluation of different parameter settings for a preemptive scheduling strategy.

In particular, we address a specific kind of gang scheduling to be used in the management system of the IBM RS/6000 SP2, a widely available commercial parallel computer. Gang scheduling has already been subject of many studies, see e.g. Feitelson and Rudolph [5, 7], and a significant number of manufacturers, like Intel, TMC or SGI, have included gang scheduling into their operating systems. A gang scheduling prototype for the SP2 has also been presented [11, 20]. The performance of this prototype has already been analyzed by Wang et al. [21]. Although these results were in favor of gang scheduling for the SP2, typical installations do not include it yet.

In this paper we present a new scheduling strategy consisting of a combination of gang scheduling together with a First-come-first-serve approach. Moreover, we show that the performance of gang scheduling is dependent on the selected parameters of the scheduler and that significant gains are achievable. In addition, we address the problem of finding a suitable criterion for measuring the scheduler performance.

To this end we first derive a machine model and a job scheduling model for the IBM RS/6000 SP2 based on the description of Hotovy [13]. Next, we describe the workload data obtained during a period of 11 months from the Cornell Theory Center (CTC) SP2. Then, various scheduling objectives are discussed. Based on those objectives we suggest a new *fairness* criterion. In Section 5 our new scheduling concept is introduced and its parameters are explained. Finally, we present our simulation results and discuss some of them in detail.

2   The Model

2.1   The Machine Model

We assume an MPP architecture where each node contains one or more processors, main memory, and local hard disks while there is no shared memory. The system may contain different types of nodes characterized e.g. by type and number of processors, by the amount of memory or by the specific task this node is supposed to perform. An example for the last category are those nodes which provide access to mass storage. In particular, IBM SP2 architectures may presently contain three types of nodes: *thin nodes*, *wide nodes*, and *high (SMP) nodes*. A wide node usually has some kind of server functionality and contains more memory than a thin node while there is little difference in processor performance. Recently introduced high nodes contain several processors and cannot form a partition with other nodes at this time. However, it should be noted that most installations are predominantly equipped with thin nodes. In 1996 only 48 out of a total of 512 nodes in the CTC SP2 were wide nodes while no high nodes were used at all. Although in most installations the majority of nodes have the same or a similar amount of memory, a wide range of memory configurations is possible. For instance, the CTC SP2 contains nodes with memory ranging from 128 MB to 2048 MB with more than 80% of the nodes having 128 MB and an additional 12% being equipped with 256 MB. For more details see the description of Hotovy [13]. For these reasons we use a model where all nodes are identical.

Fast communication between the nodes is achieved via a special interconnection network. This network does not prioritize clustering of some subsets of nodes over others as in a hypercube or a mesh, i.e. the communication delay and the bandwidth between any pair of nodes is assumed to be constant. The network aspect and its consequences on job scheduling will be further discussed in the next subsection.

In our model the computer further supports gang scheduling by switching simultaneously the context of a subset of nodes. This context switch is assumed to be executed by use of the local processor memory and/or the local hard disk while the interconnection network is not affected except for synchronization [20]. Here, we use gang scheduling (preemption) without migration, that is no change of the node subset assigned to a job will occur during job execution. Any context switch may result in a time penalty due to processor synchronization, draining the networks of not yet delivered messages, saving of job status, page faults, and cache misses. In the simulation this penalty is considered by adding a constant time delay to the execution time of a job for each time the job is preempted. In our model no node of an affected subset is able to execute any part of a job during this time delay. Note that our scheduler deviates substantially from the prototype scheduler presented in [20] and analyzed in [21].

2.2   The Job Model

Our job model is also derived from Hotovy's description [13]. For the simulation we restrict ourselves to batch jobs as for interactive jobs the execution time cannot be assumed to be independent of the starting time and of the number of preemptions. Therefore, we just consider the batch partition of the CTC SP2 which comprises 430 nodes. As highly parallel interactive jobs are rather unlikely our scheduling schemes have little or no effect on the interactive partition as will become clear from the description of the scheduling algorithm in Section 5.

At the CTC SP2 a job is assigned to a subset of nodes in an exclusive fashion once it is supposed to be executed. This subset is described by the number of nodes it must contain from each type of node. Any subset matching this description is assumed to require the same time for execution of the job as the interconnection network does not favor any specific subset. Therefore, free variable partitioning [6] is supported. Once a job is started on a subset it is run to completion or canceled if its time limit has expired.

As we are using gang scheduling our model deviates from the description above. We require that at any time instant any node executes at most a single job while a second job may have been preempted and now waits for resumption of its execution. However, on each node there may only be a single preempted job at any moment. Note that data and status of the preempted job can be stored on the local hard disk of a node in the same way as the disk is presently used for swapping. Further, gang scheduling requires that at any time instant either all nodes allocated to a job run this job or none of them does.

The scheduling policy of the CTC is described in detail by Hotovy [13]. Here, we just want to give a brief summary of it: A user specifies the resource requirements of his batch job and assigns it to a batch queue. The batch queues are defined by the maximum job execution time (wall clock time), that is the permitted time limit of a job. The resource requirements include the maximum and the minimum number of nodes the job needs. This feature is disregarded in our simulation as we do not know from the workload traces how the execution time of a job would change with a different number of nodes allocated to the job. Hence, we assume that for each job the size of the subset is invariable and given by the trace data. Using the terminology of Feitelson and Rudolph [8] we therefore do not allow moldable jobs. As already mentioned, our simulation is based on a machine with identical nodes, although in general the simulator is able to handle specific resource requests as well. Jobs can be submitted at any time. Note that our model allows a combination of space and time sharing.

3   The Workload Data

As already mentioned, we use the workload traces originating from the IBM SP2 of the Cornell Theory Center. The data were compiled during the months July 1996 to May 1997. The original data include the following information:

- Number of nodes allocated to the job
- Time of job submission
- Time of job start
- Time of job completion
- Additional hardware requests of the job: Amount of memory, type of node, access to mass storage, type of adapter.

Further data like the job name, class (LoadLeveler class), type, and completion status are presently of no relevance to our simulation experiments.

For the simulation we need the node requirements, the submission time, and the execution time of a job. The execution time is determined by the difference between start and completion time of a job as nodes are assigned exclusively to a job in the batch partition. As stated in Section 2, the additional hardware request of a job is not used at the moment. But it can easily be considered in the simulator and may provide valuable information for choosing the best configuration of an MPP.

The CTC uses a batch partition with 430 nodes. As will be further explained in Section 6.1, in our simulation we assume batch partitions of 128 and 256 nodes respectively. Hence, jobs with an node allocation exceeding 128 or 256 nodes are ignored as we do not want to change individual job data. Table 1 shows that this only results in a small reduction in the total number of jobs.

	Total number of jobs	Jobs requiring at most 256 nodes		Jobs requiring at most 128 nodes	
Jul 96	7953	7933	99.75%	7897	99.30%
Aug 96	7302	7279	99.69%	7234	99.07%
Sep 96	6188	6180	99.87%	6106	98.67%
Oct 96	7288	7277	99.85%	7270	99.75%
Nov 96	7849	7841	99.90%	7816	99.58%
Dec 96	7900	7893	99.91%	7888	99.85%
Jan 97	7544	7538	99.92%	7506	99.50%
Feb 97	8188	8177	99.87%	8159	99.65%
Mar 97	6945	6933	99.83%	6909	99.48%
Apr 97	6118	6102	99.74%	6085	99.46%
May 97	5992	5984	99.87%	5962	99.50%

Table 1. Number of Jobs in the CTC Workload Data for Each Month (Submission Time)

4   The Scheduling Policy

If the amount of requested nodes for a job exceeds the nodes available on the parallel computer, a scheduling policy is used to settle those resource conflicts.

This policy is supposed to reflect the objectives of the owner of the parallel computer as well as the wishes of the users. As jobs may be submitted at any time, often some kind of First–come–first–serve (FCFS) strategy is used. Especially for parallel computers which do not support preemption and if no knowledge of future job arrival is available, various versions of FCFS strategy are frequently used. This also includes modifications like backfilling [17]. Also, an FCFS strategy reflects the notion of fairness which is probably the reason for being more or less accepted by most users. If several queues are used, FCFS may be applied separately to each queue or it may span several or even all queues. For instance, the CTC uses a modified FCFS approach for all batch queues with the exception of a queue for short running jobs (less than 15 minutes). This last queue receives a slightly higher priority.

A scheduling policy is evaluated by use of some scheduling criteria. In order to satisfy the user, his objectives must be reflected in those criteria. It can be safely assumed that a small job response time is desired for many jobs. However as already mentioned, it is typically not possible to execute each job immediately due to limited resources. In this situation most users would expect some kind of fairness policy which is a reason for the frequent use of FCFS. Of course, there may always be jobs which must be executed immediately or whose execution can be postponed to the night or the weekend. In return those jobs should be associated with some kind of either higher or lower costs. Also, a part of the parallel computer may be reserved exclusively for a specific group of jobs [13].

In the theoretical scheduling community the criteria most frequently used in this context are either makespan (=completion time of the last job in all queues) or the sum of the completion or flow/response times (= completion time - submission time) of all jobs [9]. The makespan is closely related to the utilization throughput and represents an owner centric point of view [8]. Adding the completion or flow time corresponds to a consideration of the individual user criteria 'minimization of the turnaround time'. Note that the completion time is of very limited interest in a practical setting where individual jobs are not submitted at the same time. Further, it must be emphasized that addressing only the makespan or only the flow time criterion is often not good enough, as an optimal makespan will not necessarily guarantee a minimal or even small sum of flow times and vice versa [18].

Apart from these general criteria, there may be some specific priority criteria based upon the intentions of the owner of a parallel computer. The owner may wish to prioritize highly parallel jobs over mostly sequential jobs or the other way around (throughput maximization) [9]. Also, some users may receive a larger allocation of compute time while others are only allowed to use selected time slots. Altogether, it is possible to think of a large number of different strategies. Some of these strategies can be implemented by using weights in connection with each job resulting in a weighted flow time criterion. In this case, the priority strategy must still be linked with the necessary selection of job weights. Hotovy [13] pointed out that in a real machine environment the selection of a priority strategy and its implementation is a complex and iterative process. But the overall goal of the policy established by the CTC is never explicitly stated and the final strategy is the result of several experiments which were evaluated with respect to backlog and average waiting time. Lifka [17] addressed a similar problem by describing the properties of his *universal scheduler*.

In our simulation, we use the following three criteria:

1. Makespan of the whole schedule
2. Sum of flow times over all jobs
3. Sum of weighted flow times over all jobs with a special selection of the weights

Note that the simple adding of flow times (second criterion) does not consider the resource use of a job. In order to minimize the sum of flow times it is preferable to immediately schedule a large number of jobs requiring few nodes and running only for a short time and postpone all highly parallel jobs which require a long time to execute. Thus, this criterion indirectly prioritizes small jobs over others. While it may also increase throughput, the application of this criterion may contradict the purpose of a parallel computer to run long and highly parallel jobs. Moreover, it is beneficial for a user to split a parallel job into many sequential jobs even if this results in increased resource usage.

Therefore, we suggest to consider the objectives fairness and resource consumption by selecting weights appropriately. In particular, we define the weight of a job by the product of the execution time of the job and the nodes required by the job. This weight can also be used as the cost of the job for the purpose of accounting. This way there is no gain in splitting a parallel job into many sequential jobs or in combining many independent short jobs into one long job or vice versa. Only the overhead of a parallel job in comparison to its sequential version must be paid for. Using this type of weight (cost) for the purpose of accounting has the additional advantage that the user is only charged for the actual resource consumption instead of the projected value. This is especially important for long running jobs which fail immediately due to the lack of an input file or a similar cause. As the execution time of a job is not certainly known before the termination of the job, the actual weight is not available at the start of a job. Therefore, the scheduling algorithm cannot take the actual weight of a job into account when making its decisions. Only the maximum weight is provided due to the time limit of a job. A theoretical analysis of a scheduler based on this kind of weight selection is given in [19].

5   The Algorithm

We already mentioned the close relation between FCFS and fairness in the previous section. Note however that while FCFS guarantees that jobs are started in the order of their arrivals the same property does not necessarily hold for the completion of the jobs due to differences in job execution times. A fair schedule strategy can also be defined as a strategy where the completion time of any job does not depend on any other job submitted after it. Lifka's backfilling [17] method tries to obey this kind of fairness principle as only those jobs are moved

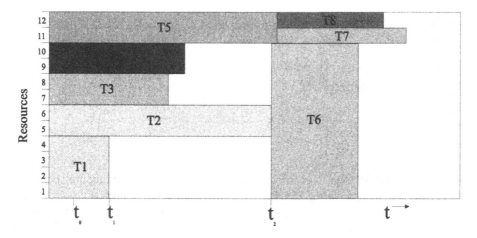

Fig. 1. Example for Fragmentation in FCFS by Wide Jobs

up in the queues which are supposed not to affect the execution time of any job submitted before them. However, if job execution times are not known, this notion of fairness can only be preserved by aborting those backfilled jobs which would delay the start of a job submitted before then. Also, a preemptive schedule will not be fair in general even if the jobs are started in FCFS order. In this paper we therefore use a more general fairness notion called κ–fairness which has been introduced in [19]:

A scheduling strategy is κ-fair if all jobs submitted after a job i cannot increase the flow time of i by more than a factor κ.

Note that the term κ-fairness is not closely related to other schedule criteria. Therefore, we are looking for a scheduling strategy, which produces schedules with small deviations for makespan, sum of (weighted) flow times, and κ from the optimal values.

Since it is much harder to approximate the optimal total weighted flow time than the optimal total weighted completion time, as shown by Leonardi and Raz [16], many theoretical researchers focused on the completion time problem. This may be justified as both measures differ from each other by only a constant. Therefore, it is sufficient to consider just one of both criteria for the purpose of comparing two schedules.

For the sake of completeness we now repeat a few theoretical results which were already presented in other publications.

Using a pure FCFS schedule will obviously minimize κ. If all jobs are sequential it will also guarantee small deviations from the optimum values provided our weight selection is used with respect to the total weighted completion time. Here we denote by h_i and w_i the execution time and the weight of job i respectively. The following theorem can be derived from [15, 12, 10] and has been stated in this form in [19]. The makespan and the total completion time of a schedule S are described by m_S and c_S, respectively.

Theorem 1. *For all FCFS schedules S with only sequential jobs i and $w_i = h_i$ the following properties hold*

1. $m_S < 2 \cdot m_{opt}$,
2. $c_S < 1.21 \cdot c_{opt}$, *and*
3. S *is 1-fair.*

For the parallel case, it is usually assumed that FCFS scheduling may possibly generate big deviations for the makespan and the sum of flow times from the optimal values because fragmentation may occur and lead to a large number of idle nodes. The amount of fragmentation grows if jobs require large subsets of nodes, see Fig. 1. In the displayed example, job T6 cannot be started before time t_2 although it became the first job of the FCFS queue at time t_0. However, if the maximum degree of parallelism is restricted, FCFS still guarantees small deviations from the optimal case for parallel job systems with limited resource (node) numbers. Here we use r_i to denote the required nodes. Further R is the maximum number of nodes. The following results are also presented in [19].

Theorem 2. *For all FCFS schedules with $r_i \leq \frac{R}{2}$ and $w_i = r_i \cdot h_i$ there is*

1. $m_S < 3 \cdot m_{opt}$,
2. $c_S < 2 \cdot c_{opt}$, *and*
3. S *is 1-fair.*

From Table 1 we can see that highly parallel jobs are only a very small part of the workload. This explains the acceptable performance of FCFS schedulers in commercial MPPs in contrast to the bad behavior predicted by theoretical worst case analysis [19]. However, if more jobs with a small degree of parallelism are moved from MPPs to SMP workstations, it can be assumed that FCFS performance will suffer more severely.

As the percentage of idle nodes caused by jobs that require only a few nodes is rather small, our new scheduling strategy, called preemptive FCFS (*PFCFS*), especially cares for the highly parallel jobs. While in FCFS scheduling idle nodes must stay idle until the next job in line is started (with the notable exception of backfilling), we allow highly parallel jobs to interrupt the execution of currently running jobs.

Intuitively, we can describe PFFS by using two different schedules for small and for highly parallel jobs, which are then partially interleaved.

It is shown in [19] that PFCFS generates good theoretical results for makespan and completion time.

Theorem 3. *If the execution times of all jobs are unknown and $w_i = r_i \cdot h_i$ holds for each job and $n \to \infty$ and $\delta \geq \Delta$, then for all schedules S produced by the PFCFS Algorithm there is*

1. $m_S < (4 + 2\bar{p})m_{opt}$,
2. $c_S < (3.56 + 3.24\bar{p})c_{opt}$, and
3. S is $(2 + 2\bar{p})$-fair.

For this concept to be applied in practice, theoretical analysis is not sufficient. Therefore, parameters must be chosen to fine tune the strategy. In particular our new strategy and its parameters can be described as follows:

1. Any job requiring less than $x\%$ of the total number of nodes in the batch partition (in the following called *small job*) is scheduled in an FCFS fashion.

2. Any job requiring at least $x\%$ of the nodes (*wide job*) will preempt other running jobs under the following conditions:
   (a) The wide job is the next job to be started in FCFS order.
   (b) No other previously submitted wide job is still active.
   (c) A time span of δ seconds has passed since the moment the previous two conditions became valid.
3. If a wide job has been determined to start in a preemptive fashion a suitable subset of nodes (*preemptive subset*) is selected.
4. Once the machine is in a preemptive mode caused by a wide job, there is a context switch in the subset every Δ seconds up to a maximum of n context switches.

Note that not all currently running nodes must be preempted by a wide job. A wide job only preempts enough running jobs to generate a sufficiently large preemptive subset. Those small jobs are selected by a simple greedy strategy to preempt as few jobs as possible. The strategy also tries to adjust the size of the preemptive subset as much as possible to the requested node number. If n is odd, the wide job will be run to completion after the maximum number of context switches is exhausted. Otherwise those small jobs which are allocated to nodes of the preemptive subset all complete before the wide job if the latter has not finished at the last permitted context switch. Whether the size of the preemptive subset may change during the preemptive mode depends on the implementation. Altogether, the strategy is characterized by the selection of the four parameters x, δ, Δ, and n. It is the task of our simulation experiments to determine the best parameter set.

Fig. 2 gives an example for such a schedule. The system is executing jobs T1 - T5 with wide job T6 being due to execution at time t_0. That means T_6 is the next job to be scheduled in the FCFS queue. After a time delay $\delta = t_1 - t_0$, a sufficient large resource set to execute T6 is selected. The delay is introduced to prevent a possible starvation of smaller jobs if many wide jobs arrive in succession.

At this time t_1, all small jobs in the selected preemptive subset are interrupted. In the example, wide job T6 requires 9 resources for which jobs T1 to T4 must be preempted. After the preemption the wide job is started in the now available node subset. The wide job runs for a parameterized amount of time $\Delta = t_2 - t_1$. Next, we preempt the wide job and resume the execution of the

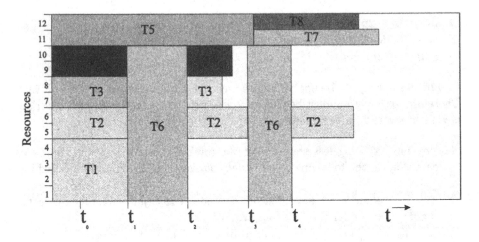

Fig. 2. Example for Gang Scheduling of a Wide Job (T6) without Migration

previously preempted jobs (t_2). This cycle between the wide job and the small job gang will be repeated until a gang has been completed. In the example, T6 completes at t_4 after which the remaining jobs T1 and T3 of the smaller gang are immediately continued.

Intuitively, a schedule produced by rules outlined above can be described as the interleaving of two non preemptive FCFS schedules, where one of the schedules contains at most one wide job at any time instant. Note again that only a wide job can cause preemption and therefore increase the completion time of a previously submitted job. However, as the subset of a job is invariably determined at the starting time, it is also possible that the preemptive mode will actually increase the completion time of the wide job causing the preemption.

6   Simulation

6.1   Description of the Simulation

For obtaining information on the influence of the parameters and to determine good parameter values, various simulations have been done. For each strategy and each month we determined the makespan, the total flow time, and the total weighted flow time using our weight selection and compared these values with the results of a simple non-preemptive FCFS schedule. To compare the algorithm performance with a non-FCFS strategy, we made simulations with a backfilling scheduling policy.

Further, we examined variations on the specification of wide jobs. We also simulated with different gang lengths x and start delays δ before the start of the preemption.

The work traces of the Cornell Theory Center reflect a batch partition comprising 430 nodes. There are only very few jobs in these traces that use between

x	n	Δ	δ
Wide job spec.	Maximum preemptions	Start Delay	Gang Length
40%	1	60 sec	1 sec
45%	2	120 sec	60 sec
50%	3	240 sec	Δ
55%	10	600 sec	
60%	11	1800 sec	
		3600 sec	

Table 2. Different Parameter Settings for Simulation Experiments

215 ($\frac{R}{2}$) and 430 nodes, as seen in Table 1. A reason is the tendency to use a number of processors which is equal to a power of 2. Taking into account that a noticeable gain by PFCFS can only be expected for a suitable number of wide jobs, we assume parallel computers with 128, respectively 256 resource. This is also reasonable as most installations only have a smaller number of nodes, and it can be assumed that there the percentage of wide jobs will be larger than for the CTC. This approach prevents the direct comparison of the simulation results with the original schedule data of the CTC.

In order to evaluate our scheduling strategy we assume a homogeneous MPP, that is a computer with identical nodes. As already mentioned, the batch partition of the CTC SP2 consists mainly of thin nodes with 128 or 256 MB memory. Therefore, our reference computer is almost homogeneous in this respect. Special hardware requests of the jobs are currently ignored. Although it is easy to consider those requests in the scheduler, it is not helpful in determining basic properties of the new strategy. Those requests can be taken into account in future studies.

As the CTC schedule itself is not suitable for comparison due to these deviations, we use a simple FCFS schedule for reference in this analysis.

Table 2 shows the parameter spectrum of our simulations.

The theoretical analysis [19] suggests $x = 50\%$. We chose several values around 50% to determine the sensitivity of the schedule quality on this parameter. While good theoretical results require a potentially unlimited number of preemptions we wanted to determine whether in practice a restriction of this parameter is sufficient. The time period between two context switches Δ is selected to span a wide range. However, to prevent a significant affect of the preemption penalty a minimum value of 60 seconds was used. The theory also suggests to set $\delta = \Delta$. We additionally used two fixed values for δ.

Finally, we ignored any preemption penalty in our simulations although it can easily be included into the simulator.

Moreover, as migration is not needed and only local hard disks are used for saving of job data and job status, the strategy allows gang scheduling implementations with a relatively small preemption penalty. Note that a preemption

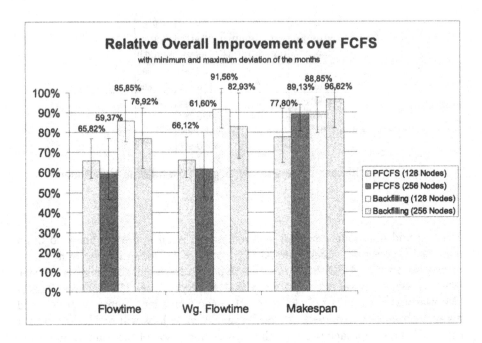

Fig. 3. Comparison of PFCFS with FCFS for Different Criteria

penalty of 1 second as assumed in [21] will still be small compared to the minimal value of Δ.

Finally, our experiments were conducted for each month separately to determine the variance of our results. This is another reason why the CTC schedule data could not be used for comparison as in the original schedule there are jobs which were submitted in one month and executed in another.

6.2   Analysis of the Results

Fig. 3 shows that the preemptive FCFS strategy was able to improve FCFS for all scheduling criteria if the best parameter setting was used, see Table 3. The

Resources	128	256
Wide job spec. x	40%	45%
Max. preemptions n	1	1
Start delay δ	60 sec	60 sec
Gang length Δ	not applicable	

Table 3. Parameter Setting for the Results Shown in Fig. 3

preemptive FCFS strategy also outperformed the backfilling scheduling policy. This algorithm does not utilize preemption, but requires the user to provide a maximum execution time for a each job.

However, it can be noticed that the effect on the flow or weighted flow time is more pronounced for a 256 node parallel computer while the smaller 128 node machine achieves a better result for the makespan criteria. It can also be seen that in every month a noticeable gain can be achieved with this set of parameters although the actual gains depend on the workload. Note that in the selected setting there is no time period between two context switches as with $n = 1$ a wide job will interrupt some small jobs and then run to completion. A similar approach was also subject of another publication ([1]) in a different context with dynamic jobs.

Also, there is only very little difference between the weighted flow time and the flow time results. This can be attributed to the large amount of short running jobs which do not require a large number of nodes. The stronger emphasis of larger highly parallel jobs in weighted flow time criterion does not have a significant impact on the evaluation of the strategy. However, this can be expected to change if the number of those jobs would increase.

Next, we examine the result for different limits on the number of preemptions. The results in Fig. 4 and Fig. 5 show that there are always improvements for odd values of n. Note that an odd n gives preference to the execution of the wide job once the maximum number of preemptions is reached. However, the gains change only little if the number of preemptions is increased. This indicates that the desired improvement of the scheduling costs can already be obtained by using a simple preemption for a wide job. On the other hand, even values of n result in significantly worse schedules in comparison to FCFS. This is due to the fact that the completion time of the wide job may actually be further increased over the FCFS schedule as its node allocation is fixed at the start time of the job and no job migration is allowed. This may then lead to a larger degree of fragmentation.

The schedule quality is not as sensitive on the other parameters. Theoretical studies [19] indicate that $x=50\%$ would be the best choice to separate wide jobs from small ones. Fig. 6 and Fig. 7 show that the schedule cost increases for all three criteria if x is selected to be larger than 50%. For real workloads a further slight improvement can be obtained by selected values for x which are less than 50%.

Δ is irrelevant if n is selected to be 1. For all other odd values of n the schedule cost varies only little with Δ. There, $\Delta = 120$ sec is frequently the best choice. If n is even, the results improve with a larger Δ as the chances to reach the preemption limit become smaller.

As the choice of Δ has little influence on the schedule quality, it is sufficient to just consider the cases $\delta= 1$ sec and $\delta=60$ sec. From theory we would expect a better makespan for $\delta= 1$ sec as fragmentation will be reduced if wide jobs are executed as early as possible. On the other hand, $\delta= 60$ sec will permit some short running small jobs to complete before they are interrupted by a wide job.

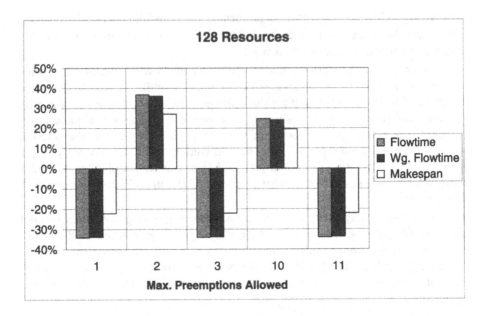

Fig. 4. Results for Different Limits on the Number of Preemptions for the 128 Node Machine

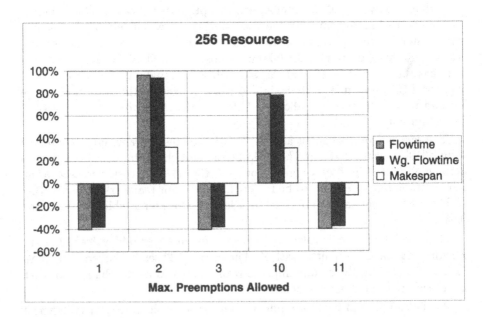

Fig. 5. Results for Different Limits on the Number of Preemptions for the 256 Node Machine

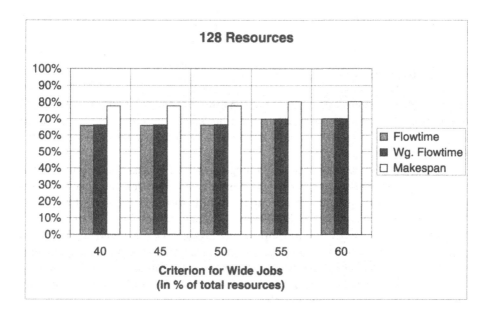

Fig. 6. Results for Different Characterizations of Wide Jobs for the 128 Node Machine

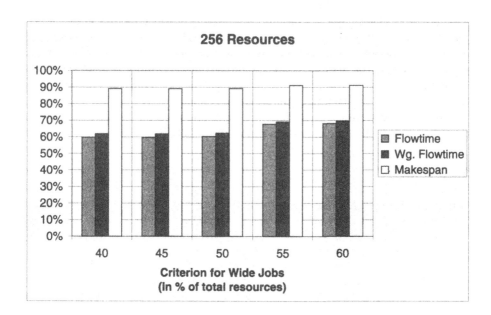

Fig. 7. Results for Different Characterizations of Wide Jobs for the 256 Node Machine

However, in our simulation, switching from 1 sec to 60 sec changed the schedule costs by less than 0.01%. Therefore, δ can also be ignored.

7   Conclusion

In this paper we presented a new scheduling method called PFCFS for batch jobs on MPPs. This strategy uses gang scheduling and is able to produce significant improvements of up to 40% in flow time and 22% in makespan for real workload data over FCFS.

It has been shown that the scheduling algorithm is sensitive to some of the scheduling parameters and should be carefully adapted for the specific workload. Nevertheless, it is possible to apply default settings that seem to increase schedule quality compared to FCFS. For instance, it may be sufficient to start execution of a wide job by preempting a suitable node set and let it run to completion. Based on our simulation this is sufficient to significantly improve the flow time and increase the machine utilization. For better results, we suggest that the parameters are determined on-line in an adaptive fashion from the workload results of previous months.

The implementation of the scheduling algorithm can also be improved, e.g. by allowing the start of new small jobs during gang scheduling. It may also be beneficial to check that the preemption cycle is only initiated, if more resources are utilized after the start of the wide job than before. Both modifications are not used in the presented simulations.

The PFCFS strategy is especially interesting since it has only limited requirements on the preemption support of the MPP. It uses no migration and at any time instance at most 2 jobs are resident on any node. Therefore, it can be assumed that the algorithm can be implemented on most systems with preemption capabilities. Also, there is no need for users to provide additional job information like an estimate of the execution time.

Acknowledgment The authors are especially grateful to Steve Hotovy for providing them with the workload data of the CTC SP2.

References

[1] S.-H. Chiang, R.K. Masharamani, and M.K. Vernon. Use of application characteristics and limited preemption for run-to-completion parallel processor scheduling policies. In *Proceedings of ACM SIGMETRICS Conference on Measurement of Computer Systems*, pages 33–44, 1994.

[2] D.G. Feitelson. Packing schemes for gang scheduling. In D.G. Feitelson and L. Rudolph, editors, *IPPS'96 Workshop: Job Scheduling Strategies for Parallel Processing*, pages 89–110. Springer–Verlag, Lecture Notes in Computer Science LNCS 1162, 1996.

[3] D.G. Feitelson and M.A. Jette. Improved utilization and responsiveness with gang scheduling. In D.G. Feitelson and L. Rudolph, editors, *IPPS'97 Workshop: Job Scheduling Strategies for Parallel Processing*, pages 238–261. Springer–Verlag, Lecture Notes in Computer Science LNCS 1291, 1997.

[4] D.G. Feitelson and B. Nitzberg. Job characteristics of a production parallel scientific workload on the NASA Ames iPSC/860. In D.G. Feitelson and L. Rudolph, editors, *IPPS'95 Workshop: Job Scheduling Strategies for Parallel Processing*, pages 337–360. Springer–Verlag, Lecture Notes in Computer Science LNCS 949, 1995.

[5] D.G. Feitelson and L. Rudolph. Gang scheduling performance benefits for fine-grain parallelization. *Journal of Parallel and Distributed Computing*, 16:306–318, 1992.

[6] D.G. Feitelson and L. Rudolph. Parallel job scheduling: Issues and approaches. In D.G. Feitelson and L. Rudolph, editors, *IPPS'95 Workshop: Job Scheduling Strategies for Parallel Processing*, pages 1–18. Springer–Verlag, Lecture Notes in Computer Science LNCS 949, 1995.

[7] D.G. Feitelson and L. Rudolph. Evaluation of design choices for gang scheduling using distributed hierarchical control. *Journal of Parallel and Distributed Computing*, 35:18–34, 1996.

[8] D.G. Feitelson and L. Rudolph. Towards convergence in job schedulers for parallel supercomputers. In D.G. Feitelson and L. Rudolph, editors, *IPPS'96 Workshop: Job Scheduling Strategies for Parallel Processing*, pages 1–26. Springer–Verlag, Lecture Notes in Computer Science LNCS 1162, 1996.

[9] D.G. Feitelson, L. Rudolph, U. Schwiegelshohn, K.C. Sevcik, and P. Wong. Theory and practice in parallel job scheduling. In D.G. Feitelson and L. Rudolph, editors, *IPPS'97 Workshop: Job Scheduling Strategies for Parallel Processing*, pages 1–34. Springer–Verlag, Lecture Notes in Computer Science LNCS 1291, 1997.

[10] A. Feldmann, J. Sgall, and S.-H. Teng. Dynamic scheduling on parallel machines. *Theoretical Computer Science*, 130:49–72, 1994.

[11] H. Franke, P. Pattnaik, and L. Rudolph. Gang scheduling for highly efficient distributed multiprocessor systems. In *Proceedings of the 6th Symp. on the Frontiers of Massively Parallel Computation*, pages 1–9, 1996.

[12] M. Garey and R.L. Graham. Bounds for multiprocessor scheduling with resource constraints. *SIAM Journal on Computing*, 4(2):187–200, June 1975.

[13] S. Hotovy. Workload evolution on the Cornell Theory Center IBM SP2. In D.G. Feitelson and L. Rudolph, editors, *IPPS'96 Workshop: Job Scheduling Strategies for Parallel Processing*, pages 27–40. Springer–Verlag, Lecture Notes in Computer Science LNCS 1162, 1996.

[14] J. Jann, P. Pattnaik, H. Franke, F. Wang, J. Skovira, and J. Riordan. Modeling of workload in MPPs. In D.G. Feitelson and L. Rudolph, editors, *IPPS'97 Workshop: Job Scheduling Strategies for Parallel Processing*, pages 94–116. Springer–Verlag, Lecture Notes in Computer Science LNCS 1291, 1997.

[15] T. Kawaguchi and S. Kyan. Worst case bound of an LRF schedule for the mean weighted flow-time problem. *SIAM Journal on Computing*, 15(4):1119–1129, November 1986.

[16] S. Leonardi and D. Raz. Approximating total flow time on parallel machines. In *Proceedings of the 29th ACM Symposium on the Theory of Computing*, pages 110–119, May 1997.

[17] D.A. Lifka. The ANL/IBM SP scheduling system. In D.G. Feitelson and L. Rudolph, editors, *IPPS'95 Workshop: Job Scheduling Strategies for Parallel Processing*, pages 295–303. Springer–Verlag, Lecture Notes in Computer Science LNCS 949, 1995.

[18] U. Schwiegelshohn. Preemptive weighted completion time scheduling of parallel jobs. In *Proceedings of the 4th Annual European Symposium on Algorithms*

(ESA96), pages 39–51. Springer–Verlag Lecture Notes in Computer Science LNCS 1136, September 1996.

[19] Uwe Schwiegelshohn and Ramin Yahyapour. Analysis of First-Come-First-Serve Parallel Job Scheduling. In *Proceedings of the 9th SIAM Symposium on Discrete Algorithms*, pages 629–638, January 1998.

[20] F. Wang, H. Franke, M. Papaefthymiou, P. Pattnaik, L. Rudolph, and M.S. Squillante. A gang scheduling design for multiprogrammed parallel computing environments. In D.G. Feitelson and L. Rudolph, editors, *IPPS'96 Workshop: Job Scheduling Strategies for Parallel Processing*, pages 111–125. Springer–Verlag, Lecture Notes in Computer Science LNCS 1162, 1996.

[21] F. Wang, M. Papaefthymiou, and M.S. Squillante. Performance evaluation of gang scheduling for parallel and distributed multiprogramming. In D.G. Feitelson and L. Rudolph, editors, *IPPS'97 Workshop: Job Scheduling Strategies for Parallel Processing*, pages 277–298. Springer–Verlag, Lecture Notes in Computer Science LNCS 1291, 1997.

Expanding Symmetric Multiprocessor Capability Through Gang Scheduling

Morris A. Jette

Lawrence Livermore National Laboratory, Livermore, CA 94550, USA
jette@llnl.gov
http://www--lc.llnl.gov/global_access/dctg/gang

Abstract. Symmetric Multiprocessor (SMP) systems normally provide both space-sharing and time-sharing to insure high system utilization and good responsiveness. However the prevailing lack of concurrent scheduling for parallel programs precludes SMP use in addressing many large-scale problems. Tightly synchronized communications are impractical and normal time-sharing reduces the benefit of cache memory. Evidence gathered at Lawrence Livermore National Laboratory (LLNL) indicates that gang scheduling can increase the capability of SMP systems and parallel program performance without adverse impact upon system utilization or responsiveness.

1 Introduction

Parallel computer systems have been in use at LLNL since the introduction of a 126 processor BBN TC2000 computer in 1989. Subsequent deployments of Meiko CS-2, Cray C90, Cray T3D, IBM SP, and Digital Alpha systems have encouraged parallel application program development. The majority of LLNL's workload consists of numerical analysis programs designed for 16 to 256 way parallelism with memory requirements in excess of one gigabyte, disk space requirements in the 10 to 10000 gigabyte range, and execution times in the 1 to 40 hour range.

While Massively Parallel Processing (MPP) systems are well suited for execution of existing programs, the scheduling mechanisms available on some systems make program development somewhat difficult. Once a parallel program on the Meiko CS-2 or IBM SP begins execution, processors are dedicated to the program until its termination. Multiple parallel programs may execute concurrently on distinct processors, but will not time-share any processor. In order to provide good responsiveness for program development at LLNL, small numbers of processors are placed in a partition available only to programs with short execution times and small processor counts. Larger programs may experience delays of many hours in order to execute outside of program development partitions.

SMP systems normally have multiple processors sharing a common workload and memory. Distinct programs may execute on each processor and a program's threads of execution may migrate between processors to provide good responsiveness and high system utilization. Many of our customers find the programming

Dror G. Feitelson, Larry Rudolph (Eds.): JSSPP'98, LNCS 1459, pp. 199–216, 1998.
© Springer-Verlag Berlin Heidelberg 1998

environment on Digital Alpha computers to be particularly appealing with a large memory space shared by eight to 12 processors. The Digital Alpha processor performance is also excellent and attracts interest for execution of small to moderate size applications. Some applications require faster throughput than can be provided by a single processor and utilize multitasking to achieve this. Multitasking a program can provide some performance enhancement, but performance can vary widely with system load.

There are some UNIX scheduler implementation differences, but most systems maintain one or more queues of runnable threads [1,2]. Whenever a processor becomes available, the highest priority thread is selected to execute. The thread's priority may be based upon a history of recent processor utilization, reason for last relinquishing a processor (eg. waiting for I/O completion), process nice value, and priority class (real-time or time-sharing). The thread continues execution for some time quanta which is dependent upon the process' priority and priority class. This algorithm tends to maximize system utilization and responsiveness. In most cases, no effort is made to concurrently schedule the threads which comprise a single parallel program. On a computer without concurrent scheduling and more runnable threads than processors, the components of a parallel program may experience synchronization delays due to poor overlap in scheduling. Many tightly synchronized programs continuously poll semaphores at synchronization points (spin-wait) rather than relinquishing the processor. Unless the program's threads of execution can be provided with processors in a synchronized fashion, this spin-wait time can consume substantial resources without advancing the application's progress.

Figure 1 shows the behavior which might be experienced by a six thread parallel program executing on an eight processor multiprogrammed computer without gang scheduling. Processor use for only a portion of the parallel program's execution time is shown. Other running programs consume the remainder of processor resources and this is not shown. Most SMP systems fail to provide synchronized compute resources for parallel programs and even slight levels of competition for processors can severely impact the program's performance. The problem is most severe for programs with large thread counts on heavily utilized systems.

Gang scheduling groups a program's parallel threads of execution into a gang, then concurrently schedules an independent processor to each thread in the gang [5]. A thread here is broadly defined as being a path of program execution which can proceed concurrently with others. Included in this definition are processes generated by fork system calls, MPI (Message Passing Interface) and PVM (Parallel Virtual Machine) programs, as well as Pthreads. MPI and PVM threads may span multiple computers. Multiple programs may execute independently on distinct processors at the same time, referred to as *space-sharing*. Time-sharing is supported by providing the gang scheduled program access to processors as well as removing that access concurrently. Time-sharing is used to prevent starvation of any program or achieve other resource distribution criterion. The gang scheduled program is provided with the perspective of dedicated resources dur-

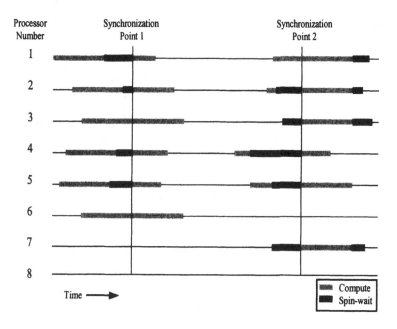

Fig. 1. Parallel program performance without gang scheduling

ing its periods of execution, with the exception of memory and I/O bandwidth. Figure 2 shows the dramatic reduction in spin-wait overhead which the sample program might experience with gang scheduling on the Digital Alpha. While perfect synchronization can not be provided with the Digital UNIX system's infrastructure, it can provide quite good synchronization as explored later in the paper. The program's throughput can be significantly improved by reducing spin-wait time without significant impact upon either overall system throughput or responsiveness. Gang scheduling is one of those rare circumstances when it is possible to get something for (almost) nothing.

Several studies of scheduling algorithms indicate that gang scheduling is a relatively good policy [5,9,14]. Gang schedulers have been implemented on a variety of computer platforms including Cray T3D [6], Cray T3E [12], CM-5, and Silicon Graphics multiprocessor workstations [3]. This paper describes a gang scheduler implementation for Digital computer systems and its performance characteristics both on a single computer and across a cluster.

2 Digital UNIX

LLNL has two clusters of Digital Alpha 8400 computers. The cluster for un-classified work includes eight computers with a total of 80 440 MHz processors, 56 gigabytes of memory, and 800 gigabytes of local disk. These computers are

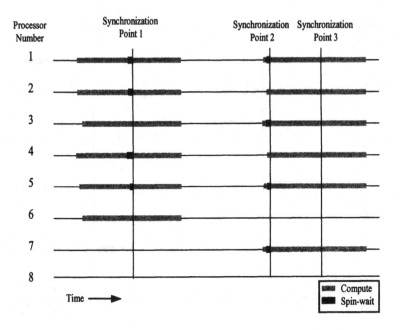

Fig. 2. Parallel program performance with gang scheduling

interconnected with a Digital *memory channel* with performance that permits high-performance problems to effectively span a cluster. The memory channel has a latency of 3 microseconds and bandwidth in excess of 100 megabytes per second. This compares with 0.5 microsecond latency and bandwidth in excess of 500 megabytes per second for the computer's bus. A comparably sized cluster exists exclusively for classified work.

The Digital UNIX 4.0D operating system includes a very fine grained fair-share scheduler called a *class scheduler*. Each process and its threads may be associated with a specific class and each class has a target resource allocation. If class scheduling is configured, each process is by default associated with the class *default*. For example, consider an eight processor system with two classes defined: *default* and *gang.job.1*. One might associate a four thread program with *gang.job.1* and target the class at 50 percent of resources to provide it with four processors. The remaining 50 percent of resources, or four processors, would be available to processes in the *default* class and managed through normal UNIX scheduling.

Modifications to the class scheduler database are performed via an Application Program Interface (API) to a class scheduler daemon. The class scheduler daemon's database is propagated to the operating system kernel immediately when a process is added or removed from a class. Changes in a class' target resource allocations are propagated to the kernel at configurable intervals of one second or longer. The kernel then maintains precise resource utilization statistics for each class. These statistics are used in conjunction with normal UNIX process scheduling priority to assign a runnable thread to a processor available for scheduling. Threads belonging to classes exceeding their target resource allocation will either be scheduled only to prevent a processor from becoming idle or will be completely prevented from executing, depending upon a configurable parameter. Executing threads are not preempted prior to completion of their normal time quanta nor are classes assured of achieving their target resource allocation on a short-term basis, so a gang scheduler's ability to concurrently schedule threads is imperfect.

While the class scheduler infrastructure may be less than ideal for implementing a gang scheduler, it does offer some interesting capabilities. If a parallel program is unable to fully utilize its target resource allocation, those resources (processors) can be automatically reallocated to other programs in order to sustain high overall system utilization. This minimizes the negative impact of unbalanced parallel applications and those with significant I/O components. Processes run by user *root* are exempt from class scheduling constraints, which insures that system functionality will be maintained at a cost of reduced control for the gang scheduler. Since changes in a class' target resource allocation require on the order of one second to propagate into the kernel, gang scheduling with this mechanism necessitates time-slice durations at least this large to be effective.

Class scheduling makes no attempt to bind specific processors to specific threads. Digital UNIX does calculate the highest priority thread for each available processor and the last processor used by each thread is a factor in this calculation. This algorithm limits movement of threads between processors and reduces the overhead of refreshing a processor's cache. The overall rate of context switches for a parallel program on a heavily utilized computer is reduced by about 50 percent with this gang scheduler compared with normal Digital UNIX scheduling. Thread migration between processors is reduced by a similar amount. The binding of threads to processors may very well reduce cache refresh overhead, but at a cost of reduced processor scheduling flexibility. Investigation of this issue has been deferred.

Table 1 illustrates the speedup actually achieved by a gang scheduled compute bound benchmark on a multiprogrammed computer. Efficiency here is defined as the speedup divided by the benchmark's thread count. This twelve processor system provided excellent speedup despite interference from about twenty other runnable threads throughout the testing period (the computer was in normal production use at this time with a heavy interactive load). Near perfect efficiency was achieved at low levels of parallelism. High levels of parallelism experienced less efficiency and greater variation in results, apparently due to difficulties faced by the class scheduler in managing far more runnable threads than processors.

Table 1. Speedup achieved with gang scheduling on a busy computer

Thread Count	Speedup	Percent Efficiency
1	1.000	100.0
2	1.983	99.1
3	2.998	99.9
4	3.989	99.7
5	4.992	99.8
6	5.968	99.5
7	6.928	99.0
8	7.876	98.4
9	8.791	97.7
10	9.665	96.6
11	10.511	95.6

3 Gang Scheduler Design

The gang scheduler developed by LLNL for Digital clusters is an evolution of earlier ones developed for the BBN TC2000 [7,8] and Cray T3D [6,10,11] systems. Both implementations were very successful at adding a time-sharing capability to these MPP systems, which otherwise provided both space-sharing and concurrent scheduling of resources. The Cray T3D was able to sustain weekly CPU utilization over 96 percent while the aggregate interactive workload slowdown was only 18 percent (amount by which elapsed time exceeded run time). One important feature of this design is the classification of each program in terms of scheduling requirements. The following prioritized job classes are supported in the Digital implementation:

Express jobs are deemed by management to be mission critical and are given rapid response and optimal throughput. Programs may be placed into the express class only by system administrators.

Interactive jobs require rapid response time and very good throughput during working hours. The response time and throughput may be reduced at other times for the sake of improved system utilization or throughput of batch jobs.

Batch jobs do not require rapid response, but should receive very good throughput outside of working hours.

Standby jobs have low priority and are suitable for absorbing otherwise idle compute resources. Programs are normally placed into the standby class after the user or his group have consumed more resources than desired by management.

Users may submit programs to the interactive, batch, and standby classes. The class of a program may be altered to a lower priority class by the user at any time. The system administrator may set any program to any job class.

The implementations for BBN and Cray systems were able to take advantage of vendor supplied parallel job initiation software to perform gang scheduling without application modification. The Digital environment lacks a single parallel job initiation mechanism, making the application interface more complex. At least four distinct parallel job initiation mechanisms exist: MPI, PVM, Pthreads, and fork calls. These mechanisms are utilized through compilers, libraries, and/or explicit user request. It is also common to combine multiple mechanisms in a single program, such as a PVM program spanning multiple computers but using Pthreads within each computer for improved performance.

For the Digital gang scheduler implementation, minor application or library changes were deemed necessary to register each program and process to be gang scheduled. These functions are provided through an API which issues Remote Procedure Calls (RPC) to one or more the gang scheduler daemons. The program registration function includes the job class and for each computer to be used: desired processor count, minimum processor count, desired real memory space, and desired disk space. This RPC contacts the gang scheduler daemon on each computer to be used and returns a single global job ID. For process registration, each process ID to be associated with a global job ID is specified. These calls were embedded into LLNL's version of the MPICH library and automate gang scheduling for users of that library with the setting of an environment variable. Other programs must have the necessary modifications made directly to the code, typically 20 to 50 lines of code. While this entails some programming effort, it can function with any combination of programming models and communications mechanisms within a computer or across multiple computers. A simple example of program and process registration is shown in the appendix. Additional API calls can be used to dissociate a process from a program, changes a program's class, modify resource requirements, gather resource utilization information, and query a computer's load. API functions are provided for both C and FORTRAN programs, which each account for roughly half of our workload.

The API writes the program's request into a file of a global file system and communicates with the gang scheduler daemons using sockets and a well known port. The RPC contains user identification and the file's location. Daemons receive the RPC, confirm the file's ownership for authentication, perform the requested action, and reply over the socket. This mechanism provides good security, flexibility, and performance.

Program and computer status information is written to a globally readable file at the start of each gang scheduler time-slice. An x-window program, *xgang*, reads this file and reports computer and program status as shown in fig. 3. Limited program modification capabilities are also provided by xgang. A user may modify a program's class, suspend, resume, or kill it across all computers with the push of a button. xgang has also proven quite useful for monitoring overall system performance.

The class scheduler provides a reasonable infrastructure for gang scheduling, but some performance enhancing tactics are used. A class is created by the gang scheduler for each registered parallel program on every computer the program will use. When processes are registered as a component of the program, their process IDs are added to the class. A class is allocated zero resources to stop the program, but this may not be completely effective if idle processors exist on the computer. In order to more effectively stop a program, the SIGUSR1 and

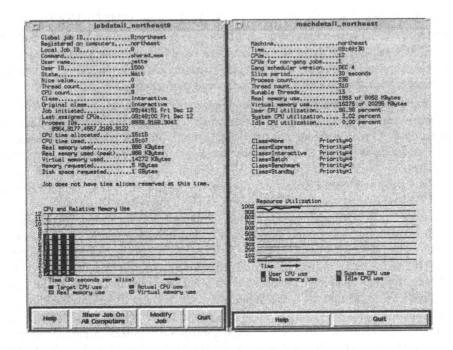

Fig. 3. Gangster display of Digital program and machine status

SIGUSR2 signals are optionally used to pause and continue programs. The API permits an application to explicitly disable gang scheduler use of these signals if they are required by the program for other purposes, but doing so will reduce concurrency and may reduce its performance. These signals also permit a more tightly synchronized stopping of a program at the end of a time-slice than can be achieved by the class scheduler alone. Rather than waiting up to one second to propagate new scheduling information to the kernel, these signals can stop a program immediately. Rather than allocating resources to a class in proportion to the number of processors desired, a higher target is specified and better overlap is achieved. This tactic effectively schedules auxiliary threads, which consume few compute cycles but are common on many applications. For example, a four thread program on an eight processor computer might be targeted to receive 60 percent of the resources rather than 50 percent. The actual percentage used varies system load and has been tuned to maximize parallel program overlap without causing significant reduction in responsiveness. The maximum resource allocation to all gang scheduled programs is limited to a configurable level. This may be used to insure that one or more processors are available to maintain overall system responsiveness.

Any gang scheduled program failing to utilize any CPU cycles for a configurable period of time, currently 10 minutes, will cease being gang scheduled and will revert to normal UNIX scheduling. Should the program resume consumption of CPU cycles, it will resume gang scheduling. This mechanism effectively addresses programs waiting for input, network traffic, or otherwise stopped. Any program faining to use any CPU cycles for an extended period, currently configured at 2 hours, is completely removed from the gang scheduler database.

One gang scheduler daemon executes on each computer. Programs spanning multiple computers contact the appropriate gang scheduler daemons to be preallocated specific time-slices on each computer. An Ousterhout [13] matrix is used to record these preallocated resources as shown in table 2. Each processor is represented by one column of the matrix and each row represents one time-slice. At prearranged times, the gang scheduler daemons allocate resources as specified in the Ousterhout matrix. The last row in the matrix, time slice 4, is followed by repeating the cycle from the top, time slice 1. In this gang scheduler implementation, the Ousterhout matrix describes a one hour schedule with the first time-slice occurring on the hour and subsequent time-slices at intervals configured when gang scheduler is built. All computers clocks must be synchronized to within a fraction of one second for concurrent scheduling to occur. LLNL uses a Network Time Protocol (NTP) for clock synchronization, although the Distributed Time Service (DTS) and other systems would equally satisfactory. The gang scheduler daemon uses an alarm to awake at the appropriate time and runs as user *root* to avoid being subject to class scheduling constraints.

Table 2. Sample Ousterhout matrix

| Time | Computer East | | Computer West | |
Slice	CPU 1	CPU 2	CPU 1	CPU 2
1	Job A	Job A	Job B	Job B
2	Job C	Job C	Job C	Job C
3	Job A	Job A	Job B	Job B
4	Job D	Job D	Job D	Job D

The gang scheduler is designed to provide each program with access to a similar quantity of processor cycles whether registered for gang scheduling or not. The number of time-slices, or entries in the Ousterhout matrix, allocated to a program spanning multiple computers is based upon the load on each computer at program initiation time. The program is allocated a percentage of Ousterhout matrix entries equal to its proportion of threads on the most heavily loaded computer. For example, a program registering with the gang scheduler for four-way parallel on an eight processor computer with 12 other runnable threads should be allocated 25 percent of Ousterhout matrix entries on that computer, or four processors every other time-slice. A gang scheduler sub-system periodically may increase or decrease the number of time-slices pre-allocated to a program spanning multiple computers as system loads vary.

For programs which execute exclusively on one computer, scheduling decisions are made at the beginning of each time-slice. These programs lack entries in the Ousterhout matrix, but make use of available entries based upon current conditions. This permits the gang scheduler to rapidly respond to changes in the workload.

Time-slices are configured to be rather long, 30 seconds. While such a long time-slice reduce program responsiveness, it was necessitated by two factors. Class scheduler resource allocation targets require on the order of one second to be propagated to the kernel, resulting in unsatisfactory parallel program over-lap for time-slice durations less than about 5 seconds. Second, many programs exceed one gigabyte in size and while context switching the processor may be performed in milliseconds, the time to refresh the cache may be on the order of hundreds of milliseconds and the time to context switch memory (paging one program from memory to disk and paging another program in the reverse direction) may be several seconds. In order to provide faster responsiveness, the execution of a newly initiated program may commence prior to the beginning of a new time-slice, if appropriate for the given workload. Also note that programs not registered for gang scheduling are not subject to these time-slices, but are scheduled using normal UNIX scheduling algorithms and compute resources not allocated to gang scheduled jobs.

4   Application Benefits

The most obvious benefit of gang scheduling to the application is the concurrent scheduling of required resources. Tightly synchronized threads of execution typi-cally perform spin-wait at synchronization points rather than relinquishing their processors. Concurrent processor scheduling largely eliminates spin-wait time.

A second benefit of this gang scheduler implementation is that resources are allocated for much longer time periods than normally provided by Digital UNIX, permitting more efficient use of memory systems. Cache memory typically must be refreshed between context switches. By decreasing the frequency of context switches about 50 percent, the overhead of cache refreshing will be reduced. The applications typical of the LLNL workload utilize substantial memory resources. When several such applications are running concurrently, paging adversely im-pacts the performance of each.

While computer systems in which the number of executable threads never exceeds the number of processors can achieve similar performance for individual programs without the use of gang scheduling, this is difficult to achieve in prac-tice. Computers designed as batch systems will have a regulated workload, but without some level of processor oversubscription, I/O bound programs will waste compute resources and even large compute-bound programs typically have I/O bound pre- and post-processing periods. A processor oversubscription rate of 50 percent (threads of queued work initiated on a computer equal to 150 percent of the processor count) largely eliminates idle processors for our workload. This will result in some competition for processors and even slight competition for processor resources can result in dramatic reduction in parallel program perfor-mance.

5 Application Consequences

While gang scheduling can provide the synchronization required by many applications, it can adversely impact performance of others. Reduced performance has been observed for both I/O bound programs and programs with severe memory contention. Most uniprocessor and SMP schedulers assign a high scheduling priority to processes waiting for I/O completion. This scheme maximizes the throughput of I/O bound programs without substantial impact upon processor availability. Since gang scheduling blocks the program's access to processors for some time-slices, the rate at which I/O requests can be issued and the overall program throughput is reduced. If the program is primarily compute bound, the Digital UNIX class scheduler will merely reallocate processors during periods of synchronous I/O and maintain high system utilization without substantial impact upon the individual program. Contention for the system's memory banks can also reduce a program's performance, particularly if its threads of execution are repeatedly writing to the same memory bank. This problem has been observed in only one parallel program performing repeated write instructions to a single memory location. The program was modified to eliminate the memory contention bottleneck and an overall improvement in throughput resulted. Since gang scheduling is provided only to programs explicitly registering for the service, gang scheduling may be easily avoided when appropriate. When in doubt, it is a simple matter of performing timing tests and comparing results to assess the benefit of gang scheduling.

6 Results

Performance characteristics of several benchmarks developed by Brooks and Warren [4] were utilized to assess the impact of gang scheduling. All benchmarks are tightly synchronized and compute bound, as is typical of the LLNL workload as a whole. The benchmarks were executed on a 12 processor Digital Alpha 8400 with 440 MHz clock and eight-way memory interleave. Twelve single-threaded application programs were running concurrently with these timing tests to simulate interference which might expected in a normal production environment. Table 3 and fig. 4 show the performance of a 70 CPU second Gaussian elimination benchmark. Twenty executions were made at each thread count, alternating between gang and UNIX scheduling. Both mean and standard deviation values are report for MFLOP measurements based upon CPU time used. This benchmark experiences superlinear speedup due to the scaling of the cache size with processor count and high cache hit rates. Gang scheduling provided consistent program performance and scaling with increasing thread counts. Without gang scheduling, performance is good with small thread counts, but significant variation in performance occurred in each execution. Higher thread counts in some cases result in reduced program performance and the standard deviation in performance exceeds 10 percent in many cases. Gang scheduling benefits this benchmark partly through the synchronized processor allocation, but also through reduced the cache refresh overhead. The time period between synchronization points is inversely proportional to the thread count, at six threads the time is 1.10 seconds.

Table 3. Gaussian elimination benchmark performance

Thread	Gang Scheduled		UNIX Scheduled	
Count	MFLOPS	Speedup	MFLOPS	Speedup
1	28.2 ± 0.4	1.00	29.9 ± 0.4	1.00
2	148.2 ± 2.1	5.25	127.4 ± 10.4	4.26
3	253.3 ± 3.4	8.98	163.6 ± 35.3	5.47
4	319.6 ± 2.3	11.33	287.4 ± 20.8	9.61
5	389.5 ± 7.5	13.81	280.1 ± 36.3	9.37
6	454.2 ± 8.2	16.11	268.7 ± 23.3	8.99
7	538.9 ± 13.7	19.11	226.0 ± 48.1	7.56
8	604.1 ± 9.8	21.42	104.5 ± 6.0	3.49
9	691.1 ± 10.4	24.51	136.6 ± 16.4	4.57
10	772.5 ± 9.0	27.39	145.3 ± 18.0	4.86
11	832.2 ± 10.5	29.51	191.9 ± 30.1	6.42

The second benchmark investigated is a 15 CPU second matrix multiply benchmark. The memory requirements are sufficiently large to eliminate significant benefit of improved cache management. Benefit is provided primarily through synchronized processor assignment and reduced spin-wait time. The time period between synchronization points is inversely proportional to the thread count and is 2.67 seconds at six threads. Table 4 provides a summary of the results, but the results of individual timing tests are quite interesting. As expected, gang scheduling provided consistently good performance results. For most benchmark executions, normal UNIX scheduling provided similar performance to gang scheduling, but on occasion provided dramatically worse performance. This benchmark was executed twenty times at each thread count, alternating using UNIX and gang scheduling. An excerpt from the five thread benchmark log follows:

```
UNIX   615.16 MFLOPS
Gang   620.91 MFLOPS
UNIX   110.55 MFLOPS
Gang   623.83 MFLOPS
UNIX   110.64 MFLOPS
Gang   612.33 MFLOPS
UNIX   612.33 MFLOPS
```

Clearly the processes being managed by UNIX scheduling can result in substantial variation in spin-wait overhead. The timing tests at many thread counts demonstrated one or more abnormally low performance results.

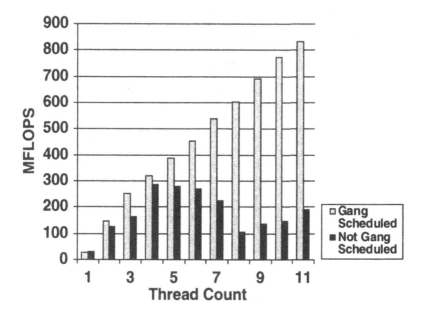

Fig. 4. Gaussian elimination benchmark performance

Most of our numerical analysis programs do benefit significantly from the cache and their performance characteristics seem to be best reflected by the Gaussian elimination benchmark. Typical parallel application programs executing in LLNL's normal production computing environment experience throughput improvements of five to 100 percent through gang scheduling. The CPU time required to execute some applications has decreased by up to 50 percent and the customer response has been very positive. This gang scheduler has been in production use on some of LLNL's compute servers since July of 1997. No reduction in system utilization has been observed. During working hours, idle time is typically zero, system time only a few percent, and user time is in excess of 95 percent. System responsiveness is not noticeably reduced, although this has not been quantified.

In order to offload some work from MPP systems, a very popular Arbitrary Lagrange-Eulerian (ALE) hydrodynamics application was ported to the Digital cluster. Performance requirements dictated that this application be executed over sizable numbers of processors. Performance results for this application are shown in table 5 and fig. 5 for both single computer and multiple computer executions. The Digital memory channel interconnect provides performance across the cluster similar to that on a single computer. The application displays near linear speedup with gang scheduling even for large thread counts spanning 8 computers.

Table 4. Matrix multiply benchmark performance

Thread Count	Gang Scheduled MFLOPS	UNIX Scheduled MFLOPS
1	114.0 ± 0.4	111.8 ± 0.4
2	226.2 ± 0.9	227.5 ± 0.8
3	350.4 ± 0.2	347.8 ± 0.2
4	475.2 ± 2.7	469.7 ± 2.7
5	604.0 ± 4.8	403.1 ± 75.7
6	740.3 ± 5.7	737.5 ± 6.4
7	873.3 ± 8.7	728.6 ± 87.5
8	1002.4 ± 10.3	965.3 ± 23.7
9	1175.2 ± 12.8	1147.0 ± 23.5
10	1329.9 ± 16.8	1100.1 ± 124.9
11	1441.1 ± 14.8	1357.3 ± 72.5

Table 5. ALE hydrodynamics application performance

Thread Count	Run Time (seconds)			
	1 Computer	2 Computers	4 Computers	8 Computers
1	2313	–	–	–
2	1235	1257	–	–
4	632	656	668	–
8	308	323	346	343
16	–	157	164	172
32	–	–	78.5	85.4

7   Conclusion

Gang scheduling can provide substantially improved performance for tightly synchronized parallel programs in multiprogrammed environments, particularly those with large thread counts and substantial cache use. This can be accomplished without reduction in system utilization or noticeable reduction in responsiveness. Gang scheduling also provides the means of harnessing the power of an SMP cluster to address large-scale problems without sacrificing a multiprogramming capability. These results were achieved without binding threads to specific processors, although the benefit of this warrants further investigation.

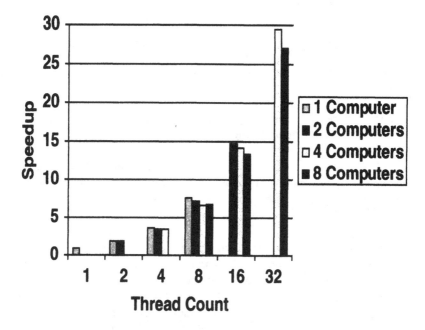

Fig. 5. ALE hydrodynamics application performance

8 Acknowledgments

Tony Verhulst of Digital Equipment Corporation developed the class scheduler infrastructure. Programs developed by Eugene Brooks, Mike Collette, Scott Futral, Karen Warren, and the ALE3D code group were utilized to generate the performance results.

9 Appendix

The sample program shown below illustrates the program modifications required for gang scheduling. Equivalent FORTRAN subroutines are also available.

```
#include <string.h>
#include <strings.h>
#include <unistd.h>
#include "GangUserAPI.h"
#define CPU_COUNT 2
```

```
main(int argc, char *argv[])
{
    int i;
    char host[MAXHOSTNAMELEN];

    gsRetVal rc;
    struct GangJobId my_job_id;
    struct GangResources gang_resources[1];
    struct GangResources *gang_resource_list[2];

    /* Clear job_id on first call, otherwise the calls will */
    /* apply to an existing program.  Resource requirements */
    /* of a program may be modified during its execution.   */
    bzero(&my_job_id, sizeof(my_job_id));

    /* Define resource requirements for each computer used  */
    /*    machine   = Computer's name                       */
    /*    cpu_count = CPU count desired                      */
    /*    cpu_min   = Minimum CPU count acceptable           */
    /*    mega_mem  = Megabytes of memory (optional)         */
    /*    giga_disk = Gigabytes of disk (optional)           */
    gethostname(host, sizeof(host));
    strcpy(gang_resources[0].machine, host);
    gang_resources[0].cpu_count = CPU_COUNT;
    gang_resources[0].cpu_min   = CPU_COUNT;
    gang_resources[0].mega_mem  = 5;
    gang_resources[0].giga_disk = 1;

    /* NULL terminated list of computers and resources      */
    gang_resource_list[0]      = &gang_resources[0];
    gang_resource_list[1]      = NULL;

    /* Register the program and get job id                  */
    rc = GangJobRegister(&my_job_id, CLASS_INTERACTIVE,
                         gang_resource_list);
    if (rc != gsSuccess) {
        printf("GangJobRegister Error: %s\n", GangErrMsg(rc));
        exit(1);
    } /* if */
    printf("GangJobRegister completed successfully\n");

    /* Fork processes as needed */
    for (i=1; i < CPU_COUNT; i++) {
        switch (fork()) {
        case -1:          /* Error */
```

```
                printf("Error forking process\n");
                exit(1);
        case 0:          /* Child */
                cpu_count = 0;
                break;
        default:         /* Parent */
                ;
        } /* switch */
    } /* for */

    /* Register each process */
    rc = GangProcAdd(&my_job_id, PROC_ID, getpid());
    if (rc != gsSuccess) {
        printf("Error from GangProcAdd: %s\n", GangErrMsg(rc));
        exit(1);
    } /* if */

    /* Run each process */
    printf("Running process %d \n", getpid());
    Parallel_Code();
    exit(0);
} /* main */
```

References

1. AT and T: UNIX System V Release 4 Internals, Vol. 1. AT and T, (1990) 2.4.1–2.4.21
2. Bach, M. J.: The Design of the UNIX Operating System. Prentice-Hall Inc. (1986) 247–268.
3. Barton, J. M. and Bitar N.: A Scalable Multi-discipline, Multiple-processor Scheduling Framework for IRIX. Job Scheduling Strategies for Parallel Processing, Edited by: Feitelson, D. G.; Rudolph, L., Springer Verlag (1995) Lecture Notes in Computer Science, Vol 949, 45–69.
4. Brooks, E. D. III and Warren K. H.: A Study of Performance on SMP and Distributed Memory Architectures Using A Shared Memory Programming Model. Proceedings of SuperComputing (Nov 1997).
5. Feitelson, D. G.: A Survey of Scheduling in Multiprogrammed Parallel Systems. Research Report RC 19790 (87657), IBM T. J. Watson Research Center (1994).
6. Feitelson, D. G. and Jette, M. A.: Improved Utilization and Responsiveness with Gang Scheduling. IPPS '97 Workshop on Job Scheduling Strategies for Parallel Processing, (Apr 1997) 238–261.
7. Gorda, B. and Wolski, R.: Timesharing massively parallel machines. International Conference on Parallel Processing, volume II, (Aug 1995) 214–217.
8. Gorda, B. C. and Brooks E. D. III: Gang Scheduling a Parallel Machine. Technical Report UCRL-JC-107020, Lawrence Livermore National Laboratory (Dec 1991).
9. Gupta, A., Tucker, A. and Urushibara, S. : The Impact of Operating System Scheduling Policies and Synchronization Methods on the Performance of Parallel Applications . Proceedings of ACM SIGMETRICS (May 1991) 120–132.

10. Jette, M., Storch, D. and Yim, E.: The Gang Scheduler - Timesharing the Cray T3D. Cray User Group (Mar 1996) 247–252.
11. Jette, M.: Performance Characteristics of Gang Scheduling in Multiprogrammed Environments. Proceedings of SuperComputing (Nov 1997).
12. Lagerstrom, R. N. and Gipp, S. K.: PScheD Political Scheduling on the CRAY T3E. Proceedings of Workshop on Job Scheduling Strategies for Parallel Processing Job Scheduling Strategies for Parallel Processing, Edited by: Feitelson, D. G.; Rudolph, L. , Springer Verlag. Lecture Notes in Computer Science, Vol 1291, (1997) 117–138.

13. Ousterhout, J.: Scheduling techniques for concurrent systems. Proceedings of the Third International Conference on Distributed Computer Systems, (Oct 1982) 22–30.
14. Seager, M. K. and Stichnoth, J. M.: Simulating the Scheduling of Parallel Supercomputer Applications. Technical Report UCRL-102058, Lawrence Livermore National Laboratory, (Sep 1989).

Overhead Analysis of Preemptive Gang Scheduling

Atsushi Hori[1], Hiroshi Tezuka[1], and Yutaka Ishikawa[1]

Tsukuba Research Center
Real World Computing Partnership
Tsukuba Mitsui Building 16F, 1-6-1 Takezono
Tsukuba-shi, Ibaraki 305-0032, JAPAN
TEL:+81-298-53-1661, FAX:+81-298-53-1652
{hori,tezuka,ishikawa}@rwcp.or.jp

Abstract. A preemptive gang scheduler is developed and evaluated. The gang scheduler, called SCore-D, is implemented on top of a UNIX operating system and runs on workstation and PC clusters connected by Myrinet, a giga-bit class, high-performance network.

To have high-performance communication at the user-level and a multi-user environment simultaneously, we propose *network preemption* to save and restore network context as well as process contexts when switching distributed processes. We also developed a high-performance, user-level communication library, PM. PM and SCore-D collaborate for the network preemption. When user processes are gang-scheduled, communication messages are first flushed, then the messages and pending messages in the receive and send buffers are saved and restored. Unlike CM-5's All-Fall-Down mechanism, our gang-scheduling scheme is all software; no special hardware support is assumed. Also there is no limitation on network topology and partitioning.

The overhead of the gang scheduler is measured on our new PC cluster, which consists of 64 PentiumPros connected by Myrinet. NAS parallel benchmark programs are used for the evaluation. We found that the message flushing time and network preemption time depends on the communication patterns of the application programs. We also found that the time of saving and restoring network context occupies more than two third of gang scheduling time. Evaluation shows that the slowdown of user program execution due to the gang scheduling is less than 9 %when the time slice is 100 *msec*.

1 Introduction

Gang scheduling is efficient for the scheduling of frequently communicating processes[Ous82, GTU91, FR92]. Gang scheduling also enables time sharing scheduling, which provides shorter response times and interactive parallel programming. However, despite the benefits of gang scheduling, there have been few implementations (Table 1).

Dror G. Feitelson, Larry Rudolph (Eds.): JSSPP'98, LNCS 1459, pp. 217–230, 1998.
© Springer-Verlag Berlin Heidelberg 1998

Table 1. Gang schedulers on distributed memory parallel machines

Scheduler	Platform	Comm. Level	Pre-emptive	Hardware Support
(anonymous)[FR92]	Makbilian	OS	Yes	Yes
CMOST[Thi92]	TMC CM-5	User	Yes	Yes
Medusa[OSS80, Ous82]	Cm*	OS	Yes	Yes
Meiko CS-2	Meiko CS-2	OS	Yes	N/A
MPCI GangScheduler[GW95]	BBN TC2000	N/A	No	Yes
OSF-1 AD[ZRB+93]	Intel Paragon	OS	Yes	No
PScheD[LG97]	Cray T3E	User	Yes	N/A
SCore-D[HTI+96, HTI97b]	Workstation Cluster	User	Yes	No
SHARE[FPR96]	IBM SP-2	User	No	No

In this paper, *parallel process* is defined as a set of UNIX processes that are execution entities of a parallel program. A parallel process is a unit of gang scheduling. The frequency of communication in a parallel process can be much higher than that of distributed processes. At the same time, communication interface hardware is getting faster every year causing problems with system call overheads. To tackle this problem, there are several *user-level communication* proposals which allow users to access communication interfaces directly[PLC95, vEBV95, THIS97, CMC97].

User-level communication provides high-performance communication, however, it introduces a new problem when implementing gang scheduling. First, the network interface status must be saved and restored when switching processes. Second, some messages that should be received by a process before being switched may be received by another process after being switched. There should be some mechanism to avoid this situation.

We proposed *network preemption* to tackle the problem when implementing a gang scheduler, SCore-D[HTI+96, HTI97b], with a user-level communication library, PM[THIS97]. Network preemption can utilize gang scheduling without sacrificing user-level communication performance. PM is designed not only for providing high-performance communication, but also provides the required functions for network preemption. Our gang-scheduling scheme is all software; no special hardware support is assumed. SCore-D is designed for workstation and PC clusters, and is implemented as a set of daemon processes running on top of the UNIX operating system. SCore-D explicitly controls (schedules) user processes via UNIX signals. Thus, no kernel modification is required at all. With the network preemption, network status is saved and restored when switching parallel processes. However, the implemented gang scheduling overhead was evaluated with some simple programs, and was not analyzed[HTI+96, HTI97b].

In this paper, we evaluate the SCore-D gang scheduling overhead with more realistic applications, NAS parallel benchmark programs[BBLS93]. NAS parallel benchmark is a set of numerical programs, each of them is a component of CFD calculation. Thus they are expected to exhibit some aspects of real world problems. The gang scheduling overhead is analyzed, and we found that the time of saving and restoring network context occupies more than two third of gang scheduling time on the applications with 64 processors.

2   Related Work

CM-5 has a hardware support for network preemption called *All-Fall-Down* [Thi92]. In the All-Fall-Down mode, all messages in the network fall down to the nearest node regardless of destination. To restore the network context, the fallen messages are reinjected into the network. Since the CM-5 network was not designed to preserve message order, the disturbance of message order by All-Fall-Down does not cause a problem. When the All-Fall-Down takes place, message order is not preserved, and message sending by the user program may fail since the message sending operation is not an atomic operation. The user program must handle these situations and extra communication overhead is introduced.

SHARE is a gang scheduler on IBM SP-2 [FPR96]. SHARE saves and restores network hardware context, however, it has no message flushing mechanism. Each message has a tag to identify the process receiving the message. If a message is delivered to the wrong process, then message sending fails. Since failure recovery must be handled by software, it introduces additional communication overhead.

We propose *network preemption* to tackle the problem when implementing a gang scheduler with user-level communication. Network preemption can provide high-performance communication to its user and can utilize gang scheduling without sacrificing communication performance. The proposed network preemption for user-level communication not only enables gang scheduling, but also provides a method to tackle some distributed process problems, such as; distributed termination detection, consistent checkpointing, and global garbage collection[HTI97b].

3   Cluster Software System

We have been developing a cluster software system for workstation and PC clusters. Figure 1 shows the software structure of our cluster software system. SCore-D is a gang scheduler on top of the UNIX operating system. PM is a low-level, high-performance communication library. In our cluster system, PM plays an important role for both providing high-performance communication to its user and implementing gang scheduling. One unique feature of SCore-D is that it is written in MPC++[Ish96], a multi-threaded C++. The distributed control structure objects are linked with MPC++ global pointers. The MPI communication library is also implemented[OHT+97].

3.1   SCore-D

Figure 2 shows the process structure of SCore-D and user processes. Here, *parallel process* is defined as a set of processes invoked from a single parallel program.

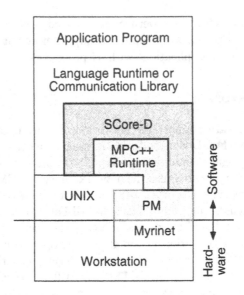

Fig. 1. SCore-D Software Structure

Each process of an SCore-D parallel process is running as a daemon process on every processor in a workstation cluster. Users can invoke their parallel program from their workstations. This invoked process on user's workstation is called the *Front End Process* (*FEP*). The FEP is a client for the SCore-D parallel computation server. Each process of a user parallel process is forked and execed by SCore-D processes. SCore-D can control user processes via UNIX signals.

Figure 3 shows an example of the SCore-D control structure to manage a user parallel process. Each user parallel process has a control structure tree. This control structure is distributed over a cluster to avoid a bottleneck. The root of the tree is a parallel process object, and the leaves are element process objects. Each element process object represents a UNIX process in a user parallel process. When a gang scheduler decides to stop a parallel process, then the stop command goes down the control tree, and finally every element process object sends a SIGSTOP signal to its corresponding process. The stopped state of each user process is caught by an element process object with a wait() system call, and the stopped event is forwarded to its super node. Each control node object synchronizes the events from its subnodes, and then forwards the event to its super node. When a parallel process object receives the events, it is guaranteed that all user processes are stopped. Along with the distributed control structure, commands are broadcasted and events are synchronized. Thus processes of a user parallel process change their states in a gang. The tree structure in Figure 3 is a binary tree. Actually, a hexadecimal-tree is used in SCore-D, because hexadecimal-tree is the fastest structure.

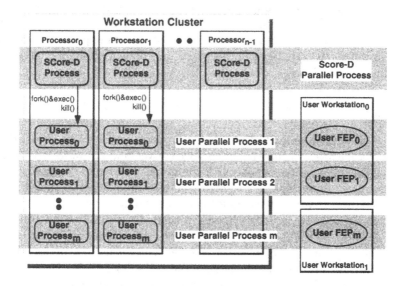

Fig. 2. SCore-D Process Structure

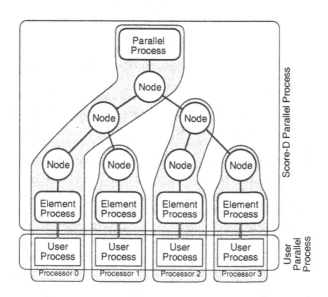

Fig. 3. Distributed Control Structure

One can implement any kind of scheduling policies and mechanisms with SCore-D. Actually, we have implemented a time sharing and space sharing scheduler, called DQT[HIK+95, HIN+95]. With DQT scheduling, sequential workload is treated as an exceptional case in that parallel process requires only one processor. However, all evaluations in this paper were done with simple time sharing scheduling for simplicity.

3.2 PM

PM is a low-level communication library for Myrinet[BCF+95]. PM[THIS97] consists of a software library, a software device driver, and firmware. It is designed to exploit the full potential of the Myrinet interface. PM is also designed so that a gang scheduler can be implemented on top of it. In this section, we will introduce two PM features that are designed for gang scheduling.

The first feature is multiple *channels*. A channel essentially consists of a pair of send and receive FIFO buffers. Those buffers are memory mapped to the address space of a process that opens the channel. This memory mapping technique reduces the number of memory copies and protects those buffers from access by other processes. While PM provides a connection-less communication model, the set of processors that can communicate with each other can be restricted when the channel is open. Inter-channel communication is not allowed. A channel is associated with a channel descriptor, and the descriptor can be passed to other processes like file descriptors in UNIX. SCore-D opens two channels; one for SCore-D itself and the other for user processes. The opened user channel descriptor is passed to the user process. PM also supports a blocking receive using receive interrupts. SCore-D waits for incoming message with blocking receive, and user processes wait for an incoming messages by polling. Thus the executions of SCore-D threads and a user process are interleaved at the SCore-D thread level.

The second feature of PM is its flow-control protocol. Myrinet supports hardware flow-control. However, relying on hardware flow-control can cause a deadlock because message sending region is locked until the end of the transmission, but the transmission is blocked by a hardware flow-control. PM's flow control protocol is called *Modified Ack/Nack*[THIS97]. PM provides an asynchronous message sending model. At the receiver processor, PM first determines if there is a enough room to hold the message in the receive buffer. If so, PM returns an *Ack* message. Otherwise PM returns a *Nack* message. On the sender side, when PM acknowledges with an Ack response, it frees the corresponding send buffer region. However, if a Nack message is received, PM resends the message and leaves the buffer region as is. Actually some Ack and Nack messages are merged into one to reduce message traffic. Refer to [THIS97] for more details. PM's channel and flow-control protocol introduces some important characteristics that must be considered when implementing gang scheduling.

Channel independence: When a receiver process falls into an infinite loop because of a program bug, it becomes so busy that it cannot handle the messages in the receive buffer; therefore the sender process on the other processor eventually will be unable to send any message. On PM, however, communications through the other channels will take place normally. This is because PM's modified Ack/Nack protocol never stops the flow of messages. In this case, the Nack messages and resent messages are actually exchanged. This channel independence is very important when implementing a gang scheduler. To schedule processes in a gang, each scheduler process must be synchronized in some way. Having two network interfaces may provide two independent communication channels, but this requires extra investment in hardware. PM's multiple channel support and its channel independence avoid this.

Steady state of a channel: On a PM channel, if all Ack or Nack messages corresponding to all sent messages from a processor are received by the sender processor, then this means that there is no message being sent from the processor in the network. When a channel of a processor satisfies this condition, then the channel is referred to as being "in a *steady state*". When all processes associated with a parallel computation satisfy this condition, then there is no message associated with the computation in the network.

Waiting for a steady state is different from waiting for transmission completion. The returning of a Nack message means that the message transmission has failed. When a receiver process is stopped, messages in the receive buffer are never consumed. Thus waiting for transmission completion may continue until the receiver process is resumed. When the transmission completion is applied to gang scheduling, a receiver process may be stopped by a signal, and the message flushing can last forever.

4 Gang Scheduling

Figure 4 shows the procedure for switching parallel processes in SCore-D. Parallel process switching consists of four phases.

Freeze Phase: Stopping user processes by sending SIGSTOP. SCore-D processes wait for stopped state of each user process with a wait() system call, and then wait until the user channels are in a steady state. Synchronizing the steady states of all the user channels guarantees that there are no messages from any user process in the network.

Save Phase: SCore-D saves the channel status of the user processes.

Restore Phase: SCore-D restores the channel status of the new user processes.

Run Phase: After being restored, SCore-D then sends SIGCONT signals to the new user processes. Eventually the user parallel job begins to run.

The entire set of channel contexts are called a *network context*, and the procedure described above is called *network preemption*, because SCore-D saves and restores network contexts. PM is designed to be preemptive, so that SCore-D can send signals to control user processes at any time. Thus user parallel processes can be preempted or killed by SCore-D at any time.

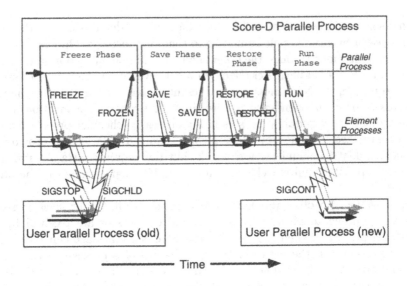

Fig. 4. Network Preemption

All broadcast and synchronization in the above four phases are propagated along with the distributed control structure in SCore-D. Thus, it takes order $log(N)$ time, where N is the number of processors, for each phase.

The network context is a snapshot of the network status that can be observed by software. Network preemption solves not only the problem of gang scheduling with user-level communication, but also helps for solving the following communicating distributed process problems.

Distributed termination detection: The detection of *no running process* in a set of distributed processes is well known as as the *distributed termination problem* and a number of algorithms have been proposed to tackle this (among these, [Mis83, CL85] are the most famous). The biggest difficulty of this problem comes from checking for the existence of messages in the network. With network preemption, this can be done by simply counting the number of messages in the saved network context. Distributed termination detection using network preemption has already been implemented in SCore-D-D[HTI97a]. SCore-D has also been successful in detecting deadlocked user processes.

Consistent checkpointing: When processes are gang-scheduled, the process contexts and channel contexts can be saved in permanent storage systems such as disks. Execution can be resumed by restoring those contexts. No additional mechanism is required to have a consistent state in the distributed processes.

Global garbage collection: Global garbage collection is difficult because of the references included in transmitted messages[KMY94]. As in the case of consistent checkpointing, network preemption gives a clear consistent state timing and a chance to investigate the messages in transmission. Here, channel contexts are added to the root set of a global garbage collection. Thus network preemption makes the "marking of live objects" in a global garbage collection easy.

5   Evaluation

The overhead of the implemented gang scheduler was evaluated on our PC cluster II (Table 2). The PC cluster II consists of 64 PentiumPros (200MHz) connected by Myrinet (160MB/s bandwidth).

Table 2. RWC PC Cluster II

Number of Processors	64
Processor	PentiumPro
Clock [MHz]	200
Cache [KB]	512
Memory [MB]	256
I/O Bus	PCI
Network	Myrinet
Operating System	NetBSD 1.2
Min. Latency (PM) [μs]	7.5
Max. Bandwidth (PM) [MB/s]	117.6
Min. MPI Latency [μs]	12.0
Max. MPI Bandwidth [MB/s]	36.8

Table 3 shows the times to save and restore a PM channel context. In this table, "receive buffer full" means that the receive buffer holds 511 messages (65,408 bytes in total), and "send buffer full" means that the send buffer holds 255 messages (61,200 bytes in total). The saving time is larger than the restoring time, because read operations from PCI memory region takes longer than write operations.

The network context switching time depends on the number and the amount of messages in the network and in the receive and send buffers when gang scheduling takes place. Having larger receive and send buffers contributes to communication performance, however, it also increases the required network context switching time. The relation of buffer sizes to network context switching time is similar to the case of process context switching. The larger the register file size, the slower the process context switching.

NAS parallel benchmark programs (version 2.3, MPI)[BBLS93] are used for the evaluation of SCore-D gang scheduling. We selected EP, FT and CG from the benchmark (class A). EP is an embarrassingly parallel program; there is almost no communication. FT is a 3-D FFT program and is a communication bound

Table 3. Channel Context Save/Restore Time

Recv. Buffer	Send Buffer	Save [msec]	Restore [msec]
Empty	Empty	0.62	0.18
Empty	Full	1.96	1.56
Full	Empty	2.16	1.59
Full	Full	3.70	3.19

program. CG is a conjugate gradient method program; there are large amount of communication, but not so much as in the FT program. In short, these three programs exhibit different communication patterns.

In the current SCore-D implementation, SCore-D does not check if the next process to be scheduled is the same as the currently running process, and SCore-D naively switches one parallel process. Thus submitting one program is enough to measure gang scheduling overhead. Through the evaluation, there is no running process, but SCore-D and the process submitted via SCore-D.

Figure 5 shows the times of freeze, save and restore phases on the applications, measurement is for processors 8, 16, 32 and 64, with a time slice of 100 msec. The freeze phase time depends on the channel context sizes. And the times of all three phases depend on the number of processors, because each phase contains a broadcast and a barrier synchronization. In the EP program, there is almost no communication. Thus most of the processing time of each phase can be thought of as a base overhead of a broadcast and a barrier synchronization along with the distributed tree control structure.

With FT and CG programs, save and restore phase times are larger than that of EP programs. This comes from the size of channel contexts and is due to the larger amounts of communications. Since FT program is a communication bound program, the total gang scheduling times (sum of save, restore and freeze times) are the highest in all cases. Thus gang scheduling time depends on communication pattern of an application program running under SCore-D.

As described in Section 4, SCore-D gang scheduling consists of process context and network context switches. In the SCore-D implementation, these two context switching are mutually dependent and are not divisible. The time necessary for switching process contexts is reasonable (approximately 40 μsec) when compared with the time needed for switching network contexts. The time of saving and restoring network context occupies more than one third of gang scheduling time on applications in most cases.

The gang scheduling overhead observed by an application O is defined as

$$O = (T_{Gang} - T_{NoGang})/T_{NoGang}$$

Here, T_{Gang} is the execution time under the SCore-D gang-scheduler, and T_{NoGang} is the execution time with an infinite time slice. However, the calculated overhead is subject to measurement error if the differences in execution times are small.

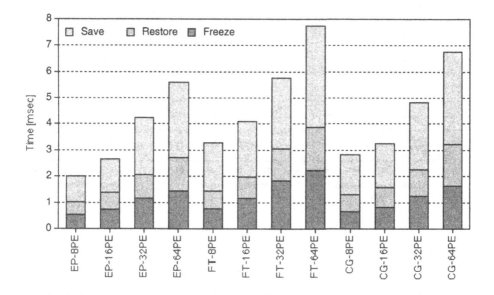

Fig. 5. Breakdown of Network Preemption

So we evaluated the gang scheduling overhead with smaller time slices (from 50 to 200 *msec*) to obtain larger elapsed time differences.

Figure 6 shows the gang scheduling overhead observed at each application. Here, the time slice of gang scheduling is set to 50, 100 and 200 *msec*, and the number of processors are 8, 16, 32 and 64. When the time slice is doubled, the slowdown is approximately halved.

The slowdown of program execution due to gang scheduling comes from a variety of reasons: SCore-D scheduling overhead, the cache effect, UNIX operating system overhead, co-scheduling skew[ADV+94], etc. Also scheduling overhead depends on the communication pattern of a user program.

Slowdown observed at the application level and the overhead measured at the SCore-D level can be different. One reason for this is that SCore-D can only detect the status changes of a user process with a `wait()` system call. There can be delay between signal sending and the detection of status change of process by the signal. Also co-scheduling skew can not be observed by SCore-D.

Comparing Figure 5 and Figure 6, we find that the overhead (slowdown) of the CG program is the highest, while the gang scheduling time of FT programs is the longest. We are now investigating these points.

6   Concluding Remarks

U-Net[vEBV95] and AM-II[CMC97] support *endpoints* similar to PM's channel to provide multiplexed, virtualized networks. If there were a sufficient number

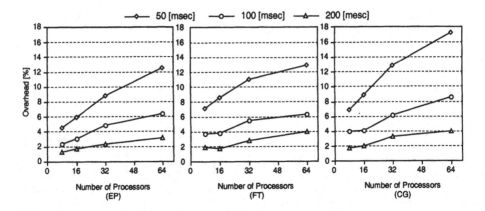

Fig. 6. Slowdown due to gang scheduling

of channels (endpoints), there would be no need of network preemption when gang-scheduling. However, one must guarantee that there is no message in all those channels involved in the parallel process in the network before the channel is reused. This means that the number of channels should be larger than the number of generated processes in the lifetime of the scheduling system. Therefore a message flushing mechanism is still needed.

Having a large number of channels degrades communication performance. User-level communication libraries have to check channels ready to send. The larger the number of channels, the larger the sending overhead. In AM-II, this problem is avoided by introducing endpoint scheduling[CMC97]. In contrast, PM limits the number of channels to four and provides channel context switching facilities. Simple round-robin scheduling for polling send buffers is used in PM. As described in Section 3.2, network preemption using channel context switching can be applied to a variety of problems in parallel processing.

Through the evaluation of our implementation on a PC cluster II, we confirmed that slowdown is less than 9 %with a 100 $msec$time slice. With a compute bound application, such as EP, the overhead is less than 7 %. We also confirmed that the overhead can be further reduced by increasing the time slice.

We found that much of the gang scheduling overhead comes from saving and restoring network context. Basically, saving and restoring network context is just copying memory between message buffers and the network context save area. It is expected, therefore, that gang scheduling overhead can be reduced by using a computer having a higher memory-copy performance.

It is normally assumed that gang scheduling overhead is quite high, and consequently time slice is longer than that of UNIX (Table 1). Although the overhead incurred by SCore-D gang scheduling is not small, we believe that it is acceptable. We have already confirmed that users can run interactive parallel programs on SCore-D[HTI97b].

Currently SCore-D is running on SunOS, NetBSD and LINUX. Our cluster software system including SCore-D, MPC++, PM, and MPI with PM is available at `http://www.rwcp.or.jp/lab/pdslab/dist/`.

References

[ADV+94]   Remzi H. Arpaci, Andrea C. Dusseau, Amin M. Vahdat, Lok T. Liu, Thomas E. Anderson, and David A. Patterson. The Interaction of Parallel and Sequential Workloads on a Network of Workstations. UC Berkeley Technical Report CS-94-838, Computer Science Division, University of California, Berkeley, 1994.

[BBLS93]   D. H. Bailey, J. T. Barton, T. A. Lasinski, and H. D. Simon. The NAS Parallel Benchmarks. NASA Technical Memorandum 103863, NASA Ames Research Center, 1993.

[BCF+95]   Nanette J. Boden, Danny Cohen, Robert E. Felderman, Alan E. Kulawik, Charles L. Seitz, Jakov N. Seizovic, and Wen-King Su. Myrinet: A Gigabit-per-Second Local Area Network. *IEEE Micro*, 15(1):29–36, February 1995.

[CL85]   Mani Chandy and Leslie Lamport. Distributed snapshot: Determining global states of distributed systems. *ACM Transactions on Computer Systems*, 3(1):63–75, February 1985.

[CMC97]   Brent N. Chun, Alan M. Mainwaring, and David E. Culler. Virtual Network Transport Protocols for Myrinet. In *Hot Interconnect'97*, August 1997.

[FPR96]   Hubertus Franke, Pratap Pattnaik, and Larry Rudolph. Gang Scheduling for Highly Efficient Distributed Multiprocessor Systems. In *Frontier'96*, pages 1–9, October 1996.

[FR92]   Dror G. Feitelson and Larry Rudolph. Gang Scheduling Performance Benefits for Fine-Grain Synchronization. *Journal of Parallel and Distributed Computing*, 16(4):306–318, 1992.

[GTU91]   A. Gupta, A. Tucker, and Shigeru Urushibara. The Impact of Operating System Scheduling Policies and Synchronization Methods on the Performance of Parallel Applications. In *ACM SIGMETRICS*, pages 120–132, 1991.

[GW95]   Brent Gorda and Rich Wolski. Time Sharing Massively Parallel Machines. In *1995 International Conference on Parallel Processing*, volume II, pages 214–217, August 1995.

[HIK+95]   Atsushi Hori, Yutaka Ishikawa, Hiroki Konaka, Munenori Maeda, and Takashi Tomokiyo. A Scalable Time-Sharing Scheduling for Partitionable, Distributed Memory Parallel Machines. In *Proceedings of the Twenty-Eighth Annual Hawaii International Conference on System Sciences, Vol. II*, pages 173–182. IEEE Computer Society Press, January 1995.

[HIN+95]   Atsushi Hori, Yutaka Ishikawa, Jörg Nolte, Hiroki Konaka, Munenori Maeda, and Takashi Tomokiyo. Time Space Sharing Scheduling: A Simulation Analysis. In S. Haridi, K. Ali, and P. Magnusson, editors, *Euro-Par'95 Parallel Processing*, volume 966 of *Lecture Notes in Computer Science*, pages 623–634. Springer-Verlag, August 1995.

[HTI+96]   Atsushi Hori, Hiroshi Tezuka, Yutaka Ishikawa, Noriyuki Soda, Hiroki Konaka, and Munenori Maeda. Implementation of Gang-Scheduling on Workstation Cluster. In D. G. Feitelson and L. Rudolph, editors, *IPPS'96 Workshop on Job Scheduling Strategies for Parallel Processing*, volume 1162 of

Lecture Notes in Computer Science, pages 76–83. Springer-Verlag, April 1996.

[HTI97a]   Atsushi Hori, Hiroshi Tezuka, and Yutaka Ishikawa. Global State Detection using Network Preemption. In D. G. Feitelson and L. Rudolph, editors, *IPPS'97 Workshop on Job Scheduling Strategies for Parallel Processing*, volume 1291 of *Lecture Notes in Computer Science*, pages 262–276. Springer-Verlag, April 1997.

[HTI97b]   Atsushi Hori, Hiroshi Tezuka, and Yutaka Ishikawa. User-level Parallel Operating System for Clustered Commodity Computers. In *Proceedings of Cluster Computing Conference '97*, March 1997.

[Ish96]   Yutaka Ishikawa. Multi Thread Template Library – MPC++ Version 2.0 Level 0 Document –. Technical Report TR–96012, RWC, September 1996.

[KMY94]   Tomio Kamada, Satoshi Matsuoka, and Akinori Yonezawa. Efficient Parallel Global Garbage Collection on Massively Parallel Computers. In *Supercomputing Conference*, pages 79–88, 1994.

[LG97]   Richard N. Lagerstrom and Stephan K. Gipp. PScheD Political Scheduling on the CRAY T3E. In D. G. Feitelson and L. Rudolph, editors, *Job Scheduling Strategies for Parallel Processing*, volume 1291 of *Lecture Notes in Computer Science*, pages 117–138. Springer-Verlag, April 1997.

[Mis83]   J. Misra. Detecting termination of distributed computations using markers. In *Second ACM Symposium on Principles Distributed Computing*, pages 290–294, August 1983.

[OHT+97]   Francis O'Carroll, Atsushi Hori, Hiroshi Tezuka, Yutaka Ishikawa, and Mitsuhisa Sato. Performance of MPI on Workstation/PC Clusters using Myrinet. In *Proceedings of Cluster Computing Conference '97*, March 1997.

[OSS80]   John K. Ousterhout, Donald A. Scelza, and Pradeep S. Sindhu. Medusa: An Experiment in Distributed Operating System Structure. *Communications of the ACM*, 23(2):92–105, February 1980.

[Ous82]   John K. Ousterhout. Scheduling Techniques for Concurrent Systems. In *Proceedings of Third International Conference on Distributed Computing Systems*, pages 22–30, 1982.

[PLC95]   Scott Pakin, Mario Lauria, and Andrew Chien. High Performance Messaging on Workstations: Illinoi Fast Messages (FM) for Myrinet. In *Supercomputing'95*, December 1995.

[Thi92]   Thinking Machines Corporation. *NI Systems Programming*, October 1992. Version 7.1.

[THIS97]   Hiroshi Tezuka, Atsushi Hori, Yutaka Ishikawa, and Mitsuhisa Sato. PM: An Operating System Coordinated High Performance Communication Library. In Peter Sloot Bob Hertzberger, editor, *High-Performance Computing and Networking*, volume 1225 of *Lecture Notes in Computer Science*, pages 708–717. Springer-Verlag, April 1997.

[vEBV95]   Thorston von Eicken, Anindya Basu, and Werner Vogels. U-Net: A User Level Network Interface for Parallel and Distributed Computing. In *Fifteenth ACM Sumposium on Operating Systems Principles*, pages 40–53, 1995.

[ZRB+93]   Roman Zajcew, Paul Roy, David Black, Chris Peak, Paulo Guedes, Bradford Kemp, John Lo Verso, Michael Leibensperger, Michael Branett, Faramarz Rabii, and Durriya Netterwala. An OSF/1 UNIX for Massively Parallel Multicomputers. In *San Diego Conference Proceedings of 1993 Winter USENIX*, pages 449–468, January 1993.

Dynamic Coscheduling on Workstation Clusters

Patrick G. Sobalvarro[1], Scott Pakin[2], William E. Weihl[1], and
Andrew A. Chien[2]

[1] Digital Systems Research Center
130 Lytton Avenue, Palo Alto, CA 94301 U.S.A.
{pgs, weihl}@pa.dec.com
http://www.research.digital.com/SRC/staff/{pgs, weihl}/bio.html
[2] Digital Computer Laboratory
University of Illinois at Urbana-Champaign
1304 W. Springfield Avenue
Urbana, IL 61801 U.S.A.
{pakin, achien}@cs.uiuc.edu
http://www-csag.cs.uiuc.edu/individual/{pakin, achien}

Abstract. Coscheduling has been shown to be a critical factor in achieving efficient parallel execution in timeshared environments [12, 19, 4]. However, the most common approach, gang scheduling, has limitations in scaling, can compromise good interactive response, and requires that communicating processes be identified in advance.
We explore a technique called *dynamic coscheduling* (DCS) which produces emergent coscheduling of the processes constituting a parallel job. Experiments are performed in a workstation environment with high performance networks and autonomous timesharing schedulers for each CPU. The results demonstrate that DCS can achieve effective, robust coscheduling for a range of workloads and background loads. Empirical comparisons to *implicit scheduling* and uncoordinated scheduling are presented. Under spin-block synchronization, DCS reduces job response times by up to 20% over implicit scheduling while maintaining fairness; and under spinning synchronization, DCS reduces job response times by up to two decimal orders of magnitude over uncoordinated scheduling. The results suggest that DCS is a promising avenue for achieving coordinated parallel scheduling in an environment that coexists with autonomous node schedulers.

1 Introduction

Coordinated scheduling of parallel jobs across the nodes of a multiprocessor is well-known to produce benefits in both system and individual job efficiency [12, 18, 4, 5, 17, 3]. Without coordinated scheduling, the processes constituting a parallel job suffer high communication latencies because of *processor thrashing* [12]. While multiprocessor systems typically address these problems with a mix of batch, gang, and timesharing scheduling (based on kernel scheduler changes), the problem is more difficult for shared workstation clusters in which stock operating systems kernels must be run.

Dror G. Feitelson, Larry Rudolph (Eds.): JSSPP'98, LNCS 1459, pp. 231–256, 1998.

With clusters connected by high performance networks that achieve latencies in the range of tens of microseconds [13, 20, 21, 9, 7], scheduling and context switching latency can increase communication latency by several orders of magnitude. For example, under Solaris, CPU quanta vary from 20 ms to 200 ms [10]; consequently uncoordinated scheduling can increase best-case latencies ($\sim$ 10 microseconds) by three to four orders of magnitude, nullifying many benefits of fast communication subsystems. Uncoordinated scheduling can also decrease the efficiency of resource utilization. Coordinated scheduling reduces communication latencies and increases system efficiency by reducing spin-waiting periods and context switches.

Coscheduling for clusters is a challenging problem because it must reconcile the demands of parallel and local computations, balancing parallel efficiency against local interactive response. Ideally a coscheduling system would provide the efficiency of a batch-scheduled system for parallel jobs and a private timesharing system for interactive users. In reality, the situation is much more complex, as we expect some parallel jobs to be interactive. Furthermore, in a cluster environment, there are advantages to be had in using existing commercial operating systems, so we restrict ourselves here to approaches that involve augmentation of existing operating system infrastructure.

The approach to coordinated scheduling that we use is a form of demand-based coscheduling called dynamic coscheduling (DCS) [17, 16], which achieves coordination by observing the communication between threads. This is a bottom-up, emergent scheduling approach that exploits the key observation that only those threads which are communicating need be coscheduled. This approach can achieve coscheduling without changes to the operating system scheduler or applications programs.

Our implementation of dynamic coscheduling is based on the Illinois Fast Messages communication layer which delivers low latency and high bandwidth user-space to user-space communication [13, 14]. We augmented this system with blocking communication primitives, and implemented dynamic coscheduling with changes to a device driver, network interface card firmware, and the communication library. The device driver influences the operating system scheduler's decisions through kernel interfaces, based on the communication traffic it observes on the network interface card.

Experiments using a variety of workloads (with different synchronization characteristics) and competing background loads are used to compare dynamic coscheduling against the unmodified Solaris 2.4 scheduler with spinning and spin-block synchronization. These results indicate that dynamic coscheduling, spin-block, and the combination of dynamic coscheduling with spin-block synchronization can effectively achieve coscheduling. The effectiveness of spin-block has been previously documented in [3] (where it was called *implicit scheduling*), and our measurements confirm their results. In addition, our work demonstrates that DCS achieves coscheduling with both spinning and spin-block synchronization, where implicit scheduling requires processes to block awaiting message arrivals for coscheduling to happen. Interestingly, coscheduling based on spin-block alone does not obtain a fair share of the CPU for parallel jobs, requiring a process to have blocked before communication can be treated as a demand for coscheduling. DCS can potentially treat all message arrivals as a demand for coscheduling, and obtains a fair share of CPU time.

The successful coscheduling approaches accrue benefits of higher system throughput and lower response time for jobs. However, one must be chary of drawing broad conclusions based on a modest set of experiments. The dynamics of schedulers and workloads are complex, and we have only begun to understand the benefits and limitations of demand-based coscheduling approaches. Important limitations of our study include use of only a single parallel job[1] and a modest sized cluster[2]. Both of these limitations are being remedied in future studies.

However, parallel jobs are only one possible application of DCS — we believe that DCS-like approaches can be used to implement coordinated resource management in a much broader range of cases, including:

- real-time and proportional-share processor scheduling
- multimedia and other quality-of-service-sensitive applications
- coordinated access to input/output devices
- coordinated memory management
- efficient parallel computing with demand-paged virtual memory

Most of these areas are still to be explored, and a discussion of specific approaches to them is beyond the scope of this paper. For the remainder of this paper we confine ourselves to a focus on achieving low latency, fairness, and efficiency for tightly-coupled parallel jobs. We found that DCS performs quite well in these cases. Our results show that under spin-block synchronization, DCS reduces job response times by up to 20% over implicit scheduling while maintaining fairness. Under spinning synchronization, DCS reduces job response times by up to two decimal orders of magnitude over uncoordinated scheduling with only a slight reduction in fairness.

The remainder of the paper is organized as follows. Section 2 summarizes the relevant related work. Section 3 describes the idea behind dynamic coscheduling briefly and our prototype implementation. Section 4 outlines our experiments and empirical results which provide evidence for the viability of dynamic coscheduling. A discussion of the results and their implications as well as limitations of our experiments are discussed in Section 5, along with some promising directions for future work. Finally, Section 6 briefly summarizes our results.

2   Related Work

There has been a wide variety of work on coscheduling, beginning with Ousterhout's seminal paper [12] which identified the need. The larger challenge can

---

[1] A limitation of our FM infrastructure.
[2] A limitation of our computing infrastructure.

be logically divided into three subproblems: detecting threads needing to be coscheduled, providing mechanisms for achieving coscheduling, and assessing the performance impact.

2.1   Performance Impact of Coscheduling

A variety of efforts on shared-memory machines have demonstrated and characterized the benefits of coscheduling for threads in a parallel job. Ousterhout provided a basic framework and presents a number of ways to achieve coscheduling while optimizing for system utilization [12]. Later work on the DASH multiprocessor [8, 2] demonstrated that coscheduling could be used to achieve efficiencies comparable to batch scheduling, while providing more flexible resource sharing. Specifically, coscheduling and process control (dynamic space-partitioning) performed similarly in the experiments described in [2].

2.2   Detecting Threads Requiring Coscheduling

Coscheduling implies coordinated scheduling of clusters of threads; identification of such clusters has been pursued through both explicit and implicit approaches. The shared memory workloads described in [8, 2] are parallel jobs which consist of thread collections, explicitly indicating which threads should be coscheduled. A variety of implicit schemes which do not require explicit programmer annotation have been explored. On distributed memory systems, the need for coscheduling has typically been associated with communication [17, 6, 3, 16]. Feitelson's Runtime Activity Working Set Identification (RAWSI) monitors the communication between processes or threads[3] to determine their rate of communication. Working sets of processes (which require coscheduling) are identified based on their rate of communication. RAWSI collects the information and uses a coordinated global mechanism to decide on a schedule. Both our dynamic coscheduling approach [17] and implicit scheduling [3] detect threads requiring coscheduling through their communication. However, neither system explicitly identifies the sets of processes to be coscheduled.

2.3   Mechanisms for Achieving Coscheduling

Once thread clusters have been identified, a mechanism for coscheduling must be used. In many systems, particularly those with shared memory, a gang scheduler which has the capability to achieve coordinated context switches across processors has been assumed [8, 12, 4, 6]. Such systems replace the basic process scheduler in the operating system, and schedule the related threads across the processing nodes. These schedulers can achieve high system efficiency on regular parallel applications, but have difficulty in selecting alternate jobs to run when processes block, require simultaneous multi-context switches across the nodes of the processor (which causes difficulty in scaling), and for good performance require long scheduling quanta which can interfere with interactive response, making them a less attractive choice for use in a cluster of commodity workstations. It is largely these limitations which motivate the integrated approaches.

---

[3] Feitelson's system actually addresses both distributed and shared memory systems.

2.4   Integrated Scheduling Techniques

The requirement of centralized control and the poor timesharing response of other scheduling approaches have motivated new, integrated coscheduling approaches. Such approaches extend local timesharing schedulers, preserving their interactive response and autonomy. Further, such systems have typically not explicitly identified sets of processes to be coscheduled, but rather integrate the detection of a coscheduling requirement with actions to produce effective coscheduling. An earlier paper on *dynamic coscheduling* [17] detailed analysis and simulation of an integrated coscheduling technique. Subsequently, Dusseau's *implicit scheduling* was evaluated via simulation in [3], using synthetic single-program, multiple data applications. Because dynamic coscheduling is discussed extensively in the remainder of the paper, we only describe implicit scheduling here.

Implicit scheduling uses spin-block synchronization primitives and the priority boost given by the SVR4 scheduler to threads which block on input/output to produce coscheduling. Because threads awakened when the communication completes obtain a high priority, they are likely to run when their communication peer has just sent a message (and is therefore running). To further improve performance, implicit scheduling can also modify the spin times in spin-block synchronization, adapting to developed skew between threads in a coschedule. Implicit scheduling has been demonstrated in simulations to achieve good performance on a variety of "bulk-synchronous" applications (those which perform regular barriers, possibly with other communication taking place in between barriers), specifically a synthetic workload of SPMD programs. It remains an open question whether good performance can be achieved for more varied communication, computation, and synchronization structures, as well as in actual operating environments (with attendant daemons, scheduling idiosyncrasies, and other system activity). However, it is our understanding that efforts to explore these issues are currently underway.

In contrast, our dynamic coscheduling achieves coscheduling by explicitly treating all message arrivals (not just those directed to blocked processes) as a demand for coscheduling, and explicitly schedules the destination processes when it would be fair to do so through the explicit control of scheduler priorities. While this appears quite similar to implicit scheduling for the particular case of bulk synchronous jobs using spin-block synchronization, we believe dynamic coscheduling can be used to achieve coordinated scheduling in a broader range of cases.

3   Dynamic Coscheduling

3.1   Overview

Demand-based coscheduling [17, 16] exploits communication between processes to deduce which processes should be coscheduled and to effect coscheduling. It is effective because of the key observation: the communicating (or synchronizing) processes are the ones that need be coscheduled. Thus, demand-based coscheduling produces emergent coscheduling without requiring explicit identification by programmer of the computations that need be coscheduled.

Dynamic coscheduling [17] is a type of demand-based coscheduling in which scheduling decisions are driven directly by message arrivals. If an arriving message is directed to a process that isn't running, a scheduling decision is made. This decision can be based on a wide variety of factors (e.g., system load, last time run, etc.), and is generally designed to maximize coscheduling performance while ensuring fairness of CPU allocation. Previously published modeling and simulation results [17] indicate that dynamic coscheduling produces robust coscheduling. Thus, the key elements of dynamic coscheduling are:

1. Monitoring communication/thread activity
2. Causing scheduling decisions
3. Making a decision whether to preempt

The latter two points are intimately tied to how the operating system operates. Causing scheduling decisions depends on the preemption capabilities and times context switches can occur. The decision procedure in particular can depend on fairness, and coscheduling stability concerns. The elements of DCS can be implemented in a host of different ways, and our experimental approach is described below. The details of any such implementation embody only a specific instance of a dynamic coscheduling.

3.2   Implementation Context

Fast Messages and Myrinet Our dynamic coscheduling prototype is implemented under Illinois Fast Messages (FM), a user-level messaging layer developed at the University of Illinois at Urbana-Champaign [15]. Fast Messages is a high-performance messaging layer that bypasses the operating system to provide direct access to an underlying Myricom Myrinet [1] and thereby achieve high performance. Details of FM can be found in [13, 15]. We also employ an implementation of the Message Passing Interface (MPI) built atop FM, called MPI-FM [11], for some of the benchmarks.

Implementing Spin-Block in Fast Messages Fast Messages was enhanced with a spin-block mechanism to support our experimentation. Adding a spin-block communication primitive required changes to the FM firmware, the network device driver, and the FM libraries. The firmware was modified to add an interrupt generation to wake a sleeping process upon message arrival. The device driver was modified to add a call that puts the caller to sleep, waiting for a message. Finally, the FM libraries were modified to integrate these changes.

We chose our maximum spin time of 1600 μsec based on the empirical evidence of experiments described in [16], in which the maximum delay we saw for response in the case where a context switch was required was approximately 1500 μsec. 1600 μsec is also slightly greater than twice the mean context-switch time plus the message round-trip time. It is noted in [12] that a two-context-switch maximum spin time is competitive, and in [3] it is argued that two context-switch times might be required for a processor to respond to a message if the message arrives at the beginning of a context switch to a process that is not the one to which the message is directed.

Experimental Platform Our experimental platform consists of seven SPARC-station-2's connected by a Myrinet. The SPARCstation-2's have 40 MHz processors, 16 MB of main memory, and run the Solaris 2.4 operating system. The Myrinet provides high-bandwidth communication (up to 80 MB/sec) and is coupled to Lanai Version 2.3 interface boards (20 MHz Lanai's which matched the SBUS clock speed).

Despite the obsolete workstations, Illinois Fast Messages Version 2.0 achieves user-space to user-space latencies of 40 μsec with 128-byte messages, and bandwidths of 13 MB/sec.[4] FM maps the Myrinet interface board memory and control registers into both kernel and user space, allowing direct user access to the network for high performance. The mapping into kernel space enables convenient initialization and control of the device in response to system calls by the kernel.

Sunsoft Solaris Version 2.4 The dynamic coscheduling prototype runs under the Solaris 2.4 operating system. Two aspects of the implementation are specific to Solaris 2.4 (or this family of operating system): the mechanism for implementing scheduling decisions, and the fairness mechanism. Both of these are affected by the priority-decay algorithm of the scheduler.

Solaris 2.4's dispatcher for timeshared and interactive jobs is a table-driven Unix priority-decay scheduler. The scheduler uses 60 queues for user processes; these are numbered 0 through 59. The priority of a given queue is its number; the higher the number, the higher the priority. The scheduler schedules the job at the head of the highest-priority queue that is occupied. Timeslice expiration leads to demotion to a lower-priority queue; preemption without timeslice expiration causes the job to be placed at the end of the queue. Once per second, a routine called `ts_update` increases the priorities of processes that are on run queues, but not running. The routine also sets a flag (`dispwait`) on processes that are on sleep queues; if the flag is set when the process returns to a run queue, it experiences a substantial priority boost, to the value called `ts_slpret`, as shown in Table 1. Some of the effects of this priority boost will be described in Section 5.

3.3 DCS Prototype

We describe our prototype by relating each of the high level elements of dynamic coscheduling to its implementation. This not only provides a clear perspective

---

[4] Note that recent performance numbers for Illinois Fast Messages Version 2.01 with more modern Myricom hardware and more modern Sun workstations are ≈ 11 μsec and 56.3 megabytes/second.

	Prio.	Quantum (ms)	ts_slpret
lowest priority	0– 9	200	50
	10–19	160	51
	20–29	120	52
	30–34	80	53
	35–39	80	54
	40–44	40	55
	45–49	40	56
	50–54	40	57
	55–58	40	58
highest priority	59	20	59

Table 1. Default Solaris 2.4 dispatch table

on the rather myriad low-level details required for work of this type, but it also clearly illuminates the approximations and compromises in the prototype. A simple illustration of the DCS implemenation is shown in Figure 1. Our description of the implementation is necessarily brief; further detail can be found in [16].

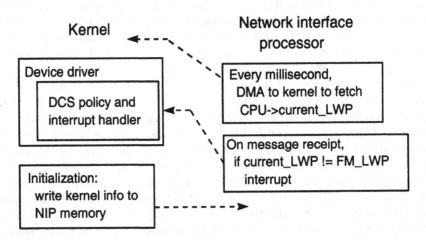

Fig. 1. Simplified DCS implementation schematic (spin-block implementation not shown).

Monitoring Communication/Thread Activity Communication and thread monitoring is performed on the network interface card. Myricom's network interface card provides a programmable processor, running the Fast Messages firmware. We modified the FM firmware to monitor the ongoing communication and thread activity. Monitoring communication is simple; the firmware is essentially a dispatch loop for each communication. The FM firmware monitors thread activity by periodically reading the host's kernel memory the address of the currently running lightweight process (LWP). Because this operation is achieved with DMA, and must cross an I/O bus bridge, is costs tens of microseconds. Thus, the firmware reads the value only once per millisecond, and hence the firmware has only an approximation of the currently running thread. However, because the scheduling quanta are 20 milliseconds or larger, this approximation is sufficient. The mechanisms used for dealing with cases where the information is inaccurate are described in [16].

Causing Scheduling Decisions Scheduling decisions are effected by a device driver for the Myrinet network interface card (NIC). This driver is invoked by interrupts from the NIC, if the message received is not for the LWP currently running. FM messages are sent to LWP's, not to individual threads within an LWP. So, in the device driver, all of the threads within the receiving process have their priority boosted as shown in Figure 2. Note that all of our benchmarks have only a single thread within the process, so this approximation is not a concern in our tests.

```
if (running_LWP != FM_LWP) {
  if (fair to preempt) {
    for each kernel thread belonging to FM_LWP {
      raise priority to maximum for user mode;
    }
    preempt currently running thread;
  }
}
```

Fig. 2. DCS scheduling decisions are affected in the device driver interrupt handler.

If the interrupt routine in the device driver finds that it would be fair to preempt the currently running process, each thread belonging to the LWP for the parallel process has its priority raised to the maximum allowable priority for user-mode timesharing processes[5] and is placed at the front of the dispatcher queue. Flags are set to ensure that the Solaris 2.4 scheduler runs on exit from the interrupt routine, causing a scheduling decision based on the new priorities. This will cause the process receiving the message to be scheduled unless the process that was running had a higher priority than the maximum allowable priority for user mode.

---

[5] With the default Solaris 2.4 dispatcher table, this is 59.

Making a Decision Whether to Preempt In dynamic coscheduling, an incoming message's process is scheduled only if doing so would not cause unfair CPU allocation. The equalization mechanism described in [17] used detailed CPU time numbers. At the time we designed our implementation, we chose to implement fairness by limiting the frequency of priority boosts.[6] Our fairness criterion is the following inequality:

$$2^E(T_c - T_p) + C \geq T_q R \tag{1}$$

where E, T_c, T_p, C, T_q, and R are defined as:

$$E = \text{Exponent}$$
$$T_c = \text{Current time}$$
$$T_p = \text{Time of previous priority boost and preemption attempt}$$
$$C = \text{Constant, in milliseconds}$$
$$T_q = \text{Length of minimum time quantum (20 msec)}$$
$$R = \text{Number of jobs in the run queue}$$

Our approach limits the frequency of the preemptions for each cycle the scheduler makes through the run queue, assuming that all jobs on the run queue are running at the highest priority. E and C are chosen empirically for individual experiments. $R \times T_q$ is the "length of the run queue in time" if the jobs on the run queue each run for an entire minimum-length timeslice (T_q). $T_c - T_p$ is the time since the last preemption. For example, a value of -1 for E would enable a preemption (priority boost) only if the time since the last preemption were at least twice the length of the run queue in time.

4 Empirical Studies

In this section, we present the results of experiments with our FM-DCS system. These experiments include a range of parallel kernels and competitive workloads. First, we describe the performance metrics, workload, and scheduling variants used. Subsequently, we describe the experimental results and give analysis.

4.1 Experimental Parameters and Metrics

Performance Metrics We chose three performance metrics which capture the scheduler's effectiveness in providing both good response times and high system efficiency.

---

[6] Only later did we learn that a direct implementation based on CPU usage information was possible. This a subject of future work.

- **Job Response Time** is the wall-clock time from job initation to completion.
- **CPU Time** is the sum of system and user CPU time for the job. In all experiments, the system time was less than 5%, so this basically captures user CPU time.
- **Fairness** is the degree to which threads are allocated equal shares of processor time. We normalize CPU share to the ideal equal share and define a fairness fraction F. An ideal fairness fraction is unity.

$$F = N\frac{T_C}{T_E} \tag{2}$$

Where T_C is the CPU time consumed by a process over its lifetime, T_E is its job response time, and N is the number of processes running on the machine.

In all graphs, the mean of several runs is shown along with 90% confidence intervals computed using Student's T-distribution. In many cases, the confidence intervals are too small to be seen on the graph.

Workload We used three distinct workloads in our experiments. These workloads consist of parallel kernels, run in competition with sequential jobs that compete for the CPU. The choice of a single parallel job is dictated by FM's current limitation to a single parallel job. The sequential competitors for the first two workloads are processes that execute a simple spin loop and run for the duration of the test; for the third workload they are real applications, as described below. The parallel kernels are designed to exercise different aspects of performance:

- **Latency** is a simple token-passing benchmark in which two nodes repeatedly exchange a 128-byte packet. Each node records the elapsed wall-clock time for each round trip, including the sending and receiving of the packet. System calls for timing add approximately three microseconds to each round trip.
- **Barrier** performs a sequence of barriers, interspersing local computation between the barriers. It provides a pattern of communication and synchronization different from the latency benchmark's. The root node initially broadcasts a "passed barrier" message to all nodes, then all nodes enter a spin loop (local computation). After the local computation is complete, each node sends an "at barrier" message to the root node. When the root node has received "at barrier" messages from all nodes, the loop begins anew.
- **Mixed Workload** consists of three programs in competition on the cluster. The parallel job is a SOR kernel, a two-dimensional Laplace's equation solver on a 128 × 128 element matrix (written in FORTRAN on an FM-based implementation of MPI [11]). The sequential jobs are GNU tar, archiving and compressing a collection of 97 files, totalling 2.1 MB, and Ghostscript, a PostScript interpreter on a 1.7 MB, 103-page PostScript file. All files were read from a remote NFS filesystem.

Program	Command line
SOR	`sor`
GNU tar (+ GNU zip)	`gtar -czhvf /dev/null` `/usr/local/Gnu/lib/gnuemacs/etc`
Ghostscript	`gs -q -dNODISPLAY -dNOPAUSE` `inputfiles/pakin-ms.ps inputfiles/quit.ps`

Table 2. Applications and arguments used for the Mixed Workload

Scheduling Variants The scheduling types used vary both the synchronization method (blocking or spinning) and whether demand-based coscheduling is included.

- ⟨**No DCS, spin only**⟩ The base Solaris 2.4 scheduler and FM using spin-based polling for incoming messages.
- ⟨**No DCS, spin-block**⟩ The base Solaris 2.4 scheduler and FM using spin-block synchronization, blocking after 1600 microseconds of spinning.
- ⟨**DCS, spin only**⟩ The Solaris 2.4 scheduler augmented with demand-based coscheduling, using spinning synchronization (without blocking). The relevant parameters are E, the exponent for the run queue length factor, and C, the offset constant.
- ⟨**DCS, spin-block**⟩ The Solaris 2.4 scheduler augmented with demand-based coscheduling, using spin-block synchronization, blocking after 1600 microseconds of spinning. The relevant parameters are E, the exponent for the run queue length factor, and C, the offset constant.

4.2 Experimental Results

To begin, we present results from our Latency and Barrier benchmarks. These kernels illuminate the behavior of DCS and the underlying Solaris 2.4 scheduler using different synchronization approaches — spinning and spin-block. Subsequently, we consider performance on the the Mixed Workload benchmark.

Latency and Barrier Benchmarks

Job Response Time. The response times for the Latency and Barrier benchmarks for a range of coscheduling approaches are shown in Figures 3, 4, 5, and 6. Note that the vertical scale in the job response time graphs is logarithmic, to accomodate the extremely long times for uncoordinated scheduling. To see the differences on a linear scale for just ⟨DCS, spin-block⟩ and ⟨No DCS, spin-block⟩, see Figures 7 and 8.

For each graph, the number of sequential competitor jobs per node varies along the X-axis and the wall-clock time to complete the benchmark varies along the Y-axis. For each number of competitors, wall-clock times for four different

scheduling approaches are presented. As mentioned above, the sequential competitors run for the duration of the test; the test ends when when the parallel
job terminates.

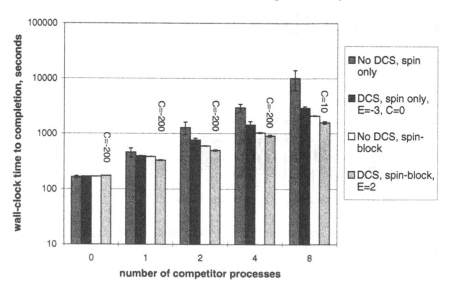

Fig. 3. Wall-clock time (job response time) in the latency benchmark for a variety of schedulers and numbers of competitors. Note the log scale; differences
are larger than they appear — see Figure 7 for fine details.

In the presence of competition, the ⟨No DCS, spin only⟩ configuration performs poorly, and especially so for the Barrier benchmark. However, either changing to spin-block or adding DCS improved the effective coscheduling for both
benchmarks. For the Latency benchmark, spin-block both with and without DCS
are clearly more effective than ⟨DCS, spin only⟩, whereas for the Barrier benchmark, ⟨No DCS, spin-block⟩ and ⟨DCS, spin only⟩ have job response times that
are quite close to each other, although ⟨DCS, spin only⟩ is slower. In all cases,
the policy ⟨DCS, spin-block⟩ produces the best coscheduling performance for
these benchmarks.

Fairness. Figures 9 and 10 contain fairness data for the Latency and Barrier
benchmarks. In each graph, the number of competitors varies along the X-axis,
and the fairness metric of Equation 2 is given on the Y-axis. As before, for each
number of competitors, data for several scheduling approaches are shown.

The fairness metric clearly distinguishes the different approaches to coscheduling. For the Latency benchmark, the base Solaris 2.4 scheduler delivers slightly

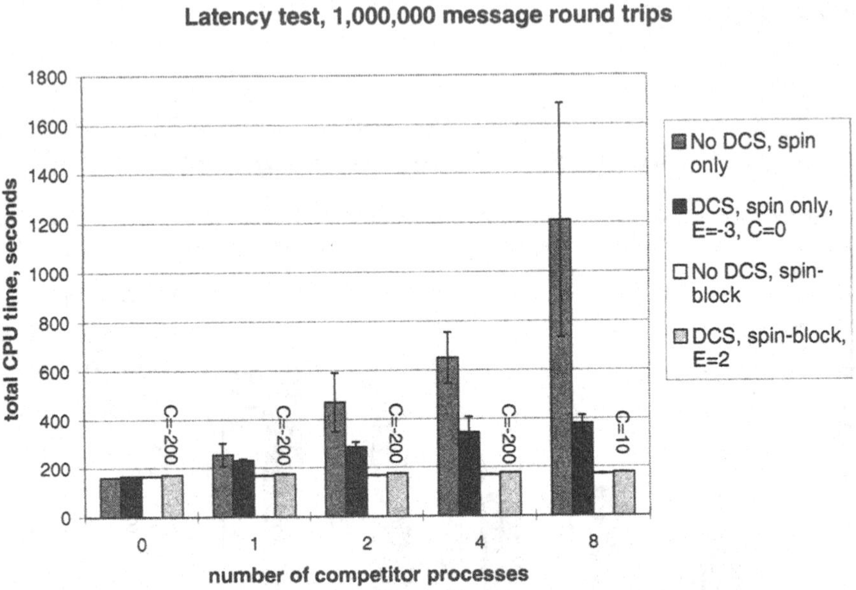

Latency test, 1,000,000 message round trips

Fig. 4. CPU time in the latency benchmark for a variety of schedulers and numbers of competitors.

more than a fair share of CPU for the parallel job. The ⟨No DCS, spin-block⟩ approach is a weak competitor, obtaining less and less than its fair share as the number of competitors is increased. However, in all cases the DCS approaches come closer to or even surpass a fair share of CPU. Thus we can see that DCS is a stronger competitor for CPU, whereas the ⟨No DCS, spin-block⟩ approach is a weaker competitor.

Mixed Workload

Job Response Time. The job response and CPU time results for the Mixed Workload benchmark are shown in Figures 11 and 12. The top four sets of bars correspond to timesharing workloads in which all jobs are started simultaneously. The response time for each job is at its right end. Batch performance is shown as a baseline at the bottom.

For the mixed workload, all three of the schedulers employing either DCS or spin-block achieved system efficiencies and therefore job response times close to that of batch. The only scheduler which produced poor performance was the ⟨No DCS, spin only⟩ version, which fails to achieve coscheduling. Amongst the other schedulers, the combination of ⟨DCS, spin-block⟩ gives the best job response time, with ⟨No DCS, spin-block⟩ and ⟨DCS, spin only⟩ not far behind.

Barrier test, 100,000 barriers, 1,000 delay iterations

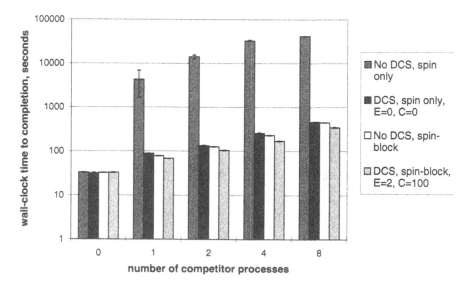

Fig. 5. Barrier Benchmark wall-clock times (job response times) under a variety of schedulers and numbers of competitors. Uniform $1,000$ delay iterations (78 μsec) used on all nodes. Note the log scale used in the job response time graphs; differences are larger than they appear — see Figure 8 for fine details.

The CPU time data (in Figure 12) clearly capture the benefits of coscheduling on parallel job efficiency. While the CPU times for the sequential jobs are fairly consistent over the four schedulers, the CPU time for the parallel job, SOR, varies widely. In the absence of coscheduling, it is nearly four times larger than in the batch case. The ⟨DCS, spin only⟩ scheduler is able to reduce this CPU time significantly, by achieving coscheduling, however the spinning synchronization still increases CPU time by nearly one half. Adding spin-block effectively eliminates the CPU time increase with the ⟨DCS, spin-block⟩ case giving best performance.

Fairness. Because jobs in the Mixed Workload test have different lifetimes, fairness is measured over the period until the first job to terminate does so; this is a shorter period than in the Barrier and Latency tests, where all processes run equally long and fairness is measured over the entire experiment. The results are shown in Figure 13. As with our Latency and Barrier benchmarks, several key characteristics are clear: the base Solaris scheduler (⟨No DCS, spin only⟩) is unfair, the ⟨DCS, spin only⟩ scheduler is least fair, the ⟨DCS, spin-block⟩ scheduler is able to use its fair CPU share, however, the ⟨No DCS, spin-block⟩ scheduler does not.

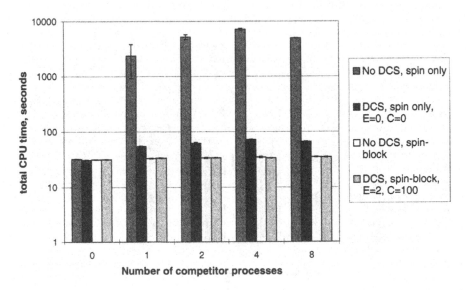

Fig. 6. Barrier Benchmark CPU times under a variety of schedulers and numbers of competitors.

4.3 Analysis

We sought in our experiments to answer the following questions:

– Can dynamic coscheduling achieve coscheduling of processes in a parallel application?
– What are the effects of using spinning synchronization versus those of using spin-block synchronization?
– What are the effects on fairness, efficiency, and response time of using DCS?

In all three workloads, DCS clearly coscheduled the parallel applications. This can be seen from both the reduced job response times and the fact that fairness could be achieved even under spin-block synchronization. More detailed evidence, in the form of histograms of message round-trip times, is presented in [16]. The unmodified Solaris 2.4 scheduler also achieved some coscheduling under spin-block synchronization, as is discussed at greater length in Section 5. However, the unmodified Solaris 2.4 scheduler (⟨No DCS, spin only⟩) failed to achieve coscheduling under spinning synchronization, as indicated by increased CPU and response times.

Under spinning synchronization, DCS significantly reduced both CPU and job response time. However, to achieve better coscheduling, it was necessary

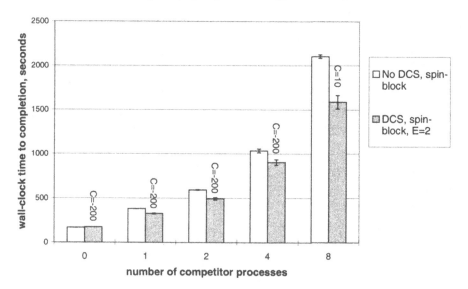

Fig. 7. Latency Benchmark wall-clock times (job response times) shown with a linear scale for the cases ⟨DCS, spin-block⟩ and ⟨No DCS, spin-block⟩. This is the same experiment as in Figure 3, with the linear scale to show detail.

to allow DCS to use up to 30% more than its fair share of CPU time. For the ⟨DCS, spin only⟩ scheduler, there is a clear tradeoff between fairness and coscheduling. It appears necessary to elevate the priority of parallel jobs to achieve coscheduling. Even with this priority elevation, efficiency declined with increasing load for ⟨DCS, spin only⟩, but not nearly as quickly as for the base ⟨No DCS, spin only⟩ scheduler.

Under spin-block synchronization, coscheduling of a single parallel job could be achieved, and DCS allows fairness to be finely controlled to almost perfect values in most cases. Without DCS, parallel jobs obtained as much as 20% less than their fair share of CPU time. In effect, this meant that parallel jobs scheduled under ⟨DCS,spin-block⟩ in the presence of competition achieved better job response times than those scheduled under ⟨No DCS, spin only⟩.

CPU times were nearly identical for schedulers which achieved coscheduling. In the case of the latency test, DCS required slightly more CPU time than the ⟨No DCS, spin only⟩ scheduler. However, we have tracked this anomaly down an extra 5 microseconds latency being required for each message transmission, because of several extra instructions performed on message receipt under DCS in the Lanai control program's main loop [16] .[7] The effect is not apparent

---

[7] This effect would be reduced with faster network controllers.

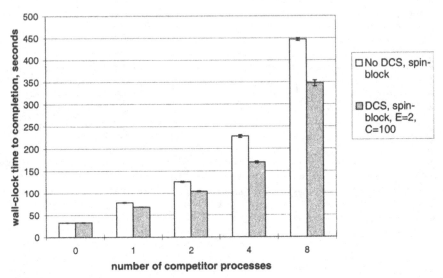

Fig. 8. Barrier Benchmark wall-clock times (job response times) shown with a linear scale for the cases ⟨DCS, spin-block⟩ and ⟨No DCS, spin-block⟩. This is the same experiment as in Figure 5, with the linear scale to show detail.

for the Barrier benchmark and Mixed Workload benchmark, because additional computation is performed which allows the overhead to be overlapped.

5   Discussion

In this section we examine the mechanisms responsible for our experimental results. We first discuss the workings of DCS and their implications; then we discuss the coscheduling effects of spin-block message receipt in schedulers that provide a priority boost on process wakeup; finally we describe directions for future work.

5.1   Mechanisms for Coscheduling with DCS

DCS achieves coscheduling for parallel processes because the arrival of a message for a process not currently running can cause it to be scheduled immediately. In programs with fine-grained communication, the sender and receiver are scheduled together and run until one of them blocks or is preempted. Larger collections of communicating processes are coscheduled by transitivity. Our experiments indicate that this basic, low-level mechanism effectively coschedules parallel processes under both spinning and spin-block synchronization.

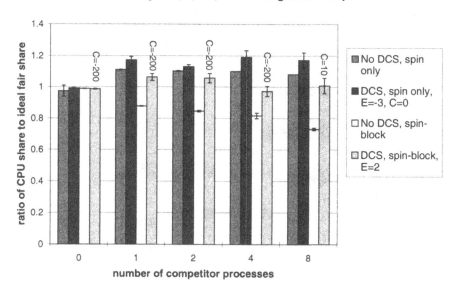

Fig. 9. Fairness metric for the Latency benchmark.

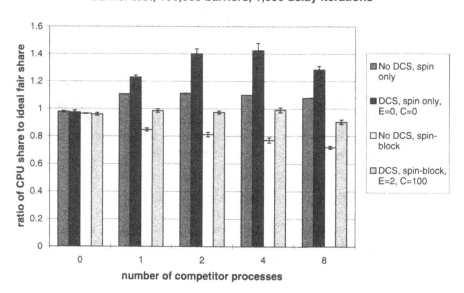

Fig. 10. Fairness metric for the Barrier benchmark.

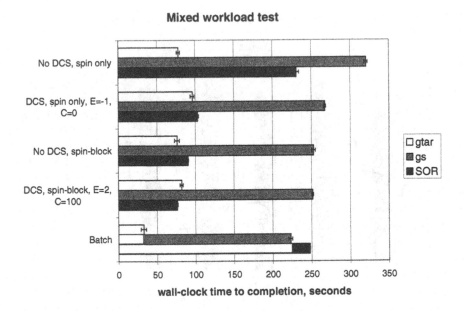

Fig. 11. Job response time in the mixed workload test. In the batch case, jobs were executed in sequence. (N.b.: axes and colors have different significance in these graphs than in the Latency and Barrier results.)

DCS enables applications with spinning synchronization to execute more efficiently and thereby achieve lower job response times when compared to the unmodified Solaris 2.4 scheduler. In effect, the coscheduling allows the use of synchronization strategies previously only viable on batch scheduled or dedicated machines. However, our experiments also show that spinning synchronization under DCS is less efficient than spin-block synchronization (further data are reported in [16]). We believe that this problem is exacerbated in Solaris 2.4 by the varying scheduling quanta used by the dispatcher (shown in Table 1), which can cause even processes that start their timeslices in synchrony to suffer long spinning phases when one ends its timeslice before others.

5.2 Coscheduling and Synchronization Mechanisms

For all three benchmarks, DCS with spin-block or spinning message receipt achieved coscheduling. The unmodified Solaris 2.4 schedule with spin-block synchronization (⟨No DCS, spin-block⟩) also achieved coscheduling, though with less success as the system load increases. Because spin-block is a weak competitor for CPU (each block yields), the parallel jobs use progressively less of their fair share of the processor with increasing load. This suggests that an

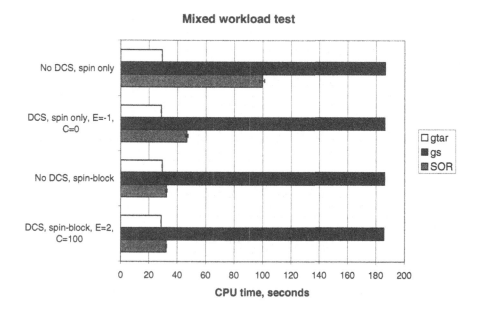

Fig. 12. CPU time in the mixed workload test.

explicit priority boosting mechanism for coscheduling may be appropriate for multitasking parallel system.

The ⟨DCS, spin-block⟩ and ⟨No DCS, spin-block⟩ schedulers were demonstrated to be most effective in achieving coscheduling efficiently (the ⟨DCS, spin-block⟩ scheduler was slightly better). We explore the surprising reasons for this in the following discussion.

Spin-block synchronization in combination with the Solaris 2.4 scheduler was reported to achieve coscheduling [3] (for a synthetic bulk-synchronous workload). The posited mechanism for this *implicit scheduling* is the following: a process spins awaiting the arrival of a message and blocks if the message does not arrive in a short period; when the message arrives, because of the priority boost described in Section 4, the process will often be scheduled immediately, resulting in coscheduling. This priority boost is a characteristic of SVR4 derived schedulers and designed to enable input/output intensive jobs to get higher priority.[8]

---

[8] Not all Unix priority-decay schedulers implement this boost in this way; for example, the OSF/1-derived Digital Unix gives a priority boost only to processes sleeping uninterruptibly in the kernel, which would exclude some ways of implementing spin-block message receipt. However, based on the results reported in [3] and our own work, it seems clear that the SVR4 approach is a very useful one for coscheduling.

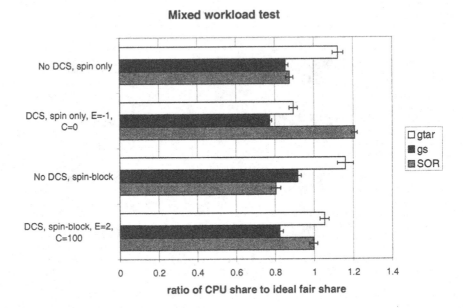

Fig. 13. Fairness in the mixed workload test. Note that fairness is shown here for competitor jobs as well.

Our experiments confirm that this priority boost is the mechanism producing coscheduling for implicit scheduling. We ran the Barrier benchmark (see Section 4.2) with an altered timesharing dispatcher table that cancels the priority boost by giving reawakened processes the same priority they had when they blocked. Specifically, in Table 1, we set the value of ts_slpret for each queue n to n. The results (see Figure 14) show that without the priority boost, no coscheduling is achieved. Job response times for spin-block are similar to those under spinning synchronization. This explains why the ⟨DCS, spin-block⟩ and ⟨No DCS, spin-block⟩ yielded such similar performance: the priority boosting performed by the Solaris 2.4 scheduler causes the processes receiving messages to be run immediately on message arrival — which is exactly how DCS works.

While the combination of the Solaris 2.4 scheduler and spin-block synchronization mimics DCS in this case, there are a wide variety of opportunities for DCS to coschedule programs with other characteristics. For example, DCS can schedule on message arrival programs that are not on sleep queues (due to polling, infrequent communication, asynchronous communication, or one-sided data movement). DCS can also be used to coschedule sets of threads, whereas the SVR4 and spin-block combination is only applicable for single thread coscheduling.

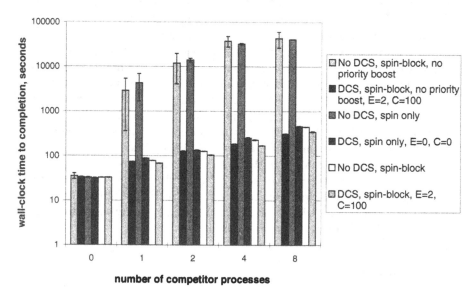

Fig. 14. Barrier test response times with the Solaris 2.4 priority boost for newly-awakened processes disabled. For comparison, times with the normal Solaris 2.4 dispatcher table are also shown.

5.3   Directions for Future Work

Experiments that vary the granularity of communication [16] indicate that spin-block message receipt paired with DCS or the unmodified Solaris 2.4 scheduler (with priority boosts on process wakeup) is less successful at coscheduling as the frequency of communication decreases. With relatively coarse-grained communication, DCS is more successful at coscheduling than the unmodified Solaris 2.4 scheduler, but no longer causes parallel processes to receive their full share of the CPU. Characterizing this sensitivity with a broader workload and exploring mechanisms to improve robustness of coscheduling (perhaps by artificially increasing communication frequency) are interesting topics for further research.

DCS with spinning synchronization is not as efficient as spin-block synchronization because processes which are not coscheduled simply spin until the end of their timeslice. Improving the efficiency of DCS with spinning synchronization is desirable, but must be achieved while maintaining fairness. We plan to explore a variety of approaches, including spin-yield synchronization, time slice size matching, or some form of shared priority for parallel jobs.

Our current prototype does not automatically achieve fairness — it isn't self calibrating. We originally thought a single setting of the fairness parameters would work for almost all cases, but in fact different parameter settings were required for individual experiments. An automatic mechanism is clearly required for any robust coscheduling system. Obviously, the widespread use of priority-decay schedulers complicates the situation — stride schedulers [22] or other proportional share schedulers would provide a better platform for DCS, by separating the concepts of execution order and processor share. Our current efforts in the context of priority-decay schedulers focus on obtaining more accurate estimates of recent run time to implement an equalization criterion [17].

The experiments described in this paper have two key limitations: a single parallel job and a cluster of only seven nodes were used in all benchmarks. Future DCS experiments must include multiple parallel jobs, larger workloads, and larger configurations. Such broadening would enable evaluation of a wide range of issues, including the viability of the epoch number mechanism [17] for multitasking parallel jobs. Such efforts are already underway as part of the Illinois High Performance Virtual Machines Project.

Most of the workloads used to study coscheduling [3, 16] are quite regular in structure, communication, and computation. Such regularity often fails to exercise the behavioral richness of dynamic systems. Study of more irregular workloads and background loads are desirable.

6   Summary

We have presented an implementation of dynamic coscheduling on a cluster of workstations using a high-performance messaging layer. Experimental results found using our DCS implementation show that dynamic coscheduling can provide good performance for a parallel process running on a cluster of workstations in competition with serial processes. Performance was close to ideal for the case of fine-grained processes using spin-block message receipt: CPU times were nearly the same as for batch processing, and DCS reduced job response times by up to 20% over implicit scheduling while maintaining near-perfect fairness. Under spinning message receipt, DCS improved efficiency and reduced job response times by as much as two decimal orders of magnitude over the uncoordinated scheduling of the base Solaris 2.4 scheduler, with only a small penalty in fairness.

Further research remains to be done, with multiple parallel processes, a larger workstation cluster, and different sorts of test workloads, but our results to date show that DCS is a promising means of achieving coscheduling in workstation clusters.

Acknowledgments

Bert Halstead, Larry Rudolph, and Chandu Thekkath have all given us valuable suggestions and comments on the work described here. Mario Lauria helped us to use his implementation of MPI on FM. Roy Campbell and Dave Raila provided the workstation cluster at UIUC that we used in our experiments.

Sobalvarro and Weihl were supported in part by the Advanced Research Projects Agency under Contract N00014-94-1-0985, by grants from IBM and AT&T, and by an equipment grant from DEC.

Pakin and Chien are supported in part by in part by DARPA Order #E313 through the US Air Force Rome Laboratory Contract F30602-96-1-0286, NSF grants MIP-92-23732, and NASA grant NAG 1-613. Support from Intel Corporation, Tandem Computers, Hewlett-Packard, Microsoft, and Motorola is also gratefully acknowledged. Andrew Chien is supported in part by NSF Young Investigator Award CCR-94-57809.

The views and conclusions contained in this document are those of the authors and should not be interpreted as representing the official policies, either expressed or implied, of the U.S. Government.

References

[1] Nanette J. Boden, Danny Cohen, Robert E. Felderman, Alan E. Kulawik, Charles L. Seitz, Jakov N. Seizovic, and Wen-King Su. Myrinet—a gigabit-per-second local-area network. *IEEE Micro*, 15(1):29–36, February 1995. Available from http://www.myri.com/research/publications/Hot.ps.

[2] Rohit Chandra, Scott Devine, Ben Verghese, Anoop Gupta, and Mendel Rosenblum. Scheduling and page migration for multiprocessor compute servers. In Proceedings of the Sixth International Conference on Architectural Support for Programming Languages and Operating Systems, pages 12–24, San Jose, California, 1994.

[3] Andrea C. Dusseau, Remzi H. Arpaci, and David E. Culler. Effective distributed scheduling of parallel workloads. In *ACM SIGMETRICS '96 Conference on the Measurement and Modeling of Computer Systems*, 1996. Available from http://www.cs.berkeley.edu/~dusseau/Papers/sigmetrics96.ps.

[4] Dror G. Feitelson and Larry Rudolph. Distributed hierarchical control for parallel processing. *IEEE Computer*, 23(5):65–77, May 1990.

[5] Dror G. Feitelson and Larry Rudolph. Gang Scheduling Performance Benefits for Fine-Grained Synchronization. *Journal of Parallel and Distributed Computing*, 16(4):306–18, December 1992.

[6] Dror G. Feitelson and Larry Rudolph. Coscheduling based on run-time identification of activity working sets. *International Journal of Parallel Programming*, 23(2):135–160, April 1995.

[7] Richard B. Gillett. Memory Channel network for PCI. *IEEE Micro*, 16(1):12–18, February 1996. Available from http://www.computer.org/pubs/micro/web/m1gil.pdf.

[8] Anoop Gupta, Andrew Tucker, and Shigeru Urushibara. The impact of operating system scheduling policies and synchronization methods on the performance of parallel applications. In *ACM SIGMETRICS Conference on Measurement and Modeling of Computer Systems*, pages 120–132, May 1991. Available from http://xenon.stanford.edu/~tucker/papers/sigmetrics.ps.

[9] D. B. Gustavson. The scalable coherent interface and related standards projects. *IEEE Micro*, 12(1), Feb. 1992.

[10] Sun Microsystems Inc. ts_dptbl(4) manual page. *SunOS 5.4 Manual*. Section 4.

[11] Mario Lauria and Andrew Chien. MPI-FM: High performance MPI on workstation clusters. Submitted to the Journal of Parallel and Distributed Computing. Available from http://www-csag.cs.uiuc.edu/papers/mpi-fm.ps.

[12] John K. Ousterhout. Scheduling techniques for concurrent systems. In *Proceedings of the 3rd International Conference on Distributed Computing Systems*, pages 22–30, October 1982.

[13] Scott Pakin, Vijay Karamcheti, and Andrew A. Chien. Fast Messages (FM): Efficient, portable communication for workstation clusters and massively-parallel processors. *IEEE Concurrency*, 1997.

[14] Scott Pakin, Mario Lauria, Matt Buchanan, Kay Hane, Louis Giannini, Jane Prusakova, and Andrew Chien. *Fast Messages 2.0 User Documentation*, October 1996.

[15] Scott Pakin, Mario Lauria, and Andrew Chien. High performance messaging on workstations: Illinois Fast Messages (FM) for Myrinet. In *Supercomputing*, December 1995. Available from `http://www-csag.cs.uiuc.edu/papers/myrinet-fm-sc95.ps`.

[16] Patrick G. Sobalvarro. *Demand-based Coscheduling of Parallel Jobs on Multiprogrammed Multiprocessors*. PhD thesis, Massachusetts Institute of Technology, 1997. MIT/LCS/TR-710.

[17] Patrick G. Sobalvarro and William E. Weihl. Demand-based coscheduling of parallel jobs on multiprogrammed multiprocessors. In *Proceedings of the Parallel Job Scheduling Workshop at IPPS '95*, 1995. Available from `http://www.psg.lcs.mit.edu/~pgs/papers/jsw-for-springer.ps`. Also appears in Springer-Verlag Lecture Notes in Computer Science, Vol. 949.

[18] Andrew Tucker. Efficient scheduling on multiprogrammed shared-memory multiprocessors. Technical Report CSL-TR-94-601, Stanford University Department of Computer Science, November 1993. Available from `http://elib.stanford.edu/Dienst/UI/2.0/Describe/stanford.cs/CSL-TR-94-601`.

[19] Andrew Tucker and Anoop Gupta. Process control and scheduling issues for multiprogrammed shared-memory multiprocessors. In *Proceedings of the 12th ACM SIGOPS Symposium on Operating Systems Principles*, pages 159–186, 1989. Available from `http://xenon.stanford.edu/~tucker/papers/sosp.ps`.

[20] T. von Eicken, D. Culler, S. Goldstein, and K. Schauser. Active Messages: a mechanism for integrated communication and computation. In *Proceedings of the International Symposium on Computer Architecture*, 1992.

[21] Thorsten von Eicken, Anindya Basu, Vineet Buch, and Werner Vogels. U-Net: A user-level network interface for parallel and distributed computing. In *Proceedings of the 15th ACM Symposium on Operating Systems Principles*, December 1995. Available from `http://www.cs.cornell.edu/Info/Projects/ATM/sosp.ps`.

[22] Carl A. Waldspurger. *Lottery and Stride Scheduling: Flexible Proportional-Share Resource Management*. PhD thesis, Massachusetts Institute of Technology, 1995. MIT/LCS/TR-667.

Author Index

Springer
and the
environment

At Springer we firmly believe that an international science publisher has a special obligation to the environment, and our corporate policies consistently reflect this conviction.
We also expect our business partners – paper mills, printers, packaging manufacturers, etc. – to commit themselves to using materials and production processes that do not harm the environment. The paper in this book is made from low- or no-chlorine pulp and is acid free, in conformance with international standards for paper permanency.

 Springer

Lecture Notes in Computer Science

For information about Vols. 1–1376

please contact your bookseller or Springer-Verlag

Vol. 1414: M. Nielsen, W. Thomas (Eds.), Computer Science Logic. Selected Papers, 1997. VIII, 511 pages. 1998.

Vol. 1415: J. Mira, A.P. del Pobil, M.Ali (Eds.), Methodology and Tools in Knowledge-Based Systems. Vol. I. Proceedings, 1998. XXIV, 887 pages. 1998. (Subseries LNAI).

Vol. 1416: A.P. del Pobil, J. Mira, M.Ali (Eds.), Tasks and Methods in Applied Artificial Intelligence. Vol.II. Proceedings, 1998. XXIII, 943 pages. 1998. (Subseries LNAI).

Vol. 1417: S. Yalamanchili, J. Duato (Eds.), Parallel Computer Routing and Communication. Proceedings, 1997. XII, 309 pages. 1998.

Vol. 1418: R. Mercer, E. Neufeld (Eds.), Advances in Artificial Intelligence. Proceedings, 1998. XII, 467 pages. 1998. (Subseries LNAI).

Vol. 1419: G. Vigna (Ed.), Mobile Agents and Security. XII, 257 pages. 1998.

Vol. 1420: J. Desel, M. Silva (Eds.), Application and Theory of Petri Nets 1998. Proceedings, 1998. VIII, 385 pages. 1998.

Vol. 1421: C. Kirchner, H. Kirchner (Eds.), Automated Deduction – CADE-15. Proceedings, 1998. XIV, 443 pages. 1998. (Subseries LNAI).

Vol. 1422: J. Jeuring (Ed.), Mathematics of Program Construction. Proceedings, 1998. X, 383 pages. 1998.

Vol. 1423: J.P. Buhler (Ed.), Algorithmic Number Theory. Proceedings, 1998. X, 640 pages. 1998.

Vol. 1424: L. Polkowski, A. Skowron (Eds.), Rough Sets and Current Trends in Computing. Proceedings, 1998. XIII, 626 pages. 1998. (Subseries LNAI).

Vol. 1425: D. Hutchison, R. Schäfer (Eds.), Multimedia Applications, Services and Techniques – ECMAST'98. Proceedings, 1998. XVI, 532 pages. 1998.

Vol. 1427: A.J. Hu, M.Y. Vardi (Eds.), Computer Aided Verification. Proceedings, 1998. IX, 552 pages. 1998.

Vol. 1430: S. Trigila, A. Mullery, M. Campolargo, H. Vanderstraeten, M. Mampaey (Eds.), Intelligence in Services and Networks: Technology for Ubiquitous Telecom Services. Proceedings, 1998. XII, 550 pages. 1998.

Vol. 1431: H. Imai, Y. Zheng (Eds.), Public Key Cryptography. Proceedings, 1998. XI, 263 pages. 1998.

Vol. 1432: S. Arnborg, L. Ivansson (Eds.), Algorithm Theory – SWAT '98. Proceedings, 1998. IX, 347 pages. 1998.

Vol. 1433: V. Honavar, G. Slutzki (Eds.), Grammatical Inference. Proceedings, 1998. X, 271 pages. 1998. (Subseries LNAI).

Vol. 1434: J.-C. Heudin (Ed.), Virtual Worlds. Proceedings, 1998. XII, 412 pages. 1998. (Subseries LNAI).

Vol. 1435: M. Klusch, G. Weiß (Eds.), Cooperative Information Agents II. Proceedings, 1998. IX, 307 pages. 1998. (Subseries LNAI).

Vol. 1436: D. Wood, S. Yu (Eds.), Automata Implementation. Proceedings, 1997. VIII, 253 pages. 1998.

Vol. 1437: S. Albayrak, F.J. Garijo (Eds.), Intelligent Agents for Telecommunication Applications. Proceedings, 1998. XII, 251 pages. 1998. (Subseries LNAI).

Vol. 1438: C. Boyd, E. Dawson (Eds.), Information Security and Privacy. Proceedings, 1998. XI, 423 pages. 1998.

Vol. 1439: B. Magnusson (Ed.), System Configuration Management. Proceedings, 1998. X, 207 pages. 1998.

Vol. 1441: W. Wobcke, M. Pagnucco, C. Zhang (Eds.), Agents and Multi-Agent Systems. Proceedings, 1997. XII, 241 pages. 1998. (Subseries LNAI).

Vol. 1443: K.G. Larsen, S. Skyum, G. Winskel (Eds.), Automata, Languages and Programming. Proceedings, 1998. XVI, 932 pages. 1998.

Vol. 1444: K. Jansen, J. Rolim (Eds.), Approximation Algorithms for Combinatorial Optimization. Proceedings, 1998. VIII, 201 pages. 1998.

Vol. 1445: E. Jul (Ed.), ECOOP'98 – Object-Oriented Programming. Proceedings, 1998. XII, 635 pages. 1998.

Vol. 1446: D. Page (Ed.), Inductive Logic Programming. Proceedings, 1998. VIII, 301 pages. 1998. (Subseries LNAI).

Vol. 1447: V.W. Porto, N. Saravanan, D. Waagen, A.E. Eiben (Eds.), Evolutionary Programming VII. Proceedings, 1998. XVI, 840 pages. 1998.

Vol. 1448: M. Farach-Colton (Ed.), Combinatorial Pattern Matching. Proceedings, 1998. VIII, 251 pages. 1998.

Vol. 1449: W.-L. Hsu, M.-Y. Kao (Eds.), Computing and Combinatorics. Proceedings, 1998. XII, 372 pages. 1998.

Vol. 1450: L. Brim, F. Gruska, J. Zlatuška (Eds.), Mathematical Foundations of Computer Science 1998. Proceedings, 1998. XVII, 846 pages. 1998.

Vol. 1451: A. Amin, D. Dori, P. Pudil, H. Freeman (Eds.), Advances in Pattern Recognition. Proceedings, 1998. XXI, 1048 pages. 1998.

Vol. 1452: B.P. Goettl, H.M. Halff, C.L. Redfield, V.J. Shute (Eds.), Intelligent Tutoring Systems. Proceedings, 1998. XIX, 629 pages. 1998.

Vol. 1453: M.-L. Mugnier, M. Chein (Eds.), Conceptual Structures: Theory, Tools and Applications. Proceedings, 1998. XIII, 439 pages. (Subseries LNAI).

Vol. 1454: I. Smith (Ed.), Artificial Intelligence in Structural Engineering. XI, 497 pages. 1998. (Subseries LNAI).

Vol. 1456: A. Drogoul, M. Tambe, T. Fukuda (Eds.), Collective Robotics. Proceedings, 1998. VII, 161 pages. 1998. (Subseries LNAI).

Vol. 1457: A. Ferreira, J. Rolim, H. Simon, S.-H. Teng (Eds.), Solving Irregularly Structured Problems in Prallel. Proceedings, 1998. X, 408 pages. 1998.

Vol. 1458: V.O. Mittal, H.A. Yanco, J. Aronis, R-. Simpson (Eds.), Assistive Technology in Artificial Intelligence. X, 273 pages. 1998. (Subseries LNAI).

Vol. 1459: D.G. Feitelson, L. Rudolph (Eds.), Job Scheduling Strategies for Parallel Processing. Proceedings, 1998. VII, 257 pages. 1998.

Vol. 1461: G. Bilardi, G.F. Italiano, A. Pietracaprina, G. Pucci (Eds.), Algorithms – ESA'98. Proceedings, 1998. XII, 516 pages. 1998.

Vol. 1464: H.H.S. Ip, A.W.M. Smeulders (Eds.), Multimedia Information Analysis and Retrieval. Proceedings, 1998. VIII, 264 pages. 1998.